JAPAN

A Global Studies Handbook

Other Titles in
ABC-CLIO's
GLOBAL STUDIES: ASIA
Series

The Koreas, Mary E. Connor

FORTHCOMING
China, Robert LaFleur
India, Fritz Blackwell
Nepal and Bangladesh, Nanda R. Shrestha
Vietnam, L. Shelton Woods

JAPAN

A Global Studies Handbook

Lucien Ellington

A B C ⬗ C L I O

Santa Barbara, California • Denver, Colorado • Oxford, England

Library of Congress Cataloging-in-Publication Data

Ellington, Lucien.
   Japan : a global studies handbook / Lucien Ellington.
      p. cm. — (Global studies, Asia)
   Includes bibliographical references and index.
   ISBN 1-57607-271-1 (alk. paper)

   1. Japan. I. Title. II. Series.
DS806 .E45 2002
952—dc21   2001007878

06 05   10 9 8 7 6 5 4

This book is also available on the World Wide Web as an e-book.
Visit abc-clio.com for details.

ABC-CLIO, Inc.
130 Cremona Drive, P.O. Box 1911
Santa Barbara, California 93116–1911

This book is printed on acid-free paper.
Manufactured in the United States of America

Contents

Series Editor's Foreword

It is imperative that as many Americans as possible develop a basic understanding of Asia. In an increasingly interconnected world, the fact that Asia contains almost 60 percent of all the planet's population is argument enough for increased knowledge of the continent on our parts. There are at least four other reasons, in addition to demography, that it is critical Americans become more familiar with Asia.

Americans of all ages, creeds, and colors are extensively involved economically with Asian countries. U.S.-Pacific two-way trade surpassed our trade with Europe in the 1970s. Japan, with the world's second-largest economy, is also the second-largest foreign investor in the United States.

American companies constitute the leading foreign investors in Japan.

The recent Asian economic crisis notwithstanding, since World War II East Asia has experienced the fastest rate of economic growth of all the world's regions. Recently, the newly industrialized Southeast Asian countries such as Indonesia, Malaysia, and Thailand have joined the so-called Four Tigers—Hong Kong, the Republic of Korea, Singapore, and Taiwan—as leading areas for economic growth. In the past decade China has begun to realize its potential to be a world-influencing economic actor. Many Americans now depend upon Asians for their economic livelihoods and all of us consume products made in or by Asian companies.

It is impossible to be an informed American citizen without knowledge of Asia, a continent that directly impacts our national security.

America's war on terrorism is, as this foreword is composed, being conducted in an Asian country—Afghanistan. (What many Americans think of as the "Mideast" is, in actuality, Southwest Asia.) Both India and Pakistan now have nuclear weapons. The eventual reunification of the Korean Peninsula is fraught with the possibility of great promise or equally great peril. The question of U.S.-China relations is considered one of the world's major global geopolitical issues. Americans everywhere are affected by Asian political and military developments.

Asia and Asians have also become an important part of American culture.

Asian restaurants dot the American urban landscape. Buddhism is rapidly growing in the United States. Asian movies are becoming increasingly popular in the United States. Asian-Americans, while still a small percentage of the overall U.S. population, are one of the fastest-growing ethnic groups in the United States. Many Asian-Americans exert considerable economic and political influence in this country. Asian sports, pop music, and cinema stars are becoming household names in America. Even Chinese language characters are becoming visible in the United States on everything from baseball caps to t-shirts to license plates. Followers of the ongoing debate on American educational reform will constantly encounter references to Asian student achievement.

Americans should also better understand Asia for its own sake. Anyone who is considered an educated person needs a basic understanding of Asia. The continent has a long, complex, and rich history. Asia is the birthplace of all the world's major religions including Christianity and Judaism.

Asian civilizations are some of the world's oldest. Asian arts and literature rank as some of humankind's most impressive achievements.

Our objectives in developing the Global Studies: Asia series are to assist a wide variety of citizens to both gain a basic understanding of Asian countries and to enable readers to be better positioned for more in-depth work. We envision the series being appropriate for libraries, educators, high school, introductory college and university students, businesspeople, would-be tourists and anyone who is curious about an Asian country or countries. Although there is some variation in the handbooks—the diversity of the countries requires slight variations in treatment—each volume includes narrative chapters on history and geography, economics, institutions, and society and contemporary issues. Readers should obtain a sound general understanding of the particular Asian country about which they read.

Each handbook also contains an extensive reference section. Since our guess is that many of the readers of this series will actually be traveling to Asia or interacting with Asians in this country, introductions to language, food, and etiquette are included. The reference section of each handbook also contains extensive information—including Web sites when relevant—about business and economic, cultural, educational, exchange, government, and tourist organizations. The reference sections also include capsule descriptions of famous people, places, and events and a comprehensive annotated bibliography for further study.

—*Lucien Ellington*
Series Editor

Preface

It is my hope that *Japan: A Global Studies Handbook* will be an informative and useful introduction for American readers to one of the world's most important countries. Americans seem to have more problems understanding Japan than is the case with other countries, particularly European ones. One pundit observed that we either see the Japanese as a threat or as unimportant for American interests. Survey research indicates that, despite improvement relative to the past, too many Americans remain ignorant of Japan.

It is crucial that we know about Japan for at least three reasons.

Although the Japanese have experienced economic problems for over a decade, Japan remains the world's second-largest economy. American companies are the leading investors in Japan while Japanese companies are the second-leading investors in this country. Millions of Americans and Japanese make their livelihoods from what some have deemed the world's most important economic relationship.

Japan is also crucially important to the United States because it has been a staunch ally since the end of World War II. As I write this preface, Japanese ships are en route to the Arabian Sea to supply American personnel in the battle against the al Qaeda terrorist network. Japan's geopolitical location in Northeast Asia near some of the world's potential hot spots makes the bilateral political relationship vital for the continued peaceful existence of, not only Americans and Japanese, but many other peoples as well.

In a world made increasingly smaller through technology it is also important that Americans become more knowledgeable of significant accomplishments of important non-Western cultures. Anyone who presumes to have a basic education in the twenty-first century should be familiar with *The Tale of Genji*, haiku, Japanese gardens, Zen, and other important elements of Japan's traditional culture. Today, Japanese architecture and animation are just two examples of Japan's contemporary contributions to world culture.

No one work can provide in-depth understanding of another culture but, hopefully, this book is a useful tool for those readers who want to begin to understand Japan. *Japan: A Global Studies Handbook* is written for the widest possible audience including businesspeople, educators, high school and university students, school teachers, tourists and virtually anyone who wants to know more about Japan.

The book has two major divisions—a narrative section and a reference section. The narrative section includes chapters on Japan's geography and history, economy, institutions, and society. Every attempt has been made to provide readers with accurate and fair information. I have studied and visited Japan since the early 1980s, and I tried very hard to integrate my own experiences with the scholarship in each of the topics I address in the narrative section.

The purpose of the reference section is to provide readers with either specific information or access to a wide range of information on a broad range of Japan-related topics. Since I believe that many of the people who read this book will either travel to Japan or interact with Japanese in this country, the very practical subjects of language, food, and etiquette are addressed. The reference section also includes brief descriptions with addresses and, where applicable, Web sites of a number of Japanese business, cultural, educational, and governmental organizations. There is also a "Significant People, Places, and Events" component of the reference section, which is organized alphabetically. The final portion of the reference section is an annotated bibliography of print and non-print sources organized by topic for those readers who need access to more specialized knowledge.

I have traveled to Japan fourteen times and attempted to

engage in systematic study of Japan for almost twenty years. Every day, I find it more fun to learn about this highly interesting nation. I hope that in addition to providing information, I have conveyed some of my enthusiasm for Japan in my prose. This book is not my creation alone although I accept responsibility for any of its weaknesses. There are so many people I could thank for this work that I will take the coward's way out and name no one, thereby not offending anyone. My one exception is ABC-CLIO editor Alicia Merritt. Without her encouragement and support all along the way, this book would have been impossible.

The book also would not have been possible without the support of family, friends, university colleagues, numerous Japanese studies colleagues, and last but not least, the employees of ABC-CLIO. This is my third published book and the helpfulness, friendliness, and most of all, professionalism of all the ABC-CLIO personnel with whom I have worked has simply been exemplary.

PART ONE
NARRATIVE SECTION

CHAPTER ONE

Japan's Geography and History

Contemporary Japanese are influenced, as is the case with any people, by the geography and history of the land upon which they live. Until the nineteenth century, the Japanese islands were difficult for others to reach, and this fact alone helped to shape aspects of Japan's culture that still cause many Japanese to be somewhat uncomfortable with foreigners. The physical geography of Japan offers a few advantages to its inhabitants, but it has often been an obstacle rather than an asset in the Japanese people's quest for economic development, safety, and security.

There has been a consistent pattern in Japan's history of periods of extreme isolation from the rest of the world alternating with eras in which the Japanese learn much from other nations. Until just a little over 130 years ago Japan was a feudal society with lords and vassals and a rigid class structure. Despite over fifty years of democratic government, remnants of these "vertical" aspects of human relations are still very much alive in Japan. The following pages will assist readers in acquiring a basic understanding of Japan's geography and history—an understanding that can lead to clearer insights about contemporary Japanese cultural patterns and institutions.

THE PHYSICAL AND HUMAN GEOGRAPHIES OF JAPAN

With its four major islands—Hokkaido, Honshu, Kyushu, and Shikoku—as well as thousands of smaller ones, Japan has a total land area of approximately 145,370 square miles. The distance from the northernmost tip of Hokkaido to extreme southern Kyushu is approximately the same as the distance

3

Tokyo's Ginza district, pictured here, is one of the most crowded sections of any Japanese city. (Library of Congress)

from Bangor, Maine, to Mobile, Alabama, in the United States. Japan has more land area than countries that many people imagine to be larger, including Great Britain and Italy.

Japan's population of over 126 million makes it the ninth-largest nation in the world. Japan's population is almost one-third larger than Germany and more than twice the size of the individual populations of Great Britain, Italy, and France.

Still, when the amount of usable land in Japan is compared with that in other nations, Japan is, in practical terms, much smaller than it looks on a map. Japan has the second-highest population density per square mile of the world's ten most populous countries, but population density statistics alone do not accurately depict the Japanese space problem. Because the islands are extremely mountainous and contain few plains, nearly the entire population lives on about one-sixth of Japan's total land area. Even though smaller countries such as Belgium and the Netherlands have higher ratios of people to total land area than Japan, in terms of habitable land, Japan is much more crowded than either of those countries.

Japan's location relative to other nations has been significant in shaping Japanese culture and attitudes. The Japanese islands are located in northeast Asia and are separated by water from other countries. To Japan's north, the nearest foreign soil is the Russian-controlled island of Sakhalin. Although China and Korea have always been important neighbors to Japan, the distances between them and Japan are relatively great. One must travel 500 miles across the East China Sea to reach Mainland China or travel 120 miles through the Korea Strait to land on Korean soil. Many writers, when considering Great Britain, emphasize how important the geographic isolation of the British from the rest of Western Europe was in shaping many of the distinctive features of English life. Yet Japan is five times further away from Korea and twenty times further away from China than the twenty-mile distance from the white cliffs of Dover to France.

Today with superspeed air travel and computers, the physical distance between Japan and other countries seems slight. Yet the habits and attitudes of the people of any nation are strongly influenced by the past, and until just a few decades ago Japan was relatively isolated compared to many other countries. Because Japan was difficult to reach, the Japanese avoided being successfully invaded from ancient times until the American occupation in 1945. Historically, the Japanese very carefully controlled the inflow of foreign influences and for long periods of time chose to have almost no contact with foreign countries. Modern Japanese culture contains foods, words, tools, and practices from other countries that were allowed into Japan in earlier times and also many uniquely Japanese objects and ways of doing things that developed during periods when Japan was extremely isolated.

Japan's early geographic and later self-imposed isolation also influenced the historic and contemporary racial characteristics of the Japanese people. The Japanese are, like their nearest neighbors on the Asian continent, a Mongoloid people. Archeological evidence indicates the earliest human settlements in what is now Japan were approximately 30,000 years ago or more. The fall in sea levels due to successive ice ages created temporary land bridges between Japan and the continent of Asia. People probably came to Japan by bridges located in what is now Manchuria in the north, the Korean peninsula in the west, and the Ryukyu island chain toward central and south China. The Ainu, a people who share some characteristics of Caucasians, also settled in early times on the present-day island of Hokkaido and on part of what is now Honshu.

Once humans moved to Japan, geographical isolation and a temperate climate meant that they usually remained. Since the eighth century C.E., there has been no major infusion of immigrants into the Japanese islands. The end product of this historical absence of immigration or migration, along with no successful foreign invasion, is a very high level of racial homogeneity in modern Japan. In fact, the Japanese are one of the most culturally and ethnically homogeneous peoples in the world. Ethnic minorities now living in Japan constitute just a little more than 1 percent of the population.

The Japanese have long been keenly aware of how culturally and racially alike they are compared with most peoples in other nations. This homogeneity has in part spawned a deep-seated notion among many Japanese that they are so unique that foreigners cannot ever really understand their language or culture. Although this sentiment seems to be receding somewhat in recent years, its continuing presence at least partially explains the difficult time many Japanese have in closely relating to anyone who is a foreigner.

While historic geographical isolation and ethnic homogeneity have been important in shaping Japan's people, the islands' climactic and physical features have also contributed to molding contemporary Japanese culture. Mountains are the most common topographical feature of Japan, with over two-thirds of the land area classified as mountainous. Japanese mountains, while not particularly high by world standards, tend to be extremely wooded and quite beautiful. Most Japanese mountains are only a few thousand feet high, although in central Honshu in the Japanese Alps there are ranges that soar as high as 10,000 feet. Mount Fuji can be found in the same general part of Honshu as the Japanese Alps. This perfectly shaped extinct volcanic cone attains a height of 12,389 feet and is probably Japan's most famous geographic symbol.

Japan's mountains, although beautiful, have been more of a hindrance than an asset to people; because of the high percentage of mountainous terrain in Japan, there are few level areas. The 120-square-mile Kanto Plain on Honshu, which includes Tokyo, is the most extensive plain in Japan. Japan is so mountainous that less than 20 percent of the land area is level enough for agricultural cultivation. Historically, the mountains were barriers to communication, trade, and political unification within Japan. Today, they still constitute largely wasted space from an economic utilization perspective.

Most Japanese are reluctant to live in the mountains for fear of volcanic activity and landslides, expense, and inconvenience. Also, few industries locate in the mountains. The result is that throughout Japan one observes homes, factories, businesses, and farms jammed next to each other on the scarce level land.

Japan is fortunate to have, by and large, a quite temperate climate. Although there are substantial climatic variations within Japan, particularly in sparsely populated and rather cold Hokkaido and in warm southern Kyushu, in general, Japanese weather is similar to that of the U.S. East Coast. However, Japan experiences more annual rainfall, and most of Japan is warmer, both in the winter and in the summer, than the northeastern section of the East Coast.

Most of Japan's great cities on the main island of Honshu enjoy weather remarkably similar to that of the American states of North Carolina, Tennessee, and Virginia. For example, the average January and August Tokyo temperatures of 38.6 °F and 79.7 °F and the humidity levels are very similar to what might be found in Nashville, Tennessee, or Norfolk, Virginia.

Because of the temperate climate, there are long growing seasons in all of Japan except for Hokkaido. Historically, scarce agricultural land could be utilized very productively to support large numbers of people. Vegetables and rice constitute Japan's largest crops. Nonirrigated fields are devoted to fruits and vegetables, and most rice is grown in fields that lend themselves to irrigation. Since farms are quite small, averaging between four and five acres, considerably less than 5 percent of total cultivable land in Japan is utilized as pastureland for beef or other animals. Animal husbandry is found chiefly in Hokkaido. Japan's large population and the small space available for farming have meant that since around 1900 Japan has been forced to depend upon foreign countries for a portion of its food. Currently, imported food accounts for approximately 63 percent of all the calories

Japanese annually consume. Japanese purchase large amounts of beans, cereals, fruit, meat, and even fish from abroad. Even though Japan is the world's second-largest economy, few Japanese probably ever forget that they inhabit a country that is incapable of feeding itself.

During the last century Japanese farm families experienced revolutionary changes. In the early 1900s farmers made up 60 percent of Japanese workers. By 2000 the percentage of Japanese employed in agriculture and forestry had declined to approximately 5 percent of the total fulltime workforce. Although Japanese agricultural production has increased in recent years, farm mechanization and the enormous expansion of industry have transformed Japan into one of the world's most urban countries. This transformation meant the end of traditional rural living and working patterns for most Japanese. By the mid-1990s only 20 percent of farm households derived all their income from farming and increasingly, larger percentages of old people were engaged in farm work. In 1996 46 percent of all farm workers in Japan were age sixty-five or older.

Cities have been part of Japan's geography since 710 C.E., when an early emperor established the city of Nara. By 1700 Tokyo, or Edo, as it was then called, had an estimated population of over 1 million people, making it possibly the largest city in the world. Still, until well into the twentieth century most Japanese have lived in rural areas. Today over 75 percent of Japanese live in cities, and an even higher percentage of the population works in urban environments.

The highest concentration of people is in the Kanto Plain in central Honshu, which includes Tokyo, Japan's largest city, and Yokohama, second-largest. Tokyo's population is over 8 million people. If Tokyo were a country, it would have a higher gross national product than China or South Korea. But Tokyo is only one of twelve Japanese cities whose population exceed a million. The 300-mile distance along the eastern Honshu coast from Tokyo south to Osaka, the third-largest Japanese city, is almost completely urbanized. Approximately 50 percent of the Japanese population lives in three great clusters: greater Tokyo (including Kawasaki, Yokohama, and Chiba), greater Nagoya (including Aichi and Mie Prefectures) and greater Osaka (including Hyogo and Kyoto Prefectures). All of these megalopoli are located on Honshu, making it Japan's most populous island by far. Although massive urbanization has been in many ways beneficial to Japan's economy, it has complicated Japan's fundamental problem of living space and caused major air and water pollution.

Since they rely on business and industry for economic growth, urban nations in particular must have access to both a great variety and amount of natural resources. The Japanese are not self-sufficient in vitally important commodities such as iron ore, petroleum, lead, zinc, copper, and timber. The energy situation is a perpetual problem, for the Japanese must import virtually all the oil they use. Mineral fuels (primarily oil) constitute, in recent years, the leading raw material import for the Japanese. Although Japan has been able to afford oil due to relatively low prices since the 1980s, in the event of a crisis or war involving the oil-producing nations, the Japanese would have every reason to fear for their economy and social fabric.

The resource picture is not completely dark for the Japanese, however, since there are two great resources with which Japan has been blessed. One is the sea. No part of Japan is over seventy miles from the sea, and Japan has a total of 16,800 miles of coastline as well as a large inland sea. In Japanese history the ocean was a great boon for transportation, and the sea has always been a wonderful source of food. Herring, cod, halibut, salmon, crab, sardines, tuna, skipjack, sea breams, mackerel, yellowtail, octopus, eel, seaweed, and squid are just some of the sea life that ends up on Japanese tables. In traditional Japanese cuisine it is most unusual to eat a meal that does not include some kind of food from the sea.

The second greatest resource within Japan is undoubtedly its people. Throughout history few peoples have proven to be more hard working, intelligent, accepting, and resourceful than the Japanese. These traits are especially important in a relatively resourceless, crowded country.

THE LIVING SPACE PROBLEM

Because much of Japan's land does not lend itself to development, lack of living space is a permanent problem that affects many aspects of human life. The space situation is worst in Tokyo but severe in most of Japan's cities. The daily task of getting from one place to another is much more problematic for the average Japanese than for the average American or European. Even though Japan has only a little over half the number of cars as in the United States, many Japanese city streets average up to ten times as many cars daily as U.S. streets. Based on the size of each nation's population, in some years the Japanese average about one-and-a-half times the number of deaths due to automobile accidents as does the United States. A major reason that Japanese streets are so crowded and dangerous for vehicles and pedestrians is that there is little room to build adequate expressways in urban areas. This incredible congestion makes it impossible for Japanese to depend upon the car to the extent that it is used in the United States.

Fortunately, the Japanese enjoy one of the best train and subway systems in the world. In a recent year almost ten times as many Japanese annually used Japan's public rail systems as Americans utilize the same kind of transport. Still, in Tokyo and other large Japanese cities, using subways and trains during rush hours can be uncomfortable at best and, because of the enormous number of users, dangerous at times.

During rush hour Tokyo subway cars often are jammed to over twice their capacity and passengers are warned not to

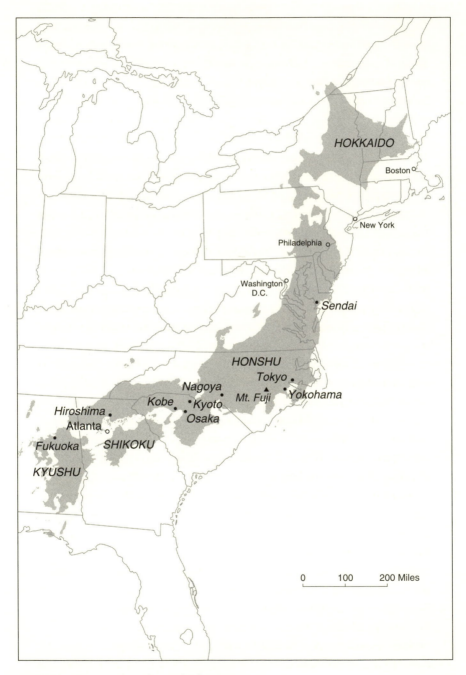

HOKKAIDO

Boston ○

New York ○

Philadelphia ○

Washington D.C. ○

● Sendai

HONSHU

Tokyo ●

Nagoya ● ▲ Mt. Fuji ● Yokohama

Kobe ● ● Kyoto

Hiroshima ● ● Osaka

Atlanta ○

Fukuoka ●

SHIKOKU

KYUSHU

0   100   200 Miles

Japan superimposed on the United States.

board subways with their arms in awkward positions because of the possibility of broken bones. In rare cases babies have suffocated on crowded Japanese subways. Windows sometimes shatter because of the crowds, and every day dozens of riders lose shoes. Station attendants on commuting trains and subways often must shove the last few people entering a car on board in order to close the doors. In winter the situation is particularly frenetic as heavy clothing increases the average rider's bulk and forces officials to employ more shovers.

In central Tokyo most Japanese can afford only the smallest apartments. Even though prices have fallen relative to a few years ago, both the price of land for a house and the price of the house itself are a major reason Tokyo is the most expensive city in the world. In a recent year, New York City residential land space cost only 4 percent as much as the equivalent Tokyo residential land space, and the price of a New York City home was, on average, only 26 percent that of a Tokyo home. Fortunately, although housing is expensive all over Japan, residential land and dwelling prices outside of Tokyo are considerably lower.

The effect of lack of adequate living space upon the daily quality of life of typical Japanese is an even more important factor than simply the high cost of housing. The average Japanese home or apartment is cramped, noisy, and very cluttered, and individual privacy is usually difficult or impossible to fully attain. The amount of space in typical Japanese homes compared to residential space in other countries makes privacy a precious commodity. Japanese homes average just 1,002 square feet, compared to 1,911 square feet for an American home and 2,160 square feet for a Belgian home. According to Japan's statistics bureau, each person in Japan has 323 square feet of floor space for housing, whereas the average resident of the UK enjoys 434 square feet and the average American takes up 691 square feet for residential space.

Use of the small space available in homes and apartments has also changed with Japan's recent economic affluence. Traditionally, Japanese utilized the limited space available in their homes in very flexible ways. Rooms would contain very little furniture. Instead of a sofa and chairs there would only be a low table in the middle of the room. Family members would sit on the floor on straw *tatami* mats, and at night the table would be pushed aside and futons, the traditional Japanese sleeping rolls, would be taken from the closet and spread out. Therefore, one room could easily be used for eating, recreation, and sleeping. In the past, traditional Japanese homes were also pleasing in appearance because of the lack of big heavy furniture.

Japanese homes are now in some ways more difficult places in which to spend large amounts of time than in years past. The rise in living standards and changes in cultural preferences mean that even though average family size is smaller and the available living space is larger now, the interiors of houses tend to look extremely cluttered. In most Japanese homes every available inch of wall space is now taken up with wardrobes, bureaus, and furniture. Typically, rooms are littered with children's toys, and a large variety of decorative objects such as stuffed animals and French dolls are likely to be found on top of television sets and pianos. Japanese urban dwellers, while usually retaining one or two traditional rooms with tatami mats, now usually own Western-style beds, sofas, and heavy chairs.

Lack of adequate home space forces Japanese to pursue a number of activities outside the house that people in other developed countries would engage in at home. For example, almost no homes have lawn space or outside play equipment for children. Because of the lack of space and high noise level at home, many students do their homework in study areas provided by their schools or in public libraries. Friends are usually entertained at restaurants or other public places. There are now even buildings in Tokyo where people who can't take the noise and congestion of their home can rent a private reading room!

Insufficient space is so widespread in Japan that primary school students are assigned the exercise of finding the best way to get from one to another section of their town or city. Japanese children learn early how to read detailed train and subway maps because it is unlikely they will be driven to school or other activities on the country's crowded roads. Lack of adequate habitable space affects how Japanese people live, travel, spend leisure time, and work.

THE HAZARDS OF BEING JAPANESE

In 1995 6,400 people were killed in an earthquake in the western port city of Kobe. The Kobe tragedy was the latest major earthquake in a country that is particularly prone to earthquakes and typhoons. Central Japan, including Tokyo, is one of the world's worst earthquake areas. Throughout Japan an average of 7,500 earthquakes are recorded annually and approximately 1,500 can be felt by people. Because of the frequency of earthquakes, tremors strong enough to gently shake a sleeper in bed often receive minor coverage in the Japanese media.

Unfortunately, several earthquakes and resultant fires have done much more than cause slight tremors. In 1657, 1703, and 1923 much of Tokyo was destroyed by earthquakes and accompanying fires. Government estimates of the dead and wounded in the 1923 earthquake were over 156,000 people, and the property damage was incalculable. From Tokyo south the earthquake destroyed sixty miles of railroad track. Over 1 million people temporarily fled the Tokyo-Yokohama area because of the disaster. Some seismologists predict a major quake in the Tokyo area early in this century.

As if earthquakes were not bad enough, the Japanese must deal annually with an average of six to seven tropical cyclones—better known as typhoons. Typhoons, most of which originate in the Philippine Sea in the late summer and early fall, can be devastating to both humans and property. In October 1959 a terrible typhoon crashed through Nagoya, Japan's fourth-largest city, killing 5,000 people and leaving 400,000 homeless. Seven days after the storm over 25,000 people were still stranded on their roofs because of the water.

Little usable land, almost no natural resources, incredible urban congestion, earthquakes, typhoons—the list of seemingly ill-fated aspects of Japanese life caused by the physical and human geography of the archipelago is long. Still, in the year 2000, an average life expectancy of almost seventy-seven years for men and almost eighty-three years for women made the Japanese one of the most long-lived people in the world. This statistic is at least partial evidence that despite the seemingly cruel hand nature dealt Japan, its people are amazingly flexible and resilient.

JAPAN'S PREHISTORY

Archaeologists have used the art of Japan's earliest known culture to name the first period of Japanese prehistory. A *jomon* was a rope pressed into a clay vessel to form a design; the clay pot was then fired to imprint the design. It is now the name given to a people who from approximately 10,000 to 300 B.C.E. lived a simple nomadic lifestyle of hunting, fishing, and gathering edibles. Evidence of Jomon culture has been found from Okinawa to Hokkaido. The only surviving evidence of early Jomon culture are remains of their pottery used as containers, but more sophisticated implements from the late Jomon period (2500 B.C.E.), such as the remains of serving bowls, have been unearthed.

By approximately 300 B.C.E. in parts of the present-day islands of Kyushu and Honshu, individuals were engaged in a much more sophisticated lifestyle than in the Jomon era. More importantly, the people of the Yayoi culture, named after an excavation site in the Tokyo area, were assured a steady food supply because they adopted wet field or irrigated rice cultivation. Agriculture enabled these early Japanese to build permanent communities and devote time to activities other than hunting for food. Even during these times the more advanced Chinese and Korean civilizations were important in Japanese development, since wet field rice cultivation almost certainly came to Japan from the Asian mainland. People during the Yayoi period produced a variety of implements, including large jars and urns; used two other Chinese imports, bronze and iron for making weapons; and established some sea trade with Korea and China. Surviving Chinese records reveal that representatives of that nation's government visited Japan as early as 57 C.E.

The Yayoi people were eventually dominated by a technologically and militarily more advanced people from the Asian mainland now known as Kofun or Tomb people, because they buried their leaders in huge keyhole-shaped tombs. By 250 C.E. Japanese culture resembled that of Korea and China more than Yayoi culture. Tomb artifacts such as textiles, pottery, coins, and mirrors indicate that regular contact was maintained with the Asian mainland. Also, the arrival of military technology from the Asian mainland, particularly the skill of riding horses, enabled some powerful families to gain power through coalitions.

One such coalition, who lived on the Yamato plain near present-day Osaka and Kyoto, extended their political power to the point they controlled all of modern Japan except Northern Honshu and Hokkaido. The Yamato rulers were in regular contact with the Chinese and built alliances with Korean sovereigns. Also, Yamato leaders, who were both male and female, established the principle of hereditary accession to the throne. The Yamato rulers were religious as well as political leaders.

By the time of the Yamato rulers, elements of religious practices that are now known as Shinto were already present. Shinto, which can be translated as "Way of the Gods," is uniquely Japanese. It has no founders, no sacred book, no teachers, no martyrs, and no saints. The religion is built around nature worship and the presence of spirits or *kami* in mountains, rocks, trees, streams, and even in certain people. Many of the physical places where kami existed during these early times are now the sites of Shinto shrines. Another major aspect of Shinto still present that dates back to the dawn of Japanese history is the emphasis on purification. Almost all Shinto ceremonies begin with the use of water. Values common to most Japanese today that originated in part through early religious practices include a love of bathing and deep reverence for nature.

Shinto also bequeathed a rich mythology to the Japanese people, with stories of gods and goddesses who possessed various magical powers. The Yamato rulers, who were originally priest-chiefs and later became the first Japanese emperors, claimed descent from Amaterasu, the Sun Goddess and a leading Shinto deity. The sun has gone on to play a central role in Japanese culture. The Japanese name for their country, Nippon, means "source of the sun." It would not be until after World War II that the formal connection between the Japanese imperial family and the Shinto religion would be broken.

EARLY MAINLAND ASIA AND CHINESE INFLUENCES

An event as historically significant as the beginnings of Shinto occurred in 552 C.E. when Buddhism was introduced to Japan from the Asian mainland. Buddhism, which originated in India and spread to China, eventually reached Korea and then Japan. According to legend, the king of the Korean state of Paekche, in the process of requesting Japanese military assistance, sent gifts to the Yamato rulers that included Buddhist sutras, a statue of Buddha, and a letter of praise for the religion.

Buddha, meaning "enlightened one," was born Prince Gautama Siddhartha in the Indian Shakya nation around 563 B.C.E. and died in 483. Siddhartha was a human and only later deified. According to the story of the founding of Buddhism, written centuries after Siddhartha's death, the young boy was brought up in luxury and protected from the evils of the world by his parents. However, Siddhartha ventured from the safe confines of the palace and encountered old age, sickness, and death. Siddhartha was extremely troubled by these ultimate realities of human existence and, abandoning his privileged life and his family, pursued the life of the wandering religious seeker.

For a number of years Siddhartha engaged in practices such as extensive fasting that almost killed him. Finally, he settled upon a middle way that preserved his life but did not lead to overindulgence in the world's pleasures. After extensive meditation under the Bodhi, or wisdom, tree, Siddhartha became enlightened and spent the rest of his life bringing his teachings to a growing number of disciples. From Siddhartha's evolution to Buddha, a world religion was born.

The Four Noble Truths constitute the essence of Buddhist teachings, though they are now greatly augmented by an entire canon of theological literature. The first Truth is that life is suffering. To be human is to suffer, and tribulations such as pain and old age are impossible to avoid. Integrated with this teaching are the notions of karma, reincarnation, and Nirvana. The principle of karma focuses upon human action and moral results. Both good and evil deeds accrue for the individual. If an individual lives a good life he or she will be born again, or reincarnated, in a better life. Still, all human life means suffering, so the ultimate spiritual goal is not to continue to be born or reincarnated again, but rather to achieve Nirvana where one transcends the repeating life cycle and is never reborn.

The second and third Truths expand upon the first Truth. In the second Truth, desire is clearly identified as the cause of human suffering. The third Truth is an injunction that if humans want to stop suffering they must extinguish desire. This goal is achieved through religious practices such as meditation and through following the fourth Truth, or Eight-fold Path, which includes right views, right intention, right speech, right action, right livelihood, right effort, right mind-fulness, and right concentration.

As Buddhism matured in India, its theology became more complex and other concepts became important to the belief system as well. One major Buddhist tenet critical to under-standing the religion is that the notion that each individual possesses a "soul" is incorrect. Because to live is to change, any individual is a compilation of his or her attributes at any given point in time. Human attributes are not permanent and change as time passes. Buddhism also divided relatively early in its history into two major sects, Theravada, which is today dominant in most of Southeast Asia, and Mahayana, which spread to China, Korea, and then Japan, and is still the gen-eral institutional framework for the many Buddhist denomi-nations in existence in northeast Asia today.

Mahayana Buddhism accentuates the notion of emptiness, or that apparent reality is empty or void and that everything is a product of mind. Only ultimate consciousness is real. The Mahayana sect is responsible for the concept of Bod-hisattvas, or enlightened ones, who delay their own acces-sion into Nirvana in order to help other humans realize this state. Also, Mahayana Buddhism encouraged the growth of devotion toward not only the Buddha but a pantheon of other Buddhas including Kannon, the Buddha of Mercy; Maitreya, the Buddha of the Future; and Amida, the Buddha of Infinite Light. The eventual effect of Mahayana Buddhism was to make the religion popular among common people who had neither the education nor the time to engage in philosophi-cal speculation and meditative practices.

The advent of the new religion in Japan, whose influence would be limited to aristocrats for hundreds of years, caused extreme controversy in Yamato ruling circles. Although two powerful clans, the Nakatomi and the Mononobe, opposed the strange new spiritual import, a third influential clan, the Sogas, who had ties to the Yamato ruler, were leading proponents of Buddhism. Buddhism had initial setbacks. After the Soga clan adopted a Buddhist image as their house kami, an epidemic occurred that the Nakatomis, who were Shinto ritualists, blamed upon the new religion. Eventually though, the Soga clan defeated the Mononobe clan in war in 587 C.E., thereby insuring Buddhism's survival in Japan.

The introduction of Buddhism in Japanese culture not only had profound eventual religious implications but also helped to increase the level of general knowledge in Japan. Japanese Buddhist priests traveled to China for religious instruction and then returned to Japan with technology and ideas ranging from better tools and weapons to governmental innovations and philosophy.

Although several important Chinese imports including wet rice cultivation, iron, and a writing system had come to Japan earlier, between the late sixth century and 838 C.E. a Chinese-based knowledge explosion occurred. The Japanese government, eager to learn from what was perhaps the world's most advanced civilization at the time, sent at least nineteen separate missions to China between 600 and 838 C.E. Missions, usually numbering more than 500 individuals, included official envoys, students, Buddhist monks, and translators. Many Japanese who braved these often-dangerous trips stayed in China for as long as twenty to thirty years.

Confucianism, another Chinese belief system that would eventually be just as influential on Japanese thinking as Buddhism, also gained the attention of those Japanese élites who were eagerly absorbing new knowledge from China. Confucius, who lived from approximately 551–479 B.C.E., was born of a minor aristocratic Chinese family during the Warring States Period of Chinese history, when the country was not unified under one dynasty. A well-educated man, Confucius greatly desired to influence public policy and advise rulers. Although he held minor bureaucratic posts and consulted with several rulers, Confucius was unable to affiliate as a high-level adviser with any Chinese sovereign.

Confucius instead turned to teaching. Though he left no writings, after his death his disciples compiled his teachings in a printed work, known as *Lun Yu* in Chinese and the *Analects* in English. Later Confucianists have produced an entire canon of Confucian texts. Confucianism is extremely difficult to categorize. Some scholars assert it is a philosophy, while others, citing the fact that there are Confucian temples in northeast Asia, classify it as a religion. However, all scholars concur that Confucianism has profoundly influenced the beliefs and actions of Chinese, Koreans, and Japanese as well as people in several other Asian cultures.

Although respectful of the spiritual and supernatural, Confucius was most concerned about the promotion of societal harmony at every level in this world. He viewed the proper maintenance of important relationships as vital to the promotion of a just and peaceful society. Specifically, Confucius identified five basic relationships that must be nurtured in appropriate ways for societal harmony: those between ruler and people, parent and child, husband and wife, older and younger siblings, and friend and friend.

Although Confucius viewed all these relationships as important, he placed special emphasis upon family relations in general and upon the absolute obedience children owe parents in particular. Confucius was an aristocrat, and his belief system is clearly hierarchical in nature. However, it is not so much oppressive as reciprocal. Subordinates are expected to obey and be loyal to superiors, but the latter are expected to be benevolent and protective toward humans below them in status.

Confucius also clearly articulated the importance of education, tradition, and virtue. He stressed the cultivation of an aristocracy based upon learning and virtue instead of blood. Confucius was basically conservative in that he idealized a more stable Chinese past than the chaotic period in which he lived. He constantly reminded disciples to be respectful of both ceremonies handed down through the generations and of their ancestors. Confucius felt that the practice of virtue, whether by a ruler or the head of a household, taught people proper moral behavior much more than did penalties or punishments.

Early Japanese political leaders valued the teachings of Confucius for its practical utility—its stress on the need for good government along with ethics, social hierarchy, harmony, duty, and respect for authority. Many influential Japanese felt that adoption of the organizing principles of the powerful Tang Dynasty in China would strengthen central government power and stabilize Japanese society.

Buddhism and Confucianism as well as other Chinese-derived ideas received a powerful boost from Prince Shotoku, who served as imperial regent from 593 until his death in 622. Shotoku was a strong advocate of the new religion and gave it official government approval. Although there was some opposition to Buddhism from Shinto priests and powerful families, Buddhism took root in Japan without the substantial bloodshed that historically accompanied the introduction of a new belief in many other countries. Although it would be centuries before Buddhism would become a popular religion with the common people, it became highly favored among the nobility, at least partially because it was known to be the religion of an advanced Chinese civilization.

As Japan moved from a land ruled by a clan to a country with an organized government, Shotoku also promoted Chinese ideas in his so-called seventeen-point "constitution" in 604, which affirmed the power of the emperor, Buddhism, and the Confucian notion of harmony. Following Shotoku's death in 622 there were blood feuds between factions for power, but in 645 a pro-China faction led by the founder of the Fujiwara family and an imperial prince engineered a coup d'état. The next year the new government initiated the *Taika,* or "Great Reforms."

The intent of these reforms, most of which were modeled after the Chinese Tang Dynasty and based on Confucian ideas, was to transfer power from clan and family leaders to the throne and its representatives. The separate domains ruled by clans became provinces, and Chinese taxation systems and law codes were adopted. All agricultural land supposedly belonged to the Yamato emperor; and bureaucrats of different ranks, who theoretically earned their positions by merit, were to run the national government.

Even as many Chinese-based reforms took root in Japan, its leaders altered some of the Chinese models and omitted aspects of China's political system that did not fit their culture. In Japan, unlike China, key government positions were awarded to members of leading families rather than meritorious applicants. Although some Japanese emperors did have actual political power, the existence of powerful families and the throne's inability to gain control over agricultural lands prevented the establishment of the tradition of an all-powerful emperor as in China. Japanese emperors have, with some exceptions, been largely symbolic leaders; individuals acting in the emperor's name have historically made important decisions.

During the years of the Taika Reforms and afterward, Japan was affected by China in ways other than politics and religion. The few literate Japanese were extremely familiar with Chinese literature. Japanese also adopted many Chinese techniques in weaving, lacquerware, metallurgy, orchestral music, dance, architecture, sculpture, and painting. Still, as in government and politics, the Japanese either changed many Chinese practices to fit their culture or rejected Chinese ideas entirely. Chinese food and eating habits were not accepted during this time in Japan. Even the emperor might have a Chinese-style palace but live in private quarters that would retain the Japanese tradition of cedar-bark roofs and pillars of plain, undecorated wood.

CLASSICAL JAPAN

Japan's first permanent capital was established in 710 to the west of the modern city of Nara, which is near Kyoto and Osaka. The capital city, called Heijo, which translates into "Capital of Peace and Tranquility," was laid out in direct imitation of the Chinese Tang Dynasty capital, Changan. Shortly after the capital's founding, the earliest two surviving Japanese books, the *Kojiki,* or "Record of Ancient Matters," and the *Nihon Shoki,* "Chronicles of Japan," were completed in 712 and 720 respectively. These books contain both mythology and historical information. The *Kojiki* attempted to use written Chinese to represent the Japanese language phonetically, but the *Nihon Shoki* was written in conventional Chinese script. It would not be until the 800s that Japanese people would devise their own written language to accompany the already centuries-old spoken language.

While Nara was the Japanese capital, one of the world's greatest architectural projects, the construction of the enormous Todaiji Temple containing the over fifty-two-foot-high Great Buddha, was completed under the leadership of Emperor Shomu, perhaps the most devoutly Buddhist sovereign in Japanese history. An estimated 10 percent of the Japanese population contributed to the project, and 50,000 carpenters and over 370,000 sheet metal workers were involved in construction. Approximately 10,000 Buddhist priests were in attendance as well as many other visitors from foreign countries during the dedication ceremony in 752.

Emperor Shomu's project probably did imperial power more harm than good, as the costs of Todaiji placed enormous strains on government finances. Also, after Todaiji was built the Buddhist temples that surrounded Nara housed many priests who attempted to intervene in politics. Partially because of a fear of the growing influence of the great Nara temples, Emperor Kammu ordered the construction of a second capital city, Heian-kyo, thirty miles to the north of Nara. The city, completed in 794 and laid out on the checkerboard pattern of Chinese cities, would later come to be known as Kyoto and remain Japan's imperial capital until 1868.

During the Heian period (794–1156) the Fujiwara clan continued to amass power through arranged marriages with the imperial family. With notable exceptions, rule by Fujiwara regents brought internal peace to Japan while the remoteness of the island nation continued to prevent it from being invaded by a foreign power. Heian Japan is important though not for politics, but for the flowering of a traditional and indigenous Japanese culture—a culture completely emanating from aristocrats. By the middle of the ninth century the imperial court aristocracy, largely free of worry about military or economic problems, was estimated to number 5,000 out of a city of 100,000.

The nobility considered cultural refinement to be of vital importance, and both people and objects had to be pleasing to others. The following description of the dress of a Heian nobleman attending a court ceremony illustrates the importance placed upon appearance: "Michitaka wore a summer tunic with a violet mantle, laced violet trousers, underwear of deep red, and a stiff unlined brilliantly white overgarment. All gentlemen carried fans with them whose ribs were lacquered in various colors with paper of brilliant red"(Sansom 1964, 192–193). This original aristocratic emphasis upon form as equal with function remains a widespread cultural proclivity in contemporary Japan.

The Heian nobility also developed an appreciation for the written word as a medium of entertainment. For centuries the Japanese had no written language, and educated people wrote in Chinese. Because spoken Chinese and Japanese sounds are completely different, it is extremely difficult to write down spoken Japanese in Chinese. In the ninth and tenth centuries the Japanese took certain Chinese characters, greatly abbreviated them, and created a phonetic system for spoken Japanese. Eventually, the Japanese developed a written syllabary, called Kana, which provided the basis for a written language.

By the latter part of the tenth century, members of the nobility were using Japanese to write books and poems. Many writers were women, since they enjoyed even more leisure time than men did and because written Japanese was still considered to be less appropriate for educated men than Chinese. The most famous of all Heian literature, *The Tale of Genji,* was completed by Lady Murasaki Shikibu early in the eleventh century. This book, considered to be a masterpiece of world literature and the world's first psychological novel, reveals much of the life of the Heian nobility. The hero, Prince Genji, epitomizes what Heian aristocrats considered to be good. He is handsome, a thoughtful lover, a poet, a musician, and he possesses impeccable taste.

As the Japanese nobility developed a sophisticated culture, the wave of enthusiasm for things Chinese clearly declined. Because of this decline in interest and because of domestic Chinese political problems, in 894 Japan ceased sending missions to China. Over the next two centuries the Japanese had relatively little contact with the continent. By the latter Heian Period the court nobility not only had less contact with the Chinese but were also isolated from both common Japanese and from increasingly powerful rural families. As the central government asked for more and more taxes, many peasants in the provinces began to band together behind these rural lords. While the Fujiwara regents and other aristocrats in the capital concerned themselves with the arts, powerful landowners were gaining experience managing large estates, amassing wealth, and becoming quite proficient at fighting on horseback. Political change was imminent.

MEDIEVAL JAPAN

As the influence of the Fujiwara clan and the central government declined, two powerful provincial families, the Taira

One of the legacies of the Kamakura Period of Japanese history is the
Great Buddha, a major Kamakura tourist attraction (Courtesy of
Lucien Ellington)

and Minamoto, warred against each other in what historians
refer to as the Gempei War. In 1185, Yoritomo, the leader of
the Minamoto family, defeated the Taira and Fujiwara clans
and obtained military control of Japan. In 1192 the emperor
"appointed" Yoritomo *shogun,* or "barbarian suppressing
general," making him the most powerful political and military leader in Japan.

Yoritomo chose not to live in Kyoto, the imperial capital,
but remained in his headquarters in the seaside town of
Kamakura, located near the modern city of Tokyo. Yoritomo's
headquarters in Kamakura, which came to be known as the
bakafu, or "tent government," became the center of power.
At the same time the weak imperial court and emperor continued to reign in Kyoto. The trend continued that those
occupying official positions of power were, in fact, relatively
powerless. This pattern of rule from behind the scenes
became even more pronounced in the power struggle follow-

ing Yoritomo's death in 1199. The family of Yoritomo's widow, the Hojo, emerged victorious. By placing Hojo family members in key positions, the family exercised actual political power. The shogunate, first occupied by a Minamoto, then by Fujiwaras, and later by princes of royal blood, became a figurehead.

Political power was quite decentralized. Yoritomo established a system throughout Japan where his vassals, or *gokenin,* and their warrior-retainers, known as *samurai,* fulfilled many of the old imperial government functions. Even though there were differences in the two systems, medieval Japanese, as did their European counterparts, developed a feudal system where landowners were responsible to overlords, who, in turn, were often loyal to higher authorities. Japanese feudalism came later than in Europe and remained longer. Although in Western Europe feudalism was declining by the 1400s, Japanese society retained many feudal characteristics until the last half of the nineteenth century.

The warrior class was the backbone of Japanese feudalism. By the late 1100s a general code of ethics for the samurai was already being observed, though it was not written down until much later. As in Europe, it was of vital importance that samurai learn techniques of war such as swordsmanship. As in Europe, heroism, honor, and loyalty were highly valued. The samurai, however, were particularly enamored with the last two characteristics. Honor of family name was something a samurai would die over, but loyalty to superiors was perhaps the most treasured of ideals.

Warriors did not usually question a superior's commands, and a warrior's obedience to a superior was expected regardless of family, all private interests, and even life itself. Thus one samurai, who had a reputation for being especially brave, was in danger from a robber and evaded the assailant in what seemed to be a cowardly manner. This samurai could not risk his life to protect his own property because he needed to preserve himself to serve his lord. Yoritomo was once presented with the head of an opponent by a samurai who had sworn loyalty to the dead opponent. The founder of the Kamakura government eventually had the samurai executed for disloyalty.

Samurai also were taught to not fear death and, as mental training, to become comfortable with the notion that death is preferable to dishonor or failure. This attitude is illustrated by words from the very first page of *Hagakure,* or *The Book of the Samurai.* Although the author wrote this classic much later than Japan's Kamakura Period, samurai were already practicing the following injunction:

> The way of the samurai is found in death. When it comes to either/or, there is only the quick choice of death. It is not particularly difficult. Be determined and advance. To say that dying without reaching one's aim is the frivolous way of sophisticates. When pressed with the choice of life or death it is not necessary to gain one's aim.
>
> We all want to live. And in large part we make our logic according to what we like. But not having attained our aim and continuing to live is cowardice. (Yamamoto 1983, 17)

The ability of many samurai to focus the mind to exhibit self-discipline, as well as their appreciation for beauty, was in part stimulated by the popularity of Zen Buddhism among the warrior caste. Though Zen was a sect that largely appealed to elites, Buddhism in general during the Kamakura years grew from a religion practiced by a few to a popular belief system. Varieties of Buddhism such as the True Pure Land sect, whose adherents believed that salvation in a Buddhist paradise was possible through faith in the Amida Buddha, became popular with common people throughout Japan. Several Buddhist sects such as the True Pure Land are still in existence today, and traditional Zen-influenced Japanese art forms such as the tea ceremony and flower arranging continue to be practiced in contemporary Japan.

Self-discipline and bravery were qualities very much in demand during Japan's Middle Ages, which were marked by strife. One of the major crises in Japanese history occurred in the late 1200s as outside invaders threatened the archipelago. Mongol nomads from the steppe lands north of China conquered central Asia, southern Russia, parts of the Middle East and Eastern Europe, Korea, and China. The Mongols tried twice to subdue Japan, sending a large seaborne force of almost 30,000 men in 1274 and a much larger contingent of 140,000 troops in 1281. In both cases the Japanese fought fiercely with the Mongols but received enormous help from nature when typhoons, which the Japanese called *kamikaze,* or "divine winds," destroyed the foreign fleets.

The Kamakura system lasted a little over fifty years after the repulsion of the Mongol invaders. The Hojo family was overthrown in 1333 by Emperor Go-Daigo, who attempted to revive imperial rule in the Kemmu Restoration. In turn, Ashikaga Takauji, the leader of a powerful family who was an early imperial ally, later broke with Go-Daigo, seized Kyoto, and installed a rival puppet emperor. Shortly afterward Go-Daigo escaped from Kyoto and established a second imperial court in Kyushu. From 1336 until 1392, when the Kyushu-based emperor was forced to return to Kyoto, Japan had two sets of emperors. However, Takauji became the major political power in Japan and in 1338 had his handpicked emperor appoint him shogun. Takauji and his Ashikaga successors ruled from Kyoto.

Feudalism became more hierarchical during the Ashikaga Period (1333–1573), as feudal lords were responsible to more powerful provincial lords, or *daimyo,* who in turn were theoretically responsible to the shogun. The actual situation during most of the Ashikaga years, however, was that power was even more decentralized than in the Kamakura era. Ashikaga shoguns were relatively weak, and powerful families fought each other and the shogun for control of Japan.

The Ashikaga Period was marked by constant strife, including the bloody Onin War, which lasted from 1467 until 1477 and was fought all over Japan. During these confused years while the Ashikaga shogunate was virtually powerless, emperors continued to reign but were very often reduced to near poverty because they had no access to stable income. It is not surprising that the Ashikaga years are considered one of the darkest political times in Japan's history.

Political problems notwithstanding, in other human endeavors the Ashikaga Period was one of excitement and growth. The Ashikaga shoguns were quite interested in Zen Buddhism and the arts. They built in Kyoto the Golden and Silver Pavilions, two of the most beautiful temples in all Japan. Many world-famous aspects of Japanese culture, such as the tea ceremony and flower arranging, were fully developed during this period. Japanese art today often emphasizes the value of the natural over the artificial, irregular shaped pottery over the symmetrical, the small over the large, and the simple over the complex. These values were a lasting result of the refined artistic taste of the Ashikaga shoguns.

Two classical forms of Japanese drama, *noh* and *kyogen,* also developed during the Ashikaga Period. Although noh's roots go back even earlier, a Shinto priest named Kan'ami (1333–1384) and his son Zeami (1363–1443) fully developed noh theater during the Ashikaga years. Noh, a musical dance drama where the characters wear masks, is still performed in contemporary Japan. Buddhist themes permeate noh plays. Noh drama usually features a meeting of a troubled spirit who is still attached to an earthly incident and either a priest or other mortal. Noh is danced more than acted, accompanied by a chorus as well as flute and drum music. The noh actor's dance is controlled, slow, and intense. The unearthly voices (due in part to the effects of the masks), intensity of the dance, spare music, and grave themes create an air of great seriousness and mystery.

Shorter kyogen plays were performed between different noh dramas as changes of pace. Kyogen translates to "mad and wild words" and is completely opposite from noh. These comic plays featured provincial bumpkins in the capital, servants who were smarter than their masters, and other such light-hearted themes. Kyogen plays are also still part of modern Japanese theater.

Technological and economic progress occurred during medieval Japan in part because Japanese again began to meet and learn from foreigners. Although after 894 there had been no official government contact between Japan and China, during the mid-1100s the Japanese government began sending "tribute" to China's Song Dynasty and receiving gifts in return from the Chinese court. By the Kamakura years Japan and China engaged in an officially condoned and very lively trade. Japanese society was enriched by Chinese imports, including silk, perfumes, sandalwood, porcelain, and copper coins; and Japanese swords, fans, and lacquerware were highly prized in medieval China.

When Portuguese traders landed off southern Kyushu in 1543, Japan was exposed to both technology and ideas significantly different from anything ever introduced from Asia. Japanese immediately became interested in European guns and in less than twenty-five years were manufacturing enough guns that in one battle between rival families, the winning side had several thousand riflemen. Also, the Portuguese and other Europeans who followed included priests and clergy, who viewed the Japanese as excellent candidates for Christian conversion. The Europeans proceeded immediately to win converts.

ISOLATION AND PEACE: TOKUGAWA JAPAN

European influence, particularly new technology, served as a partial catalyst for political change in Japan. Only a few years after Europeans introduced guns to Japan, three powerful leaders—Oda Nobunaga, Toyotomi Hideyoshi, and Tokugawa Ieyasu—used advanced firepower to achieve brilliant military successes that resulted in the political unification of Japan.

In 1568 upon the invitation of the emperor and Ashikaga Yoshiaki, an unsuccessful candidate for shogun, Oda Nobunaga and his forces occupied Kyoto and took control of much of central Japan. Nobunaga allowed Yoshiaki to hold the title of shogun until 1573 and then removed him from office, ending forever the Ashikaga family claim to the shogunate. Nobunaga was in control, although he installed a member of another family as puppet shogun. Nobunaga was extremely ruthless in attempting to unify Japan. He killed every man, woman, and child in one major Buddhist stronghold that opposed him.

After taking control of all of central Japan, Nobunaga was betrayed by one of his own generals, who surrounded the warlord and forced Nobunaga to commit suicide in 1582. With Japan again threatened by civil war, a second powerful leader emerged. Toyotomi Hideyoshi was a man of peasant origins who rose to become Nobunaga's chief general. Hideyoshi first successfully defeated rival daimyo and, after subduing Kyushu and Honshu, gained control of all of Japan in 1590. He reorganized the government, made it illegal for peasants to own weapons, and dispatched an army to attempt the conquest of Korea. Because of his lower-class background, Hideyoshi did not claim the title of shogun but instead had himself declared regent to the emperor.

When Hideyoshi died in 1598, he left a young son as an heir and a group of five powerful daimyo as collective regents. The daimyo soon divided among themselves, and the most powerful of the five, Tokugawa Ieyasu, after winning the battle of Sekigahara near Kyoto in 1600, attained virtual mastery of Japan. Tokugawa, whose original power base was a huge fief that included Edo (modern Tokyo), by 1615 defeated his last opponents at Osaka castle. A competent military man and a prudent and painstaking administrator and politician, Ieyasu assumed the title of hereditary shogun in 1603 by claiming descent from Minamoto Yoritomo. Not only did Tokugawa reunify Japan, but also his heirs would occupy the shogunate for over 250 years.

During the early part of the Tokugawa Period, castles such as this one in Matsue were constructed throughout Japan. (Courtesy of Lucien Ellington)

Ruling from Edo, Tokugawa Ieyasu and his heirs controlled a system that included a relatively strong central government and three descending ranks of daimyo, feudal lords who controlled domains and lived throughout Japan. Elite hereditary daimyo also served on several councils that, with the shogunate, shared governance of Japan. Daimyo were required to reside in Edo in alternate years so that the shogun could control them. Meanwhile, the emperor remained in Kyoto. Although Japanese emperors still had no appreciable political power, they continued to be living symbols of the nation.

Tokugawa Japan was characterized by rather rigid divisions between social groups. At the top were the samurai, who constituted about 5 to 6 percent of the total population. The Tokugawas continued Hideyoshi's policy that only samurai could bear weapons. Samurai could also not marry into the lower classes. Below the samurai were the peasants, because they produced food, which was considered to be the real wealth of the country. Below the peasants were the artisans. Because the merchants were viewed in this Neo-Confucian time as nonproducing parasites, they had the lowest status. However, as time passed and the merchant class accumulated great wealth, it was impossible to restrain their influence.

During the Tokugawa years Japan turned away from foreign influences, remaining largely isolated from the rest of the world. Religious ideas and fear of economic and political domination were the reasons behind the official Tokugawa policy of seclusion, which took effect during the 1630s. Before then for a time Christianity and trade with Europeans flourished. By the 1500s several daimyo encouraged their subjects to adopt Christianity, because they either believed in the new religion or desired more trade with Europeans. It is estimated that in 1580 there were 150,000 Christian converts in Japan, and some accounts indicate that by 1600 there were twice this number.

However, leaders such as Hideyoshi and Tokugawa Ieyasu feared the Europeans and Christianity. These leaders felt that Christians, particularly Catholics, could not be completely trusted as loyal Japanese because their true allegiance would be to the pope. Also, the Japanese leadership were aware that the Spanish had conquered the Philippines under the guise of Christianity. The Buddhist religious establishment was quick to support anti-Christian sentiments because they viewed the new religion as a threat. From 1597 until the late 1630s the government persecuted and executed thousands of Christians. By 1640, except for some underground Christians in Kyushu, the Japanese government had managed to abolish the religion in Japan. Also, the Tokugawa seclusion policies limited the only contact Japanese could have with foreigners to a few Chinese and Dutch traders who were allowed to conduct business in Nagasaki. No Japanese were allowed to travel abroad, and any Japanese persons living overseas were forbidden to return.

Even though Japan was largely cut off from the world during these years, in Tokugawa society the arts, certain kinds of economic development, and learning in areas other than science were in some ways equal or superior to that of the United States or Western Europe during the same period. The city became the focal point for many advances, concurrent with Edo's growth to over 1 million people by the 1700s. In addition to the great urban areas of Osaka and Kyoto, approximately 250 smaller cities, with populations ranging from 3,000 to 20,000, gained residents during the Tokugawa years.

Tokugawa art forms are still treasured throughout Japan and the world. Wood-block prints, or *ukiyo-e,* which featured beautiful women, actors, and scenes of travelers and natural geographic beauty, became popular. The Japanese had been interested in poetry for centuries, and its culmination came with the seventeen-syllable *haiku,* which in a few words often suggests entire worlds.

It was in the Tokugawa era that two forms of Japanese theater, *kabuki* and *bunraku,* flourished. The Chinese characters for kabuki (*ka-bu-ki*) mean song, dance, and skill, and the actors in these dramas certainly exhibited these attributes. Kabuki plays were (and are, since they are still performed), spectacles with action, romance, and elaborate sets, and they were both watched and regulated by authorities. A reoccurring kabuki theme that made Tokugawa officials particularly nervous was the conflict between feudal duty and human concerns. Often to avoid censorship, playwrights would portray actual contemporary events as occurring in the distant past. Because kabuki plays were often accompanied by disruption in the audience, authorities first banned women from acting in kabuki and then a few years later banned young men as well. Today men play both gender roles in kabuki.

While kabuki was popular in Edo, bunraku theater was the rage in Tokugawa-era Osaka. In bunraku, three male puppeteers control large wooden puppets that act while chanters tell the story accompanied by *shamisen,* stringed instruments. Bunraku was successful in part because the outstanding dramatist Chikamatsu wrote superb drama for this medium. Although originally kabuki and bunraku were theater for commoners, they are considered today, along with noh and kyogen, to be classic Japanese theater.

The peaceful Tokugawa years allowed the Japanese economy to expand. Because the country was unified, trade grew throughout Japan and some members of the merchant class acquired enormous fortunes in such activities as wholesaling, retailing, and banking. The use of money, always an indicator of societal economic sophistication, became widespread in Tokugawa Japan.

Cultural and economic development were in part due to the spread of formal learning throughout Japan. The daimyo maintained schools for the offspring of samurai, and common children attended schools operated by Buddhist temples, merchants, wealthy farmers, and local teachers. Estimates are that by the mid-nineteenth century, 40 percent of all Japanese men and 10 to 15 percent of all Japanese women could read and write, making Japan one of the world's most literate societies at the time.

Despite advances, the isolation of Japan from the rest of the world led to some stagnation, particularly in science and technology. Also, other nations took a dim view of Japan's isolationist policies. Eventually Japan's isolation contributed to the collapse of the Tokugawa government. Although the shogunate endured for fifteen more years, the real death knell for Tokugawa Japan sounded when Commodore Matthew Perry and the U.S. Navy steamed into what is now Tokyo Bay in July 1853.

JAPAN ENTERS THE MODERN WORLD

Few events in Japan's history have proven as significant as Commodore Perry and his "black ships," as the Japanese called them. In the years since Perry first arrived, Japan would become the first Asian nation to modernize, attain world power status, lose a disastrous war, and recover to develop a democratic government and the second-largest economy in the world.

The United States was interested in opening Japan for several reasons. The U.S. government wanted to expand its Pacific trade, and Japan was considered both an excellent fueling station for China-bound ships and a lucrative potential market. The American government also claimed to be concerned about the fate of sailors who were cast ashore in Japan. During his first visit, Perry presented his government's demands, including better treatment for shipwrecked sailors, the opening of ports where foreign ships could procure supplies, and trade. The commodore then left Japanese waters after promising to return the following spring with a larger and more formidable fleet.

Perry's ultimatum caused turmoil within the Japanese government, and a debate raged in the months that followed over what the appropriate Japanese response should be to this foreign threat. Although some individuals within the Tokugawa government wanted to fight, most of the leadership was painfully aware of the military technology gap. When Perry returned in spring 1854, the Japanese offered no resistance and reluctantly gave in to almost all of the American demands. The Americans and Japanese signed the Treaty of Kanagawa on March 31, 1854, granting the United States access to the ports of Hakodate and Shimoda to provision their ships and providing for the appointment of an American consul at Shimoda. The treaty did not grant the Americans trading rights, however.

Although numerous gifts were exchanged to celebrate the treaty, Japan's leaders were in no real mood to celebrate, and the debate continued over future policy toward the United States and other Western countries. The Americans were not completely happy with the Kanagawa Treaty either, since the right to trade with Japan was not included, and they began

Commodore Matthew Perry, depicted by an unknown nineteenth-century Japanese artist. Perry and his U.S. Navy squadron ended over 200 years of Japanese isolation by sailing into Tokyo Bay in summer 1853. (Library of Congress)

almost immediately to pressure the Japanese for trading concessions. Antiforeign elements, including Emperor Komei and a group of young samurai, urged the government not to grant trading rights to the United States. Nevertheless, in 1858 the Tokugawa government signed a trade treaty despite these strong objections.

The Harris Treaty, named after the American diplomat who negotiated it, did far more than simply open Japan for trade. It placed Japan, for the first time in history, under the partial control of foreign powers as Americans, and later Dutch, Russians, British, and French, obtained not only trading rights but the power to determine the tariff amounts for all imports without consulting the Japanese. Western powers set very low tariffs on the products they attempted to sell in Japan, thereby limiting Japan's ability to control its own economic destiny. Also, the United States and European powers were granted the right of extraterritoriality, which meant that foreign residents were subject to their own rather than Japanese law. The shogunate's decision to acquiesce to foreign demands, although practical considering Japan's military weakness, proved to be a major reason for the overthrow of the Tokugawa government a few years later.

By the mid-1800s the Tokugawa government was in trouble over domestic as well as foreign problems. Although public expenditures exceeded revenues, the government seemed incapable of developing adequate measures to derive more income from the growth sectors of the economy, business and manufacturing. This chronic revenue shortage forced the government to cut back as much as 50 percent the monies paid to samurai. By the latter Tokugawa Period, some samurai were living in such austere circumstances that they were reduced to pawning family armor and even putting babies to death to avoid economic destitution.

Also, as education became more widespread, increasing numbers of people became unhappy with the rigid class system. Many merchants and manufacturers felt discriminated against because even though they might attain great wealth, they were still considered socially inferior to the samurai. Lower-ranking samurai, in turn, were discontented with the system because high-ranking samurai, regardless of their qualifications, were awarded upper-level government positions.

By the 1860s a group of younger samurai and commoners, adopting the slogan *sonno-joi,* "revere the emperor and repel the barbarians," were plotting to use the throne as a symbol in an attempt to overthrow the Tokugawa government. Early in 1868 antigovernment forces took over the shogun's Kyoto palace and induced the fifteen-year-old emperor to issue a decree establishing a new government. Despite Tokugawa resistance, there was little support for the old regime, and in 1868 the revolutionaries forced the government army to surrender, ending two-and-one-half centuries of Tokugawa rule relatively bloodlessly. The new emperor, who from the beginning was a symbol rather than actual leader, took the reign name *Meiji,* or "peace and enlightenment." Meiji has also become the name for the period of Japanese history from 1868 to 1912.

The small group of men who would go on to modernize Japan were unusual in several respects. They were mainly lower-ranking samurai, and many were in their thirties. Despite earlier rhetoric about driving foreigners from Japan, Meiji leaders were pragmatic for the most part and understood the value of Western knowledge. First Japan had to use this knowledge to build a strong military, economy, and political institutions. Then the nation could rid itself of the unequal treaties and assume its own destiny.

The Meiji leaders first had to establish their authority throughout Japan, which meant drastic governmental reform. By 1871 the Meiji government had transformed the old Tokugawa domains into new administrative units called prefectures. During the Tokugawa years, farmers were allowed to pay taxes in rice rather than money, and rates were based on annual harvests instead of land values. This tax system made it impossible for the government to plan expenditures in advance. In 1873 the government solved this problem by requiring that all taxes be paid in money and basing annual collections on land value rather than harvests. Payments to samurai, which were a tremendous burden to the Tokugawa government, were first reduced and eventually terminated in 1876, when the Meiji government converted the payments to interest-bearing nonrenewable bonds. The government in the same year ended the Tokugawa class system by abolishing all samurai privileges.

Economic advancement was also vital if Japan was to become an equal to the West. Western expert Kanda Kohei wrote early in the Meiji years: "The nations that depend upon business are always rich while those that depend on agriculture are always poor. Therefore the Eastern countries are always poor and the Western ones always rich" (Duus 1976, 83). As they began to shape new economic and political institutions, Meiji leaders systematically studied various elements of European economic and political systems. The Meiji government sent a number of representatives abroad to examine institutions and practices ranging from banking to education. For several years the Japanese government also paid foreigners handsome salaries to come to Japan and serve as technical advisers and teachers.

Meiji leaders systematically studied various economic models and made the decision to adopt a Prussian-style state-directed capitalism, where the government plays a significant role in determining what is produced and allocates capital through control of the financial system. The Japanese rejected the Anglo-American *laissez-faire* model in which the market largely determines what products are produced, and banks and the stock market allocate capital.

Remaining Tokugawa internal trade barriers and most export restrictions were abolished as the government encouraged Japanese business to sell rice, copper, and raw silk abroad. In order to build the communications and transportation networks vital to any sophisticated economy, the government engaged in a widespread railroad- and telegraph-building program. Japan's first railroad line, which connected Tokyo and Yokohama, was completed in 1872; by the turn of the century, 5,000 miles of railroad track had been laid. By 1880 all major Japanese cities were linked by telegraph. The government also played a leading role in the construction of factories for textiles, ceramics, cement, and glass as well as mines, shipyards, and arsenals. Later the Meiji government sold factories to private businessmen.

By the late 1880s and early 1890s, Japan's strategy of government-aided business development was beginning to pay off. Tea and silk export profits were providing capital for industrial growth, and textile factories were supplying Japanese needs and earning profits in international markets as well. Even though as late as 1902 only 14 percent of the Japanese workforce was employed in industry, the foundation for a modern economy was firmly in place.

The new government also viewed education as a major priority. Although a variety of schools flourished under the Tokugawas, the Meiji leaders recognized several advantages for Japan in the creation of a national educational system. More educated people were needed for the new factories and government, and a national school system could be used to promote loyalty to the government. In 1872 a national educational system was created and elementary education made compulsory. The government at first allowed Japanese children to leave school after sixteen months, but by 1886 the amount of required time in school was raised to four years. The Meiji government used the highly centralized French system as an administrative model, but in the early years American curricula, textbooks, and teacher training methods were also influential in Japanese elementary schools.

The 1870s witnessed a Western craze of sorts among many Japanese, particularly in the cities, as numbers of urban Japanese began wearing Western clothes and buying diamonds and gold watches. Some Japanese believed that if foreigners could be convinced that the Japanese were becoming "civilized and enlightened," the Western powers could be cajoled into modifying the unequal treaties. Other Japanese even came to believe that the West was a superior civilization compared with Asia, and some pro-Western writers were condescending toward traditional Confucian values and enamored with Western individualism.

The spread of Western ideas had important ramifications for Japanese government and politics. By the 1870s and 1880s intellectuals had read translations of Western political tracts, and support mounted for the initiation of such foreign institutions as popularly elected legislatures and a written constitution. Although the majority of Meiji leaders viewed such democratic sentiments as a threat to their power, the idea of a constitution was attractive to some powerful factions. Those in government who favored a constitution felt the creation and adoption of such a document would give Japan greater status with the West since no Asian country to date had developed one. Other Meiji leaders saw a written constitution as an instrument for promoting national unification and increasing governmental authority.

Japan's leaders were particularly interested in Germany's constitution because that country had only recently undergone unification. One of the original Meiji leaders, Hirobumi Ito, traveled to Germany to study. Upon returning to Japan, Ito wrote a constitution that was implemented by imperial decree in 1889, making Japan the first Asian country to adopt constitutional government. Although the constitution gave some power to factions other than the Meiji oligarchs, it by no means created a democratic Japan. The constitution provided for a bicameral legislative assembly, or *Diet,* with power to enact legislation and debate and approve the annual budget. The House of Peers consisted of appointed members whereas the House of Representatives were elected. However, only 1 percent of the 1890 population, male taxpayers above a set income level, could vote in legislative elections. The cabinet consisted of several of the original architects of the Meiji revolution and was quite powerful—so much so that for many years later, this body determined who would be the Japanese prime minister. The constitution, the national school system, and the creation of a merit-based bureaucracy all contributed greatly to an increase in government power and Japanese unification.

At approximately the same time as the formulation of Japan's constitution, opposition to foreign influences was growing. Conservatives worried that Japan was becoming too much like the West. As in earlier times, Japanese first embraced many foreign ideas and customs and then returned to many traditional values. Government leaders used both Shinto and schools to promote nationalism. Promotion of Confucian teaching and loyalty to emperor and state became a primary educational objective. The emperor was described in the 1890 Imperial Rescript on Education as "being coeval with heaven and earth," and his photograph was placed in every Japanese school. The indoctrination appeared to be working, because as Japan began imperialistic adventures, the government enjoyed enthusiastic support and absolute loyalty from the majority of its citizens.

The Japanese government by the late nineteenth century was following the lead of Western powers and using military force to gain territories and foreign markets. Japan engaged in imperialism for several reasons, including a desire for equality with the West, which in 1894 was partially achieved when Western powers agreed to sign treaties ending extraterritoriality. The Japanese government also wanted more East Asian natural resources and markets and feared that if no action was taken, Western powers would gain control of the tottering Chinese and Korean governments and threaten Japan.

Korea, a country that had been loosely controlled by the Chinese empire, was the major cause of the Meiji government's first foreign war. Because of fear that Korea might be taken over by a stronger Western power, in 1894 Japan went to war in Korea with Korean and then Chinese forces and won a quick victory. In the ensuing 1895 treaty with China, Japan forced China to renounce all claims to Korea, pay a substantial indemnity, relinquish Taiwan, and turn over the Liaotung peninsula in southern Manchuria. Acting quickly, Russia, in league with France and Germany, pressured Japan to give the Liaotung peninsula back to China. The Japanese considered the Western action a humiliation and were even more humiliated when the Russians attained a lease of Liaotung in 1898.

The Japanese now viewed Russia, which had territorial ambitions in Manchuria as well as Korea, as a major threat. In 1904, after negotiations over Korea broke down, Japan engaged Russia in war by a surprise attack on the Russian fleet at Port Arthur. Most military observers thought Russia would easily win the war. However, the experts were proven wrong. The Japanese army won several land victories, and in May 1905 the Japanese fleet under Admiral Togo attracted world attention by defeating the Russian navy in the Straits of Tsushima. Shortly afterward Japan and Russia agreed to allow the United States to act as mediator at peace talks in Portsmouth, New Hampshire. The resulting 1905 treaty secured a number of Russian concessions to Japan, including a lease on Liaotung, the southern half of Sakhalin Island, Russian holdings in Manchuria, and freedom of action in Korea. Japan quickly made Korea a protectorate in 1905, and a colony in 1910.

Both the Japanese government and many Japanese people began to develop two beliefs that would later lead to much trouble. Japanese came to feel that their country had a mission to protect and civilize "backward" Asian nations. Many Japanese also began to believe their military was invincible, a feeling that would help create a climate conducive to a series of unrealistic, and ultimately disastrous, governmental decisions.

In summer 1912 the Meiji Period ended with the emperor's death, which was deeply mourned by most Japanese. The new emperor gave the name *Taisho,* or "Great Righteousness," to the years between 1912 and 1926. The emperor was an obscure ruler who was physically weak and frequently ill. Nevertheless, the times proved to be quite exciting as Japan continued to develop economically, experimented with the expansion of representative government, and became a world actor in geopolitics. Yet Japan had problems in the Taisho years. Economic development, though impressive, was erratic and worked to the advantage of some urban residents while many rural people struggled. Because European powers were preoccupied with World War I, Japan, with a smaller role in the war, began to sell products in Asian countries that had been European markets. However, European partial recapture of those markets after World War I in part contributed to a major Japanese postwar recession. Also, by the 1920s, expansion of heavy industry exhausted Japan's scarce domestic supplies of raw materials such as coal, increasing the necessity for access to cheap raw materials.

The Taisho years were prosperous times for many Japanese, and the standard of living of average Japanese families more than doubled. *Zaibatsu,* or "money cliques," were in large part responsible for economic growth. Since the Meiji Period the government had channeled financial aid to those who were believed to be best able to build a strong national economy. A few powerful families used government assistance and keen business acumen to build economic empires. Four zaibatsu—Mitsui, Mitsubishi, Sumitomo, and Yasuda—controlled a variety of enterprises including banking, manufacturing, mining, and foreign trade concerns. Although the zaibatsu served the government's needs by fueling economic growth, particularly in heavy industries vital for defense, elements of the public became concerned over the great political influence of the zaibatsu and the tremendous concentration of wealth in the hands of a few influential families.

Life for employees in these large industrial concerns became increasingly good during the Taisho years. Some male managers and industrial workers were given the benefits of lifetime employment in exchange for loyalty and service to one large firm. The majority of working women, small enterprise employees, and farmers were largely left out of the Taisho economic good times. Women factory workers in large companies enjoyed no lifetime benefits, and workers in small businesses and industries were subject to low pay in good times and layoffs during bad times. Farmers endured the most problems during this period. Although a few years were good, from the end of World War I until the 1930s there was a long-term drop in crop prices.

Many rural people in particular also felt bewildered and angry at the dizzy social change that seemed to be taking place in Japanese cities. Young people appeared to be giving up Japanese habits and values in favor of Western fads and ideas. Large numbers of people were reading adventure and love-story magazines, listening to radio, flocking to Western and Japanese movies, attending baseball games, listening to jazz music, and wearing Western clothes. The pendulum during the Taisho years seemed to have swung back again in favor of Western over Japanese culture.

Western ideas influenced politics as well during the Taisho years. Even before the twentieth century, political parties developed in Japan, and they continued to grow in influence. By 1918 the premiership was being filled by the head of the leading political party instead of by the choices of Meiji political leaders. From 1918 until 1932, Japan for the most part followed the British parliamentary model, with heads of major parties becoming premier and forming governments. Political parties tended to be corrupt, however, and they constantly made deals with local officials and big business. Some members of the educated public became increasingly dissatisfied with political corruption and in the 1920s began to work for more democratic government. In 1925 Japan appeared to be moving toward democracy when the Diet gave all men the right to vote, regardless of whether they owned property.

Unfortunately, elements from the military and other reactionary groups were powerful enough to stop the apparent movement toward a democratic and open society. The Diet passed the Peace Preservation Law, making it a crime to argue that the present government should be abolished or that private property ownership should be challenged, the same year it approved universal male suffrage. The law was designed to silence the political left, and because of it, a number of people were imprisoned or harassed.

In foreign affairs the Taisho years were marked by internal debate over what course to pursue in regard to imperial expansion and Japan's relations with the Western powers. Japan fought World War I on the side of the Allied powers, and, as a result, acquired German Pacific territories including the Marianna, Caroline, and Marshall Islands, as well as economic rights in Manchuria and China. However, elements of the military, particularly young army officers, wanted more. Even though many civilian politicians opposed the army, another international development, the worldwide Great Depression of the late 1920s and early 1930s, served to weaken the influence of civilian politicians and strengthen the power of the militaristic expansionists. The Japanese economy suffered greatly, and suddenly-impoverished small businessmen and farmers tended to blame the political parties.

Also, many Japanese were bitter toward fellow citizens who wanted Western-style political institutions for reasons that had little to do with economics. To these Japanese the Americans and Europeans were hypocritical when they talked of democracy and equality but practiced racism. At the 1919 Versailles Peace Conference the Japanese tried to convince the other major powers to include a clause on racial equality in the treaty, but they were defeated. In 1924 the U.S. Congress passed an Exclusion Act that made it almost impossible for Japanese to emigrate to the United States. Almost all Japanese, regardless of political viewpoint, considered the American law a terrible insult.

THE ROAD TO WAR

In 1926 the Taisho emperor died, and his son and successor, Hirohito, selected *Showa,* or "Enlightened Peace," as the name for his reign. Events however, would make this choice extremely ironic. By the late 1920s the Japanese army, under no constitutional restrictions, was taking direct action in defiance of civilian government. The flash point was Manchuria, controlled by China but coveted by Japan's army, who viewed it as a source for food and natural resources and wanted a buffer zone against the Soviet Union.

In 1928 young Japanese officers of the Kwantung army stationed in Manchuria bombed a train carrying a Manchurian warlord, and the army did little to bring the perpetrators to justice. Three years later, in 1931, elements of the army precipitated an even more serious international incident in Manchuria. Army officers blew up part of a railway owned by Japan and, claiming local sabotage, overran all of Manchuria. The civilian Tokyo government was helpless in the face of popular support for the army. In January 1932 the army separated Manchuria from China and created the puppet state of Manchukuo. There was world outrage at this action, and in early 1933 the League of Nations issued a report condemning Japanese aggression. Japan responded by withdrawing from the League, thereby further heightening world tensions.

The Manchurian takeover and further incidents involving Japanese army units in China strengthened the will of the Chinese government to resist Japanese expansion. Fighting began on the night of July 7, 1937, with a minor skirmish between Japanese and Chinese troops at the Marco Polo Bridge, and in the months that followed, the fighting

The 63-year reign of the late Emperor Hirohito, pictured here during his enthronement, included military disaster and economic triumph for Japan. (Library of Congress)

The Japanese army was engaged in a major war in China before the bombing of Pearl Harbor. Here, Japanese soldiers are involved in street fighting in Shanghai. (Library of Congress)

blossomed into an undeclared but full-scale war between China and Japan.

The Japanese enjoyed several early victories and in December 1937 captured the Chinese capital of Nanking. In what was to become one of the worst atrocities of the twentieth century, Japanese troops murdered, robbed, and raped hundreds of thousands of civilians in the city. Soon the Japanese army began to encounter stiff Chinese resistance, and although Japan continued to win victories, it could not score the knockout blow to end the war. Japan had become involved in a quagmire in China.

The United States by this time was increasingly using economic weapons in an attempt to get Japan out of China. In summer 1938 the United States placed an embargo on shipments of war material to Japan. In fall 1940, after Japan moved into French Indochina in an attempt to gain vital rubber and oil supplies, the United States ended all scrap iron and steel exports to Japan. Finally, in summer 1941 the U.S. government, in response to further Japanese advances into Indochina, froze all Japanese assets in the United States. At the same time the U.S., British, and Dutch East Indies governments ended oil exports to Japan. Although Japan attempted negotiations with the United States, the oil embargo, which cut off 90 percent of Japan's oil supply, pushed Japan toward a decision to fight the United States.

In late fall 1941, high officials of the Japanese government, in a last attempt to avoid war, proposed to Washington that Japan would withdraw from Indochina if the United States ended the oil embargo and assisted Japan in peace negotiations with China. The U.S. government responded that nothing less than Japanese withdrawal from China, Manchuria, and Indochina would be acceptable. The Japanese government found American demands completely unacceptable because of the belief that if Japan acquiesced, it would become a second-rate nation.

WORLD WAR II AND THE OCCUPATION

On December 7, 1941, Japanese aircraft-carrier-based planes carried out a successful surprise attack on the U.S. Pacific fleet moored in Pearl Harbor, Hawaii. The attack, which sunk or severely damaged nineteen naval vessels and killed over 2,000 U.S. sailors and soldiers, resulted in the United States' declaration of war against Japan on December 8. Many Japanese realized that the decision to attack the American fleet was an extremely bold gamble, since Japan could not match the productive resources of the United States. Japan hoped for a quick war and that victories in the Pacific and the conquest of Europe by Japan's ally, Germany, would pressure the Americans to resort to negotiations to end the war.

The atomic bombing of Hiroshima and Nagasaki forced Japan to sur-
render. This photo of Nagasaki was taken a few days after the bomb
was dropped. (Library of Congress)

The ensuing peace settlement would leave Japan dominant
in Asia.

One reason the Japanese people accepted this foolhardy
strategy was a popular belief that Japan could be a moral
alternative for all of Asia to the materialistic West. The
Japanese government clarified these sentiments early in the
war with the formulation of a plan called the Greater East
Asia Co-Prosperity Sphere. According to the plan, victory
over the United States was only the first objective in attaining the long-range goal of building, under Japanese leadership, a strong and unified Asia and Pacific community. At
first, all went splendidly for Japan, and by spring 1942 Japan
had conquered Singapore, the Dutch East Indies, and the
Philippines. The Japanese also established island bases

throughout the southwestern and central Pacific in such places as Guam, Wake Island, and the Solomon Islands. Japan grossly underestimated American determination and economic might, however, and by May 1942 the tides of war were already beginning to turn. In June 1942 a Japanese attempt to finish the U.S. Pacific fleet for good backfired when Japan lost four valuable aircraft carriers at the battle of Midway. During the rest of the year and throughout 1943 the Americans won islands back from the Japanese.

By summer 1944 U.S. forces captured the island of Saipan, allowing American planes to conduct regular bombing raids on the Japanese home islands. In October 1944 U.S. forces under General Douglas MacArthur began an effort to retake the Philippines by landing at Leyte Gulf. Japan's situation had become desperate. Still the Japanese military fought on and civilians persevered even as American bombing raids on the home islands intensified. In one terrible night alone in March 1945, the fire bombing of Tokyo left 78,000 people dead and 43,480 wounded. By 1945 young Japanese kamikaze, or "divine wind," pilots were engaging in suicide missions against the United States while civilians were training with sharpened spears to resist to the death the expected U.S. invasion of Japan.

At the July 1945 Potsdam Conference, the United States, Great Britain, and the Soviet Union, which was then not yet at war with Japan, reaffirmed their previous demand of unconditional surrender. Japan was threatened with complete destruction if the offer was refused. Just a few days later, on August 6, 1945, the United States dropped the first atomic bomb in wartime upon the Japanese city of Hiroshima, killing almost 100,000 people. Three days later a second U.S. bomb killed over 75,000 people in the city of Nagasaki. By then the Soviet Union had also declared war on Japan and sent troops into Manchuria. The Japanese government, faced with these developments, surrendered. On August 15, 1945, Hirohito addressed the nation by radio for

General Douglas MacArthur masterminded an occupation of Japan that, for the most part, ultimately benefited both Japan and the United States. This photo of MacArthur was taken in 1945 shortly after his arrival in Japan. (Library of Congress)

the first time ever with the news that the war was lost. World War II in the Pacific had resulted in nearly 3 million Japanese deaths.

The years following World War II would bring more change to Japan than any time since the beginning of the Meiji Period. Although theoretically an eleven-nation Far East Commission was responsible for the occupation, the United States under the leadership of General Douglas MacArthur was primarily responsible for what occurred. MacArthur, supreme commander of Allied Pacific forces, was a brilliant, dynamic, charismatic, and eccentric man. The general almost immediately won the respect and admiration of the

Japanese people through his dedication to duty and his regal bearing. Partially because of the influence of MacArthur, and because of a widespread feeling among the Japanese that the militarist course of action had been a disastrous one, the Japanese people were extremely cooperative toward the Americans. The result was that the U.S. occupation ranks as one of the most peaceful and orderly occupations of one country by another country in world history. Even though MacArthur was a life-long conservative Republican, his goals for Japan were liberal. MacArthur and his staff sought nothing less than a democratic and peaceful Japan and initiated sweeping reforms to achieve this goal. The wartime leadership was quickly purged from government. Despite the fact that many Americans wanted the imperial line abolished, MacArthur, after much thought, decided to allow the Japanese to retain their national symbol.

A major event of the occupation was the largely U.S.-written constitution, which went into effect in May 1947 and established a framework for democratic government. The emperor was retained but only as a symbol of state. A British-style parliamentary system and an independent judiciary were established. Universal suffrage for both sexes was guaranteed for the first time in Japanese history. The Japanese constitution also theoretically guaranteed equal rights for both sexes and for the right of labor unions to exist. Article Nine contained a renunciation of war and included the clause "land, sea, and air forces, as well as other war potential, will never be maintained." Americans would have second thoughts about this prohibition, and by 1953 Japan would again have a military.

In addition to bringing about the massive restructuring of the Japanese political system, the U.S. occupation of Japan produced major economic reforms. The zaibatsu were broken up, and the Americans made good their guarantee of labor unions by actively promoting them in the early years of the occupation. The occupation land reform policy brought about even more widespread economic change. Absentee landlordism was prohibited, and farmers could own no more than seven and one-half acres (an exception was allowed in Hokkaido). The land reform policy ended long-standing rural inequities and stimulated agricultural productivity, as that sector was the first to recover.

The Americans were not content with economic and political reform alone but wanted to change Japanese thinking so as to create the appropriate climate for democracy. In 1947 occupation authorities forced the Japanese to change their educational system radically. Japan's schools were modeled after the American six-year elementary school, three-year junior high, and three-year senior high school system. The new curriculum included social studies courses designed to foster democratic thinking. American reformers even attempted to decentralize the Japanese public school system by including locally elected school boards in the education laws.

By the late 1940s, however, the United States was becoming less idealistic about changing Japan. Originally, occupation authorities gave much higher priority to Japanese democratization than to rebuilding Japan's economy. Once the Cold War began, U.S. policymakers began to worry that an economically weakened Japan could very well fall to the communists. By 1948 Americans ceased to encourage labor unions and backed off their attempts to break up large business concerns. The new U.S. thinking was shared by a number of Japanese political leaders, including Yoshida Shigeru, prime minister during most of the occupation years. This shift in U.S. policy, the good fortune of the Japanese to be convenient suppliers of American forces during the 1950–1953 Korean War, and the hard work of the Japanese people paid off. By the early 1950s the Japanese economy was on the way to recovery.

The U.S. occupation officially ended in September 1952, following the signing of a peace treaty in San Francisco the previous year. Although the Japanese later abolished some

American reforms, such as the attempt to decentralize public schools, Japan today, as a democratic and free society,
continues to benefit from the sweeping, outside-initiated
changes of the occupation years.

It should be noted, though, that there is divided opinion
among both American and Japanese scholars on some of the
effects of the U.S. occupation upon Japanese life. There is
substantial evidence that Emperor Hirohito may have had
more to do with promoting Japanese aggression in Asia than
was earlier believed. A number of scholars make the case
that by allowing Hirohito to retain the throne and not to be
tried as a war criminal, the United States set the stage for
Japan as a whole to escape responsibility for what it had
done in Asia. Other critics of the occupation think the
Americans seriously weakened Japanese democratic growth
when in an effort to keep Japan from succumbing to communism, they allowed prewar and wartime bureaucrats back
in government.

UNPARALLELED PROSPERITY
AND NEW CHALLENGES

On February 24, 1989, on a cold, rainy day in Tokyo thousands
of mourners, including political leaders from 163 nations,
attended the funeral service of Emperor Hirohito, marking the
end of his sixty-three-year reign and the accession of his son
Akahito. Hirohito's death was symbolically significant because
it marked the end of a period of Japanese history that included
World War II and the "economic miracle."

Since the occupation, the so-called economic miracle has
been by far the most important development in Japanese history. From 1954 until the 1970s Japan led all nations in
annual economic growth rates. Although economic growth
slowed in the 1970s, Japan continued to have impressive
annual growth rates until the early 1990s. Today Japan is the
world's second-largest economy, and the lifestyle of the typi-

cal Japanese is an affluent one by the standards of any country. Japan's postwar economic boom years carried costs, however. Until the 1970s the government and private business concentrated so much on first rebuilding the nation and later fueling the economic miracle that social concerns such as adequate housing, protection against pollution, and attention to health and old-age related issues were ignored. Also by the 1970s and 1980s many Japanese, particularly male workers, were questioning the worth of sacrificing much of their personal lives to the workplace.

By the early 1990s the economic situation also began to darken, and for the rest of the century Japan endured some serious economic problems, including low productivity growth relative to the past, continuing high consumer prices, postwar record unemployment rates, and extremely high government deficits. There is a general consensus among economists that Japan has structural economic problems, including an overregulated economy, a capital allocation system in need of overhaul, and a now-archaic lifetime employment system in large companies that helps to raise product costs to unacceptable levels. Mustering the political will to make the necessary systemic economic changes, however, is a long and arduous process that the Japanese have only just begun.

The 1990s were a time of political as well as economic turbulence. In 1993 the Liberal Democratic Party (LDP) lost control over the Japanese government for the first time since its inception in 1955. Although the LDP has since returned to power in various coalition governments, Japanese domestic politics have been extremely volatile since the early 1990s. Parliamentary government after government has fallen, reflecting a general voter dissatisfaction with the economic and political status quo. Internationally, with the end of the Cold War, Japan has been groping for its appropriate role in world politics since it is no longer the junior partner of the United States in the struggle against communism.

The 1995 Tokyo subway poison gas attack by members of the Aum Shinrikyo religious cult that killed twelve people was an extreme example of what many Japanese view as mounting social problems in a postwar society that, until recently, has been extremely stable. Less dramatic but still troubling trends that surfaced in the Japan of the 1990s included rising divorce rates and some increases in certain types of crime. Still, both divorce and crime rates are much lower in Japan than in other developed countries.

Despite these problems, postwar Japan rose from defeat in World War II to develop an economy that is still strong, societal support for democratic politics, and a largely trouble-free society when compared with that of most other nations. Since the war Japan has also achieved world leadership peacefully, which is a tremendous compliment to the hard work and resourcefulness of millions of ordinary Japanese.

References
Beasley, W. G. 1999. *The Japanese Experience: A Short History of Japan.* Berkley: University of California Press.
Bester, L. Armorel, ed. 1985. *Understanding Japan 49: A Teacher's and Textbook Writers' Handbook on Japan.* Tokyo: Shobi Printing, Inc.
Buckley, Roger. 1998. *Japan Today,* third edition. Cambridge: Cambridge University Press.
Duus, Peter. 1976. *The Rise of Modern Japan.* Boston: Houghton Mifflin.
Fields, Sherry, ed. 1998. *Tora no Maki III: Lessons for Teaching About Contemporary Japan.* Washington, DC: NCSS Publications.
Harris, William, and Judith Levey, eds. 1975. *The New Columbia Encyclopedia.* New York: Columbia University Press.
Johnson, Marcia, and Linda Wojtan, eds. 1999. *Nippon Nyumon: An Idea Book for Teaching Japanese Economic Topics.* Washington, D.C.: National Council for the Social Studies.
Lincoln, Edward. 1999. *Troubled Times: U.S.-Japan Trade Relations in the 1990s.* Washington, D.C.: The Brookings Institution.
———. 1988. *Japan: Facing Economic Maturity.* Washington, D.C.: The Brookings Institution.
McCargo, Duncan. 2000. *Contemporary Japan.* New York: St. Martin's Press.
Perez, Louis G. 1998. *The History of Japan.* Westport, CT: Greenwood Press.
Pyle, Kenneth. 1978. *The Making of Modern Japan.* Lexington, MA: D.C. Heath.

Reischauer, Edwin O. 1981. *Japan: The Story of a Nation.* New York: Alfred A. Knopf, Inc.

———. 1977. *The Japanese.* Cambridge, MA: Harvard University Press.

Sansom, George. 1964. *A History of Japan to 1334.* Stanford: Stanford University Press.

Schirokauer, Conrad. 1989. *A Brief History of Chinese and Japanese Civilizations.* New York: Harcourt, Brace, and Company.

Stanley-Baker, Joan. 1984. *Japanese Art.* New York: Thames and Hudson.

Tashiro, Masami. ed. 2000. *Japan 2001: An International Comparison.* Tokyo: Kezai Koho Center.

Totman, Conrad. 1982. *Japan Before Perry.* Berkley: University of California Press.

"Typhoon!" 1959. *Life.* Issue 47. October 12, 1959.

Varley, Paul. 1973. *Japanese Culture: A Short History.* New York: Praeger, Inc.

Yamamoto, Tsunetomo. 1983. *Hagakure: The Book of the Samurai.* New York: Kodansha.

Young, Arthur Morgan. 1929. *Japan in Recent Times: 1912–1926.* New York: W. Morrow Company.

CHAPTER TWO
Japan's Economy

Despite over a decade of business and financial malaise, Japan remains one of the world's biggest post–World War II economic success stories. Japan is still the world's second-largest economy. Currently, Japan's economy is roughly seven times the size of China, and the Japanese produce 70 percent of all goods and services in East Asia. What factors accounted for Japan's dramatic latter-twentieth-century rise from marginally affluent nation to an economic superpower? Why has the Japanese economy subsequently, despite some bright spots, stagnated through the 1990s and beyond? What does the future likely hold for the archipelago's economic fortunes?

THE ROOTS OF SUCCESS

Even though Japan's spectacular economic rise did not occur until the three decades after World War II, the foundations for the so-called economic miracle were laid during the Tokugawa era. Though Tokugawa Japan was technologically backward compared with the West, when Commodore Perry and his fleet arrived, Japan was certainly no primitive economy. In the height of the Tokugawa era various kinds of businesses were flourishing, particularly in urban areas, and the use of money was widespread. By the 1850s larger percentages of Japanese were literate than was the case in most of the world's countries. The Japan that Perry visited contained an economic base for future commercial and industrial expansion, and a segment of the population well educated enough to make good use of new Western technology.

Furthermore, an economic condition was present in Tokugawa Japan that is absolutely imperative in any society if widespread economic modernization is to take place: Increasing numbers of farmers were not only engaged in subsistence agriculture but were producing crop surpluses as well. As a result, crop reserves could be sold for cash, and thus capital for business investment accrued. Because of this surplus cash due to profits from commercial agriculture, small-business growth rates were high in Tokugawa Japan.

Noneconomic aspects of Tokugawa society also helped created a good environment for economic prosperity. Because of a common language and history, the Japanese possessed a relatively high degree of national unity. Also the Tokugawa government managed to keep the peace within Japan for over 250 years, an achievement that almost always contributes to stable economic growth.

Although by the latter Tokugawa years these favorable conditions for economic modernization existed, Japan did not really begin that process until after the Meiji Restoration. In our examination of modern Japanese history we learned of the Meiji government tax reforms and comprehensive efforts to enhance the economy, including educational improvements, export promotion, importation of foreign technology, the development of factories, and encouragement of private business. Meiji Japan's successes in exporting and industrialization were particularly important because these actions helped to cause even greater economic success in the early twentieth century.

Luck was also a factor in the beginning of Japan's economic takeoff. The Japanese were extremely fortunate in the early Meiji years in that raw silk, a large peasant industry, enjoyed high worldwide demand. This demand, partially due to a disastrous European silk blight, subsequently enabled Japan to export massive amounts of silk and thereby raise the money to import equipment and raw materials for industrialization.

To aid industry, the Meiji government quickly established a national currency and banking system, which in turn greatly

Thanks to government leadership and dynamic private sector activity, by the first decade of the twentieth century Japan's cities were modernizing as may be observed in this Tokyo street scene. (Library of Congress)

facilitated the flow of savings to private industry. Meiji leaders were highly successful in establishing a national communications and transportation infrastructure. The government began large-scale economic enterprises such as coal mining and shipbuilding, which were later sold to private business.

As the twentieth century began, although the Japanese government continued its policies of economic assistance, private industry became increasingly important. World War I was a tremendous boon for the Japanese economy. Exports quadrupled and important heavy industries such as shipbuilding, and iron and steel, although still minor compared with textiles and agriculture, became substantial parts of the economy.

By the beginning of the twentieth century Japan already had developed mammoth industrial plants such as this Mitsui silk factory. (Library of Congress)

The 1920s and 1930s brought continued long-term growth in Japanese manufacturing despite major economic difficulties. In 1935 industrial production became, for the first time, more financially valuable to the total economy than agriculture. Although textiles remained Japan's leading industry, accounting for approximately half of all exports in 1920 and 1930, heavy industry grew rapidly. By 1937, thanks to the expansion of shipbuilding, Japan possessed the world's largest merchant marine fleet. In the same year, largely because of the military build-up, total heavy industrial production for the first time surpassed light industry in value.

There were great advancements also in the educational levels of the general populace in the early twentieth century as increasing numbers of Japanese moved from agricultural to industrial employment. Also, by the 1930s a few large Japanese companies were beginning to grant workers permanent employment, good pay, and health and welfare benefits.

As was true in Meiji times, representatives of Japanese government and business experienced extensive cooperative ventures during the early part of the twentieth century. As the Japanese empire expanded into Manchuria in the 1930s, government bureaucrats and private company employees gained experience in joint economic planning and even in successful foreign investment.

Although Japan incurred a tremendous human and economic cost because of World War II, it is important to understand that this catastrophe could not erase the human know-how in industrial production, management-labor relations, and government and business economic development that had been growing in Japan for decades. The cumulative knowledge of the Japanese people in these areas would prove to be of vital importance as Japan struggled to rebound from the worst disaster in the nation's history.

THE MAKING OF THE ECONOMIC MIRACLE

Despite the experience and knowledge of its people, Japan was a devastated nation at the end of World War II. Millions of Japanese were without the basic necessities of life. Approximately one-fourth of all Japanese homes, as well as a high proportion of factories and shops, had been destroyed by the war. Japan was also stripped of its entire empire,

This occupation-era scene, where reconstruction of devastated build-ings is planned, occurred throughout Japan for a decade after World War II. (Library of Congress)

which had been a vital source of low-cost raw materials, and of its investments in China and Manchuria.

Yet Japan, beginning just a few years later in the early 1950s, would grow its economy at an annual rate of approximately 10 percent for almost twenty years. By 1957 Japan's recovery from World War II was complete. Foreigners who came to Japan for the 1964 Tokyo Olympics returned to their respective countries with stories of the economic vitality of the Japanese. By the 1970s these long-term Japanese economic growth rates were commonly being referred to as "an economic miracle." Even though in the early 1970s the Arab oil shocks and other factors ended Japan's whirlwind growth, the Japanese would still lead advanced nations in economic growth until the 1990s.

Though the world took note and economists marveled as Japan led all nations again and again in economic growth rates during these decades, perhaps the best way to really understand the significance of the "miracle" for millions of ordinary Japanese is to examine the fortunes of one real-life Japanese person and his company in the years immediately before and during the high growth era.

Tanaka Sanosuke was born into a peasant family on a tiny farm near Tokyo in 1915. The Tanaka family lived an extremely hard life. Both parents and the children over eleven years of age worked long hours in the rice paddies but were forced to give up four-fifths of their annual crops to the landowner. The family lived in a tiny one-room thatch-roofed hut and usually had only rice mixed with millet to eat. When times were good—and they rarely were—the family could replace the hard millet with vegetables. On rare occasions the Tanakas ate fish, but they could never afford meat.

The village of 500 where the Tanakas lived was almost entirely cut off from the outside world. As was true with most Japanese in the early and mid-twentieth century, the villagers owned no radios to keep up with the news or cars to visit other parts of Japan. In fact, young Sanosuke was eight years old before he saw his first gas-driven vehicle, a bus.

Although Sanosuke dreamed of an education, his poverty made this impossible. After completing the eighth grade and delivering coal for a small business in a neighboring village, in 1937 he moved to Yokohama and was hired as an assembly worker by Nissan, a new company that was part of a very small Japanese automotive industry. Although Sanosuke's pay was modest, in those years he earned almost as much in a month with Nissan than he made in a whole year working in an earlier job. He was able to purchase something no one in his family had ever dreamed of owning before: a new suit.

Eleven years later, upon returning to Japan from military service during World War II and going back to work at Nissan, Sanosuke's life seemed worse than before the war. For several years this now-father of two children could not even buy enough food to keep his family alive and was forced to go to the countryside and forage for edibles. On Sundays in the months immediately following the war, Sanosuke spent his only weekly full day off from work hanging around American occupation troops, hoping to get work as a day laborer or at least scrounge scraps of food the rich Americans threw away. Then the "miracle" years began.

By 1954 Nissan profits and salaries had risen enough that Sanosuke was able to purchase a small, three-room house. It was a proud day for all five members of the Tanaka family when they could move out of their one-room house into these larger quarters. By the mid-1950s Nissan and many other Japanese companies were already rebounding from the effects of World War II and actually exceeding prewar production levels.

Sanosuke's personal standard of living continued to improve as the years passed. In 1957 he bought a television set. In 1963 he became a real member of the Japanese middle class with a purchase of the ultimate status symbol: his first car.

The great gains in wealth that Sanosuke and many other Japanese enjoyed in the 1950s and 1960s did not come easily. The nation paid an incredible price in human effort, first to rebuild Japan and then to take the economy to undreamed heights. In Sanosuke's company, Nissan, for example, each year it seemed the workers put in more and more effort to meet increasing consumer demand.

For a while car and truck production increases from one year to the next staggered the imagination. In 1957 Sanosuke and his coworkers celebrated when the company reached the stage where 5,000 cars and trucks a month were produced. Almost no Nissan workers even dreamed at that time that only three years later the monthly production figures would double to 10,000. Nissan was only one of many companies where people worked incredibly long hours and, by the early

To the Japanese the 1964 Olympics were much more than just games—they were a symbol that the economy had recovered from World War II. People from all over the world were impressed with the new Olympic facilities built in the Yoyogi district of Tokyo, which are still used today. (Library of Congress)

1960s, were somewhat awestruck at the fruits of their labor. Japan had arrived as an economic power.

What were the reasons why Tanaka Sanosuke and millions of others like him experienced dramatically positive improvements in their material well-being during the two decades of the economic miracle? Economists concur that Japan's postwar economic rise can be attributed to a number of factors.

After World War II, with its repudiation of militarism, the Japanese government made economic development the number-one national priority and continued its policy of state-assisted capitalism. The Japanese government attempted to identify potential blue-chip industries and subsidize them while discouraging foreign and even domestic competition. Although the government practice of picking industrial "winners" and aiding them had mixed results, a number of industries, such as automobiles and electronics, greatly benefited from government-imposed tariffs and informal trade barriers that kept foreign competitors out of the Japanese market.

The U.S. occupation of Japan was also, on the whole, extremely beneficial to eventual economic growth. Although the Americans initiated no Marshall Plan in Japan, occupation advisers strongly encouraged the Japanese government to initiate anti-inflation and prosavings policies in the late 1940s that stabilized the nation's currency and helped build a pool of capital for business expansion. The famous Article Nine of the U.S.-imposed constitution forbidding the establishment of armed forces has resulted in long-term, if originally unintended, economic benefits. Because of this constitutional provision, although Japan today has a large defensive armed force, the nation still spends a very low percentage of national wealth on defense compared to other nations. Therefore, these resources are free to be utilized in ways that benefit the civilian economy.

The United States, as recounted in the preceding chapter, also unintentionally helped the Japanese economy by becoming involved in the Korean War. The 1950–1953 conflict brought massive U.S. orders for Japanese goods. Another U.S. postwar international position, that of supporter of free trade, helped the Japanese economy substantially. After World War II, the United States, because of both belief and self-interest, aggressively promoted worldwide free trade. Free-trade policies helped to create a favorable situation for Japanese exports, especially in the United States, but in other nations as well.

There was also a shift in focus in the Japanese economy

from more resource-dependent to less-dependent industries that played a part in the postwar economic takeoff. Before the 1950s several leading Japanese industries, epitomized by textiles, were heavily dependent upon expensive raw materials purchased from abroad. By the latter part of the same decade, the Japanese were producing goods such as cars and radios that required fewer imports. Even though Japan's economic miracle was not export-led and the country did not begin substantial exporting until the 1960s, when the export boom did occur in Japan it made a strong economy even stronger.

As is the case with any national economic success story, capital, both human and financial, played a major role in Japan's economic rise. Economists use the term "human capital" in reference to the skill levels of the labor force. As late as 1950, with half the population still living on farms and relatively uneducated, Japan did not have an overly abundant supply of workers with high levels of human capital. Japan's dramatic postwar expansion of educational opportunities at all levels greatly increased the nation's supply of well-trained workers. New educational opportunities, coupled with a high birth rate and the mechanization of agriculture, meant that through most of the miracle years employers had the enviable situation of having a large supply of young, well-educated rural high school or junior high graduates who were no longer needed on farms and who desired industrial employment. Japan's booming industries were also aided by the population's high personal saving rates. All through the miracle years Japanese industrialists were able to obtain massive amounts of funds for expansion very cheaply.

Cultural and structural aspects of Japan's postwar workplace environments also contributed to the country's' astounding business and economic success. Japan has industrial rather than craft labor unions, which means management negotiates with one labor union rather than several. This form of union system both encourages efficient use of

One of the costs of rapid economic growth has been tremendous congestion in the many cities of Eastern Honshu. This crowded Tokyo subway is a typical part of the lives of urban Japanese. (Courtesy of Lucien Ellington)

management and labor time and facilitates clearer communication between management and labor.

The so-called lifetime employment system also contributed to the "miracle." Despite Western misconceptions, only approximately one-quarter of Japanese private sector employees have enjoyed guaranteed jobs during the postwar years. Formal permanent employment has been largely a male privilege, and those employees who have it almost all work in leading Japanese companies such as Hitachi, Toyota, and Sony. Until recently, large Japanese companies have been assured of long-term, extremely loyal, and highly productive workforces because of "lifetime" employment practices. Whether one enjoys so-called lifetime employment or not in Japan, employers in companies of all sizes have been much more reluctant to lay off workers than is the case with their counterparts in many other countries. This Japanese reluctance to downsize in hard economic times has deep cultural roots in that such action is viewed as a serious threat to societal harmony.

Even in the case of employees without guaranteed jobs, both Japanese businesses and the nation as a whole go to great lengths by the standards of many other countries to make new employees feel important and part of something larger than themselves. On April 1 of each year all over Japan, induction ceremonies for employees entering new firms are conducted with much fanfare. This account of a recent induction ceremony at Nippon Electronic Corporation (NEC) is typical of what occurs in, at least, large and medium firms: The "entering the company" ceremony, or *Nyu Sha Shiki,* for 1,400 recently hired young people is about to begin. Many Japanese consider such a ceremony as this one to be a profound moment for the individuals honored, the company, and society. There is the attendant feeling that if group harmony and teamwork are to be promoted, young employees must be celebrated by this ritual.

All the new inductees were required to be present at 8:25 A.M. before the ceremony, and roll is taken. The ceremony begins promptly at 9:00 A.M. with new inductees and assembled corporate dignitaries singing the company song accompanied by the corporate band. After speeches by corporate officials including the president, each new member reaches under his or her seat and opens a packet that contains business cards, a corporate lapel badge, and a 520-page textbook containing all kinds of information about the company, company expectations, and suggestions for employees. Then a young new female inductee, chosen to represent the entering class, comes forward and recites the new company member pledge, which is a promise to improve the daily lives of people with electronics and communication. Finally the president of the company leads the entire assembly in the company oath.

Medium and especially large Japanese companies also promote hard work, loyalty, and team work among employees by providing what amounts to a corporate welfare system for many of their workers. For example, NEC employees can look forward to annual salary increases based upon seniority. Single workers can live in the company dormitory for a rent that is 90 percent less than market rates. Employees qualify for health insurance, can vacation at NEC resorts, play on NEC sports teams, join the company union, and obtain special benefit accounts at Sumitomo Bank because NEC is a member of that bank's business group.

Particularly within large Japanese companies, specific management practices positively affected employee productivity and economic growth. In large Japanese corporations there is usually much less distinction between managers and workers than in companies in other nations. In many Japanese companies it is difficult to visually differentiate managers from workers, because everyone wears the same work clothes. Typically, Japanese executives do not have separate offices, eat in different cafeterias, or have special reserved parking places, as is true in many Western companies.

Also in Japan the difference between salaries of college-educated executives and assembly-line workers with the same experience is usually much less than in the United States. Researchers who studied chief executive pay levels at the end of the 1990s found that the average American CEO makes 157 times as much as the average factory worker with similar years of experience. In Japan the average CEO earns a little less than 30 times more than what a factory worker with the same years of experience is likely to earn. Japanese consider American salary differentials such as the example cited here to be very dangerous for company morale.

Usually Japanese assembly-line workers are much more active in company decisionmaking than are workers in other countries. In the late 1940s and early 1950s Edwards Deming, an American statistician and college professor, after unsuccessfully attempting to convince American corporate managers to involve assembly workers in production decisions, traveled to Japan for a series of lectures. A number of large Japanese companies quickly adopted quality control circles, a major idea of Deming. Quality control circles are groups of six to twelve workers in the same assembly section who meet regularly to identify, discuss, and pass on to management possible innovations for improvement of efficiency and product quality.

Today the Japanese have made Edwards Deming and quality control circles famous all over the world. Many large Japanese companies consistently produce fine products because millions of ordinary workers in quality control circles formulate useful suggestions on how to improve work processes or product quality, and these are adopted by management. In Toyota Motor Corporation alone in a recent year employees turned in 1.9 million suggestions, or an average of 39 per employee. Ninety-five percent of the suggestions were adopted by the company.

Japan's climb to world economic leadership was also greatly abetted by the domestic and foreign postwar political situation. Since its inception in 1955, with two exceptions, the pro-big business Liberal Democratic Party has elected all of Japan's prime ministers. During most of the postwar period the Japanese have enjoyed a stable domestic political situation with a party in leadership that unquestionably ranks economic development as the major national goal. U.S. involvement in the Cold War also indirectly benefited the Japanese economy. U.S. government officials considered Japan, with its close proximity to China, the Korean Peninsula, and the then Soviet Union, to be so strategically important that it largely ignored questionable Japanese trade policies in return for absolute loyalty in the long superpower confrontation. Therefore Japan was able to exclude many foreign products while selling its own products in other countries without garnering extensive foreign, especially American, criticism.

Despite Japan's good fortune and beneficial government

policy, the economic miracle would not have occurred without the incredible hard work of Japanese of all walks of life and the fierce competitiveness and entrepreneurship of business people. During all but a few of the postwar years, Japanese workers have led the world in annual number of hours worked. Successful Japanese corporate leaders have been fiercely competitive at home and abroad, pursuing economic success with extremely high levels of dedication. Perhaps the late Honda Soichiro, Honda Motor Company founder, best expressed the human spirit that made Japan the economy it is today when he made this statement at the time he established his company: "If my company becomes bankrupt because of the rate at which I expand my plant, the plant itself will remain to be used for the development of Japanese industry. So I will take the risk" (Allen 1981, 234).

Even though Japan's world-breaking economic success of the miracle years dramatically improved the lives of most Japanese, economic and social problems were created by rapid growth. Although the rest of the world knew of the resounding accomplishments of Toyota, Sony, and Hitachi, millions of Japanese did not enjoy the high wages or benefits, or the job security accrued by employees of these and other large companies. Overall, conditions in Japanese small companies were, and are, so much less desirable than life in major corporations that economists still use the terms *two-tiered* and *dual economy* when describing this phenomena. Japan's social security and pension systems are more modest than many Western countries, so life upon retirement is particularly hard for workers in lower-tier small businesses. Also, many of the small Japanese companies, particularly wholesalers and retailers, are extremely inefficient and are one factor in the high consumer prices that all Japanese pay when compared to consumers in other developed countries.

Women certainly did not share the full benefits of the Japanese economic miracle, at least not from the perspective of having anywhere near equal job and compensation opportunities. Until the late 1970s it was not considered respectable for most middle-class women to even work outside the home. Those women in the lower classes who did work enjoyed virtually none of the benefits their male counterparts received. By the 1980s attitudes had changed and work became acceptable for middle-class women. However, a majority of women are still classified as part-time workers and receive lower pay and greatly reduced benefits than full-time employees, even though "part-time" in Japan often means six or seven hours of daily work.

The rapid growth years brought tremendous social costs as well. Japan's business and political leaders were so obsessed with economic growth that mounting environmental problems were ignored. The result was that air pollution in Tokyo reached dangerously unacceptable levels by the 1960s. Air quality in the capital city became so bad that the city was unsafe for people with chronic respiratory diseases. Families feared for the health of their young children. The most concentrated Japanese industrial areas on the Pacific Coast became extremely ugly. People died and deformed babies were born in Kyushu as a result of ingestion of fish contaminated by methyl mercury from a nearby fertilizer plant. By the 1970s, however, the Japanese government significantly increased both antipollution expenditures and regulations. Today Japan's air and water quality are much improved and comparable to that of other developed countries. Still, given Japan's natural beauty, visual pollution is even more of a problem than in the miracle years because an extraordinarily large number of constant and often unneeded public works projects continue to be funded.

Many Japanese felt that something intangible was lost during the miracle years, a sense that there were more important values than making money and acquiring goods. It is only natural that a country impoverished by war would celebrate affluence, but to many social critics, most Japanese, particularly young people, seemed to excessively focus on things material. This societal concern continues today and is reflected in public debate over whether contemporary Japanese lack spiritual values and even in how education should be reformed.

THE END OF THE MIRACLE: THE BUBBLE BURSTS

Even though the "miracle" ended with the Arab oil shocks of the 1970s and ensuing rising energy prices, Japan continued to exhibit very impressive growth rates for a developed country all through the 1970s and 1980s. By the 1980s Japan had become second only to Great Britain as a foreign investor in the United States. Japan also had risen to trail only Canada as a U.S. trading partner. The United States was the leading foreign investor in Japan, making the United States–Japan economic relationship perhaps the most important bilateral business and financial relationship in the world. Americans were consuming enormous amounts of high-profile–Japanese-produced goods, such as automobiles and stereos.

By the 1980s, even though all foreign ownership of the U.S. economy totaled less than 10 percent of the gross domestic product, many Americans took seriously the absurd notion that the Japanese were going to take over the U.S. economy. This sentiment represented part of an increasingly negative reaction to Japan in both the United States and Europe. Even though the Japanese economy was doing well in the 1980s, it faced continuing hostile political reactions from its major trading partners. Memories of World War II undoubtedly played a part in these reactions, as did, quite possibly, racism. Still, research indicated that the perception that the Japanese were less than fair players in international trade had some factual basis.

The findings from impartial economic analyses in the 1970s and 1980s clearly indicated that the Japanese market was much less open to foreign firms and imports than was the case in other industrial nations and even in comparison with many developing nations. Although the Japanese sold goods and services all over the globe and became a major world investor, it was extremely difficult for foreigners to penetrate Japanese markets, particularly if they sold manufactured goods that might prove to be competitive with Japanese firms. Even though the Japanese lowered their formal tariffs, so-called informal trade barriers, ranging from environmental to consumer protection to peculiar product standards and testing regulations, managed to prevent the volumes of available foreign goods and services one might expect in a country as affluent as Japan. Several economic analysts went on to make strong cases that the Japanese government either tolerated or encouraged the industrial collusion that often was behind this wide array of regulations.

Some of the regulations written by government officials to keep foreign products out certainly bordered on the ridiculous. Metal baseball bats were excluded from Japanese stores on the grounds that they weren't as safe as wooden bats. One Japanese bureaucrat even had the audacity to suggest that foreign snow skis could not be sold in Japan because Japanese snow was different than European and American snow. Although these regulations have since been changed, the staggering amount of regulations concerning foreign products, and the waning of the Cold War, stimulated the Reagan, Bush, and Clinton administrations to pressure the Japanese to modify their behavior through various rounds of systematic trade negotiations. Although recently it has become easier for foreigners to sell goods and services in Japan, and much easier for foreign firms to invest, almost all economists think the Japanese have much work still to do in deregulating and opening markets.

Because the major developed economies were incurring merchandise trade deficits with Japan in the 1980s, they pressured the Japanese not only to open their markets but also to raise the value of the yen, which had been artificially low for some time. The Americans and Europeans hoped that a higher yen would help their trade deficits by making foreign exports to Japan cheaper, and Japanese imports more expensive. In 1985 the other so-called G-7 (Group of Seven) major industrialized nations insisted that fellow member Japan agree to policies that would raise the value of the yen. The Plaza Accords sent the yen soaring and reduced Japan's opportunity for further economic growth through running trade surpluses.

The Japanese government responded a short time later by lowering interest rates and substantially increasing the money supply in order to prevent the value of the yen from rising so high as to inhibit exports. This action led to an economic bubble that caused rapid and astronomical rises in the prices of stocks and real estate. By 1990 the bubble burst and Japan's stock market quickly lost about half its former value. Japanese real estate, which had risen to four times the value of real estate in the United States, also plummeted in value. Japan's banks were left with an unspecified but staggering amount of bad loans.

Despite repeated numerous government spending programs in the 1990s in an effort to "prime the pump," Japan has yet—as of the publication of this book—to fully recover from the bursting of the bubble. Unemployment rates remain among the highest in the postwar period, and general consumer and business confidence is still shaky relative to the past—even more than ten years since the bubble burst. Although the bursting of the bubble was the event that began this period of economic malaise, deeper long-term structural problems within the Japanese economy are responsible for the relative stagnation of recent years.

Japan is one of the world's most powerful economies and is far from economic collapse. Still, economic circumstances in the last decade of the twentieth century and the beginning of the twenty-first century have changed dramatically, and Japan's top-down, substantially government-controlled capitalism has been too inflexible to meet the new challenges. Although major international Japanese companies such as Sony and Toyota continue to do well, most economists argue it is despite the Japanese system, not because of it. Meanwhile, too many sectors of the Japanese economy have lost economic ground since 1990.

During the miracle years through the end of the 1980s, Japan had few economic competitors in Europe and the United States and virtually none in Asia. As described earlier, the United States government considered Japan so valuable an ally in the Cold War that it could tolerate Japan's inroads into a few American markets, such as electronics, steel, and autos. Also, during the period of most dramatic Japanese economic growth, the microcomputer and communication revolutions were yet to occur. Business decisionmaking time horizons were slower, which meant that government and business could be deliberate in strategy consultations without overly worrying about what plans domestic or foreign competitors might be enacting.

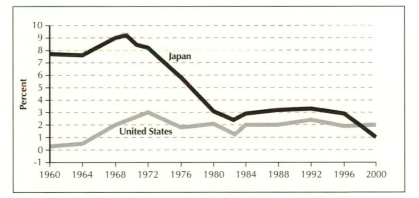

Figure 2.1: Average Annual Growth of Real GDP Per Capita over Preceding 10 Years in Japan and the United States, 1960–1999

Even though the U.S. gross national product is considerably larger than Japan's, the Japanese experienced bigger annual growth rates than the United States from 1960 until the late 1990s. Then Japan's lingering economic problems ended this trend.

Source: Management and Coordination Agency and Department of Commerce

The economic situation changed drastically in the 1980s and 1990s. By the end of the 1980s Japan had more competition in Europe than previously and faced serious competition in other parts of Asia, such as South Korea, Taiwan, Singapore, and even newly industrialized countries such as Thailand. With the end of the Cold War the United States placed even more emphasis on economic goals than in the past and began to pay more attention to Japanese market access issues.

Also, because the United States was the first county in the world to significantly employ microcomputers in business and industry, the U.S. recession of the early 1990s resulted in U.S. corporate downsizing and widespread adoption of microcomputers. This once again made many U.S. companies lean, efficient, and extremely formidable competitors. Japan's companies had not undergone such a productivity-enhancing process. The largest fundamental general problem with the Japanese economy in these new economic times is this: Japan's system is still centralized and regulation-laden whereas other nations' economies have moved toward decentralization and deregulation in response to the technology revolutions and increasing domestic and global competition.

Japanese top-down capitalism, with its myriad regulations and cartels for specific sectors of the economy, makes it difficult for companies to respond to their foreign competitors. It also keeps foreign imports from Japanese shelves, thereby raising domestic prices, and often even stifles domestic competition by keeping start-up Japanese firms out of a particular market.

Examples of government control permeate the economy. If a bank wants to establish a branch bank in a small town, it must suffer through an arduous process with the Ministry of Finance in Tokyo. In chemicals, the government controls production levels for all firms. In detergents, the government protects domestic firms from foreign competition, leaving two companies to control the market. In the extremely important glass industry, flat glass is almost completely dominated by a government-sanctioned three-company cartel. For three decades each Japanese company has controlled virtually the same respective shares of the flat glass market, and foreign share of the Japanese market is about 3 percent—despite the fact that glass prices are higher in Japan than elsewhere. Most of the domestic food processing industry, one of Japan's least successful industries by world standards, has been protected by government from foreign competition.

Largely because of government protection and discouragement of imports, only 7 percent of the processed food Japanese consumers buy comes from foreign sources. Competition in the food industry is stagnant, and low foreign imports and investment in food products means little pressure on the domestic industry. Government regulation protects inefficiency in the food-processing industry by tariffs and other anticompetitive controls. For example, tariffs on flour range, depending upon its use, from 12 percent to 160 percent above the actual price of flour. Another example is milk procurement in school lunch programs, which is under a government-imposed lack of competitive bidding. The Japanese government engages in these practices to protect not only domestic food-related industries but to benefit farmers as well. As a result, Japanese consumers spend 20 percent of their income on food, which is twice that of American consumers.

The kinds of government controls and policies in the food industry extend to many consumer products and services in Japan. These controls have contributed to the extremely high prices both consumers and many firms pay relative to citizens and companies in other developed nations. Japanese citizens pay about one-third more on average for everything than do their American counterparts. It is quite common for Japanese to go on shopping trips abroad to take advantage of lower prices. Regulations and other forms of government controls are a major reason Japanese firms now have, on average, the world's highest costs.

Productivity, the amount of output per unit of input—for example, output per labor hour—is the most important key to any nation's continued economic well-being. During the miracle years the Japanese enjoyed, along with the then West Germans, the highest annual productivity growth rates in the world. Although the United States remained the world's most productive country, by the 1980s Japan had risen to second. Now in the twenty-first century, Japan has dropped to fifth, behind the United States, France, Italy, and Germany.

Japan's economy could improve significantly if the Japanese could return to the impressive productivity growth rates they enjoyed a few years ago. The pressure of competition is vital to improving productivity. Although firms don't like it, when they are in a competitive industry, the incentive is to always improve productivity and efficiency, and the economy as a whole benefits. The most productive Japanese companies by far are the large multinational corporations, which must constantly compete in the global marketplace. One recent study indicates that Japanese manufacturers that compete internationally are 20 percent more productive than their U.S. counterparts. However, findings from the same study indicate that due to government regulation and sanctioned cartels within Japan, the intense competition that serves to stimulate firms to be more productive is absent from many areas of the domestic Japanese economy. Japanese manufacturing and service firms that are domestically oriented are only 63 percent as efficient as are U.S. firms.

Economists can measure both the productivity of labor and capital. Economy-wide, Japanese labor is 31 percent less productive than U.S. labor, and Japanese capital is 39 percent less productive than is the case in the United States.

The major drag on Japanese productivity is the continued existence of the dual, or two-tiered, economy. Japan is unique among the world's developed nations in that there is such a wide discrepancy between the high productivity levels of large industries that export and the low productivity of, usually, smaller industries that sell only to the domestic market. The electrical machinery and food-processing industries are good examples of this contrast. The electrical machinery industry managed to produce 60 percent more output during 1991–1997 than in the previous decade, with 7 percent fewer employees. By comparison, the food-processing industry, which employs more workers than auto and steel combined in Japan, could only manage 35 percent of the productivity levels of U.S. food-processing firms.

The Japanese automobile and single-family home construction industries offer another good illustration of the problem of low productivity in the second tier of the economy when compared to a leading industry. Japanese auto companies have similar productivity levels as U.S. firms, but the Japanese single-family home construction industry is 33 percent as productive as its U.S. counterpart. Due to lack of standardization in home construction and poor timetables, Japanese crews must often be tripled in the last two weeks of a job.

If reform occurred and government-imposed cartels, controls, and blockage of foreign competition and investment were eliminated in the currently inefficient industries, several effects would be noted. The most negative is that jobs would be eliminated in food processing and home construction as well as retailing and wholesaling. However, the companies that did provide these goods and services would be forced by increased competition to become much more productive. Output would increase, and consumer prices would fall. Japanese consumers would realize such savings from these more productive producers and providers that their disposable income would significantly increase. In turn, consumers would spend money for additional goods and services, causing many more jobs to be created in other sectors of the economy. One economic study indicates that if anticompetitive policies were eliminated in food processing, construction, and retailing, a half-million people would become unemployed, but 1 million jobs would be created in health care, where there is now more demand for services.

Large Japanese companies are only beginning to restructure companies to make them more efficient because of the strong societal and governmental pressure to retain lifetime employment and worker seniority. Currently, paying the salaries of surplus workers is another reason for the high costs Japanese firms incur compared to businesses in other developed countries. Estimates of even some of Japan's most successful companies indicate that top management reports the number of surplus workers range from 5 percent to almost 20 percent.

As small business booms in the "new economy" in many countries, start-ups are much more difficult for small-firm entrepreneurs in Japan. Japan's largely government-directed banking system may have greatly assisted certain large businesses to obtain capital in the past, but small firms often have difficulty obtaining funds because they lack political clout. The fact that political connections rather than business plans have traditionally influenced the loans that financial institutions make is a major reason Japan has an enormous amount of bad loans that also hurt capital flows.

Many analysts believe the U.S. economy has recently not just been doing well but has basically been reinvented to the point that the term *new economy* is an appropriate description. Although all capitalist economies are constantly changing, many attribute the significant recent U.S. productivity growth at least partially to the digital revolution. Computers both enable new goods to be produced and reduce product provision costs. The evidence is that Japan has not benefited nearly as much from the digital revolution as has the United States.

For example, Internet commerce in Japan is no more than one-fifth as large a part of the economy as in the United States. In the United States many consumers use the World Wide Web to buy goods because of both convenience and price. One Japanese Ministry of International Trade and Industry Survey in 2000 indicated that goods prices on the Web were 46 percent higher for Japanese consumers than for their American counterparts.

Even the process of Internet access in Japan remains much more of a problem than in the United States and Canada. One recent comparative calculation of Internet access at peak times indicated that it was 46.5 percent more expensive in Japan than in the United States and 73.7 percent higher than in Canada. Personal computers in offices and schools are still less prevalent in Japan than in the United States. Major reasons thus far for Japan's slow institutionalization of personal computers and the Internet are price and usage. Japan was ranked only seventeenth in both Internet price and usage in one thirty-country survey.

Japan also compares unfavorably to the United States and other countries in the extent of Internet proliferation. Not only is Internet use in Japan much less than in the United States, but studies indicate Internet use is lower in Japan than in several other Asian countries, most of which have lower per-capita incomes than Japan. For example, one recent estimate is that Japan has 20 million on-line users while South Korea has 16 million. This statistic is particularly striking given that South Korea has only slightly more than half Japan's per-capita income and a little less than half Japan's population!

Many experts put Japan currently about three years behind the United States in Internet use, and several analysts contend that the gap is widening. For example, the number of U.S. Internet users doubled between 1999 and 2000, which was roughly three times faster than was the case within the same time period in Japan. The European Union had a smaller, but very significant, 60 percent higher growth rate than Japan during the same period.

The barriers to Japan's transition to that of a "new economy" seem to be both cultural and regulatory. Many Japanese consumers don't like to use credit cards, which of course are a key medium of exchange in on-line commerce. Japanese business people have long emphasized the importance of face-to-face contact, which is not possible on the Internet and with e-mail. Also, for decades many Japanese businesses have affiliated into company groups, or *keiretsu,* and paid higher prices for each other's goods and services in exchange for the comfort of being assured stable supplies. As long as this kind of cultural preference remains, corporate Japan does not view the cost-cutting advantages of e-commerce in as favorable a light as do their Western counterparts.

Culturally, the biggest users of the Web in business throughout the globe tend to be cosmopolitan and young. Many Japanese business people have a certain amount of insularity because they have spent their working lives with one company. Also, Japan's homogeneous population means fewer foreign-born or foreign-educated residents. The latter are vital parts of the "new economy" in the United States and other Western countries. Demographically, Japan has been experiencing a baby bust that is over thirty years old and has accelerated in recent years. This has meant a disproportionately lower number of young people in Japan, who tend to be more open to the dramatic benefits of personal computers entering the workforce than is the case in other nations.

Japan's slowness to enter the "new economy" is directly related, as is the case with problems described earlier, to the thicket of regulations and government favors to particular firms that characterize the government-guided Japanese economic system. For example, policies related to Internet development and use have, until very recent government reforms, fallen under the jurisdiction of at least five ministries: the Ministry of Posts and Telecommunications, the Ministry of International Trade and Industry, the Ministry of Finance, the Ministry of Construction, and the Ministry of Agriculture, Forestry, and Fisheries.

The nurturing of the "new economy" is also difficult

because of the problems associated with an economy that is in general too regulated and anticompetition. For example, Japan's firms have been much more reluctant to buy large numbers of computers for clerical workers than is the case in the United States because regulation and industry protection means they must pay much higher unit costs for the machines. This, in turn, has kept office worker productivity from increasing in Japan, contrary to what occurred in the United States.

It is difficult to understand Japan's current economic problems without an exploration of what many observers like to label "Japan Inc." and others refer to as the "Iron Triangle," the three-way and, until recently, quite cozy relationship between the bureaucracy, much of big business, and lawmakers. Although Japan Inc. helped the economy from the 1950s until the 1980s, when the country was trying to catch the more industrialized West and the nature of economic competition was different, the bursting of the economic bubble and Japan's continued economic malaise have revealed the serious impediments the system causes.

In the United States, business and government often conceptualize each other as rivals, and business attempts to change government policies that are considered harmful while government attempts to regulate dangerous or predatory business practices. Historically and culturally the system is quite different in Japan. Since the Meiji era, for the most part, business-government relations have been cooperative in general. In the United States, government considers one of its top responsibilities to be consumer protection. In Japan, government traditionally has worked to strengthen corporations and protect their interests over consumers and workers because of the belief that such action strengthens the national economy. In the United States, since the nineteenth century, government has been quite concerned with large concentrations of economic power, and Congress pioneered antitrust legislation. The Japanese have never been uncomfortable with large concentrations of economic power. The Japanese philosophy has been that size means more wealth and that competition between a large number of small firms is disruptive rather than good for the economy.

Sociologists who study Japan consider Japanese attitudes about government-business relations and competition to be normal given that Japan is a group-oriented society. The tendency is for many Japanese to see the advantage of alliances and view competition negatively.

Throughout the twentieth century much of the direction of the economy lay in the hands of national bureaucrats in several government ministries, with the Ministry of Finance and the Ministry of International Trade and Industry having special power over economic policy. Although in the United States, the Congress has a great deal of power concerning the private sector, in Japan, the Diet's influence over business has been weak relative to the national ministries. Bureaucrats who work in national government ministries in Japan have historically enjoyed very high status. They receive their positions by passing examinations for the most prestigious universities in Japan, particularly Tokyo University, and then being employed upon graduation.

Since business is so affected by national ministry bureaucrats, corporate Japan has traditionally spent enormous amounts of time, effort, and economic resources to cultivate good relations with relevant government ministries. Many times managers in big Japanese corporations attended the same select universities as national ministry bureaucrats and after graduation the fellow graduates maintain their ties. Another weapon Japanese business uses to influence the bureaucracy is *amakudari,* or "descent from heaven." Amakudari is the private-sector practice of hiring retiring bureaucrats in associations or firms in the industries they once regulated. Even though this practice occurs in other countries to a certain extent, it is institutionalized and much more widespread in Japan. In amakudari the perceived benefits are two-way, since the national ministry also has its former "men" in the private sector and business has access to specific government ministries.

Although Diet members have less power over the private sector than bureaucrats, in recent years LDP legislators are more and more often acting as go-betweens to the ministries on behalf of business through *zoku-giin,* or "policy tribes."

Prime Minister Tanaka established policy groups or tribes in the early 1970s, supposedly to check the power of the bureaucracy and give the Diet more influence in policymaking. Each zoku-giin develops specialized expertise in the workings of a particular government ministry. Then if the particular ministry affects an industry or a group of firms, the policy support groups serve as brokers. Theoretically, the policy tribes base arguments for or against particular economic policy on expertise. However, the common practice is that the politicians provide cash gifts to bureaucrats who, though they enjoy high status, are underpaid. The legislators also provide for "life needs" of the bureaucrats, such as paying wedding costs for a bureaucrat's daughter or providing tickets for entertainment or sporting events. The policy tribes obtain the money to engage in this trading of favors for influence through business contributions.

Until very recently there has been no stigma whatsoever attached to what amounts to institutionalized bribery. Only since the bursting of the economic bubble has the situation begin to change. Throughout the 1990s, numerous stories emerged of businesses being granted special favors by government, including both access to loans and protection against competition, and of bureaucrats engaging in insider trading after being tipped off by legislators from policy tribes who obtained their information from their client companies. Some of the largest Japanese companies were involved in several well-publicized scandal stories of the 1990s. Although there have been attempted reforms of the corrupt practices that are the dark side of Japan Inc., it is too early to tell if they will be effective.

In the early years of the twentieth century with the Japanese economy still not completely recovered from the bursting of the bubble, there is one major policy question on the minds of academics, business workers, politicians, foreigners affected by Japan, and the Japanese public. It is to that question, how to restructure Japan Inc., that we now turn.

JAPAN'S ECONOMIC FUTURE

As of the end of 2000 Japan was not only secure as the world's leading robotics manufacturer but was also in the process of creating a whole new generation of robots. Matsushita Electric Company is planning the opening of a $15 million retirement home that will come equipped with loyal robots who will provide companionship and diagnostic care for elderly residents. By 2002 Japan is expected to have 370,000 industrial robots working, compared to 120,000 in the United States and 15,000 in Britain.

Robotics, automobiles, and electronics are just a few industries where, over ten years of economic troubles notwithstanding, Japanese companies remain among world leaders. Despite the problems Japanese policymakers must solve to improve the economy, it is important to keep an accurate perspective on Japan. Japan is still the world's second-strongest economy. Also, the Japanese have a recent history of rising to meet greater challenges than a few years of economic troubles. For example, the Japanese managed in the late nineteenth century to build a relatively advanced economy and military in an incredibly short time, thereby avoiding Western domination. Even more impressively, the Japanese rebuilt their nation from the ashes of World War II into a global economic power. Still, dramatic structural changes, which have begun, must be continued if Japan is to enjoy widespread prosperity in the first part of the twenty-first century.

The major general problem the Japanese must solve is how to transform a system designed in the 1950s for an industrial society that was still attempting to catch the West, but is no longer suited for a postindustrial nation. Japan is burdened by this top down system that still favors both efficient and inefficient producers over millions of consumers.

Two demographic trends that make the return of widespread economic dynamism crucial are the baby bust and

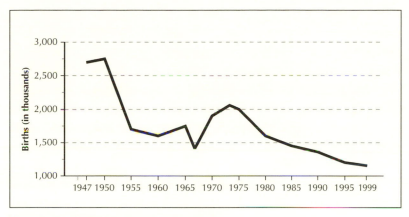

Figure 2.2: Births in Japan, 1947–1999

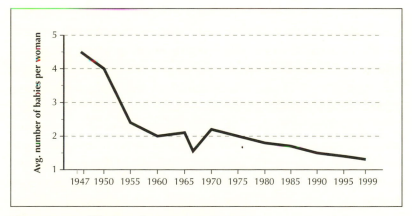

Figure 2.3: Fertility Rate in Japan, 1947–1999

As these two fertility related charts indicate, Japan now faces a shrinking number of future workers that must support one of the world's largest percentages of elderly relative to the general population.

Source: Ministry of Health and Welfare

the large growth of the elderly in Japan. For various reasons most Japanese families are having only one or at most two children. Also, by 2000 Japan trailed only Italy and Sweden in the percentage of its citizens who were 65 years or older. By 2050 Japan is expected to have the highest percentage of elderly citizens of any of the world's nations. Because of these trends estimates are that by 2025 there will be only 2.2 workers for every retired person. It is imperative that Japanese productivity again undergo impressive growth rates in order for total economic output to increase and the elderly's needs be met.

What is interesting to students of the Japanese economy is while there is disagreement over specific tactical approaches, agreement is high among both Japanese and foreign economic analysts about what Japan should do to structurally improve the system.

Widespread structural change will involve nothing less than wholesale changes in major government and corporate and financial institutions. Japan must change its political system from essentially one-party LDP rule to a more competitive system. Japan's banking system and stock market need modernization. Widespread corporate collusion should be eliminated. Japan must become a more open economy; the overregulated Japanese economy and overly powerful bureaucracy must become a thing of the past. Meanwhile, higher education should be improved.

As is the case in the U.S. and Western European democracies, Japan's political system needs to meet more of the needs of the general population and less of narrow interest groups, particularly producer groups. The virtue of a system of competitive politics is that it is much more difficult for any one party to cater to the few at the expense of the many. The introduction of genuine party competition would, for example, put much more pressure within the Diet and on the bureaucracy to stop subsidizing inefficient producers and limiting entry into particular markets. If this pressure is effective it will undoubtedly help bring down consumer prices.

Japan's financial system has been top-down and essentially government controlled since the Meiji Period. The result often is that if a company has good connections to institutions such as the Ministry of Finance, it is privy to loans. Also, in many cases if the political connections are good enough and a company loses money, it can still get more loans. Western bankers are much more likely to channel money to borrowers who they estimate will put the funds to the most efficient possible use. If a firm fails in the West it usually is not in a position to continue to obtain capital since private sector bankers are much more in control than bureaucrats. Japanese savers still have relatively few financial choices and don't obtain what is generally regarded as fair returns on their savings. If this situation is improved then Japanese banks must compete for savings with other lenders and financial institutions, which in turn provides bankers with a strong incentive to be more careful about to whom they lend money.

Before any improvement in the financial sector can occur, the Japanese government must deal with the two problems of massive government debt, which is now double the level of 1990, and the enormous number of outstanding bank loans that have been made to unproductive companies. The International Monetary Fund (IMF) estimates that Japan's bank debts now equal approximately $766 billion or about 20 percent of gross domestic product (GDP). Neither problem can be solved without painful employment effects upon millions of Japanese.

Solving the government deficit problem, created in the first place by wasteful make-work public spending, will require either higher taxes or major spending cuts. Either of these measures will depress economic short-term growth and almost immediately raise unemployment, although the economy will be eventually helped. Almost half of the outstanding bank loans are to construction, real estate, retail, and wholesale companies that are extremely unproductive. Any write-off or cessation of loans to these firms will probably mean somewhere between 1 million and over 3 million Japanese will lose their jobs. Until Japan's bad debt problem is solved, however, financial capital is blocked from flowing to more productive and job-creating enterprises.

In other developed capitalist countries the normal function of stock markets are to raise and allocate capital. In Japan, although the situation has improved somewhat, this is still not largely the case. The market has often prevented takeovers of companies because of the cross-shareholding of many Japanese companies. Also, the Japanese stock market has functioned more as a casino at times than as a rational investment medium. Because of this situation, stock and bond prices in Japan often don't serve as signals for investors to allocate or not allocate capital to a particular firm.

Japan needs to eliminate the corporate collusion that keeps prices high. Although most economic and policy analysts don't recommend that the Japanese become like Americans in their view of competition, it is important that Japanese at all levels understand that competition does have great benefits for large numbers of consumers. The more cartels, the less competition and the higher the prices for most Japanese. If this situation was significantly reversed, then an effect of lower prices would be that millions of Japanese consumers would have more disposable income than is currently the case. This in turn would stimulate more savings, job creation, and economic growth.

Another major structural economic improvement that is long overdue is for the Japanese to allow more foreign imports and foreign direct investment. Such policies also reduce consumer prices and stimulate economic growth by increasing disposable consumer income. Virtually all economists agree that widespread free trade contributes to the long-term prosperity of the populations of nations that are farsighted enough to implement the policy.

As mentioned earlier in this chapter, raising productivity is the major key to any nation's economic well-being. Although still high by world standards, Japanese productivity for over a decade has stagnated rather than grown. Several of the reforms described above, such as a more efficient capital allocation system and the introduction of competition, if implemented, should result in productivity growth increases, but more changes are needed. A general rethinking of regulation in all sectors of the Japanese economy is very much in order. Because the Japanese economy is so regulated, producer financial and time costs are high, both of which act as drags on productivity.

As described earlier, surplus employees in many Japanese companies, because of the attendant excessive labor costs, also lower productivity. Faced with either reducing their labor force or perishing, many companies have made substantial reductions through attrition, not hiring many new workers, and layoffs, but much progress is still needed.

The quality of a nation's education system can either enhance or inhibit productivity. Just as financial capital is needed to buy machines that make for more efficient production of goods, high levels of what economists call human capital, or the knowledge and skills workers possess, is also crucial to productivity growth. Japan has by many accounts the best elementary and secondary school system in the world, but there is a widespread sentiment in Japan that the elementary and secondary system overly stresses rote learning at the expense of creativity and critical thinking. It is difficult to assess the accuracy of this sentiment, but serious discussion is going on in Japanese educational policymaking circles as to how to promote deeper understanding, creativity, and critical thinking among the nation's young people.

Virtually all educational policy analysts, Japanese and foreign, agree that the one educational institution most in need of reform is the Japanese university, particularly in regard to shaping it to better meet the needs of the economy. Although about the same percentage of Japanese students as their American counterparts attend university, there is substantial evidence that the structure of the typical university causes most undergraduates to learn less than their counterparts in other countries. In Japan, the majority of students attend private universities. Although some private institutions are top-flight, most are inferior to public Japanese universities, and funding for professors, laboratories, and other facilities in private universities is quite scant compared to public universities.

Also, certain companies and government ministries tend to recruit from one or only a few public or private universities. In Japan, university entrance is primarily determined by examination, and job recruiters are usually not as interested in a student's major as in what university they were able to enter. Most Japanese students tend to relax once they are admitted to a particular university and not apply themselves very diligently in their undergraduate years. Because professors aren't very demanding as a rule in Japanese universities, students can get away with not working hard—or learning much—and still graduate.

In the United States and other countries, university research and graduate programs often directly service the needs of business and industry. This has not been the case in Japan. For a variety of reasons no Japanese university ranks among world leaders in research, and Japanese industry has long complained that the private sector is not obtaining enough benefits from the nation's university system given the resources allocated to higher education. Graduate programs in Japan, particularly those for professionals instead of scholars, are still quite scant compared to the United States. In fact, it is common practice in large Japanese companies to send bright young managerial employees to the United States for MBAs or graduate degrees in the sciences. The human capital levels of Japanese university graduates will improve considerably if higher education can be reformed.

Given the low level of disagreement about what structural changes need to be made, there has been a flurry of reform activity in Japan throughout the past several years. Although Japan has yet to return to anywhere near the prosperity of the 1980s and before, there are both signs of progress and many changes still to be made.

The fundamental reason that so much reform still needs to be enacted in Japan is that there is a very justifiable fear that restructuring will cause very high unemployment in the short term. Presently, the Japanese system is not designed to accommodate large numbers of jobless people. Unemployment benefits only have a duration of six months in Japan. If Japan restructures its economy in an attempt to solve its most serious problems, the nation's leaders must decide whether to adopt a European-style social democratic system or an American-style economy of flexible labor markets. In Western Europe taxes are high but company costs aren't excessively high, as in Japan, since governments make adequate provision for the jobless. In the United States taxes are low and companies don't have the problem of excess workers, but individuals often are forced to constantly switch jobs depending upon economic conditions. Either system is more functional in the twenty-first century than Japan's current approach of expecting private enterprise to provide jobs for unneeded employees.

In addition to economic restructuring many economists argue that Japan's business leaders need to rethink fundamental assumptions about goals and objectives. Up until the present Japanese corporations have worried more about company growth and job preservation than profits. This kind of thinking has caused companies to engage in producing too many unprofitable product lines and into embarking upon frivolous business ventures. The result has been corporate debt and, in some cases, bankruptcy or near bankruptcy. Although American companies can justly be accused of thinking too much about the bottom line, Japanese business will most probably improve by elevating the importance of profits.

As of the publication of this book the political arena appears to be the place where the least progress has occurred. The LDP continues to dominate elections and control the Diet and cabinet, despite much outcry from the press and opposing parties. Because the LDP is so tied to many elements of the status quo, as long as it is in control at least some reform that endangers vested interests will be blocked. Still, some of Japan's major multinational companies are harmed by many of the inefficiencies of Japan Inc., that the LDP has tolerated, and these corporate giants also have influence with the LDP. Even though Japan's "new economy" is growing more slowly than it should, there is steady progress being made in the information technology industry. These new companies are also strong proponents of reform and will pressure politicians to serve their interests instead of those of entrenched but inefficient old-line industries.

Although many of Japan's domestic financial institutions remain mired in bad loans and still don't appear to base loans on anticipated profitability, there has been impressive progress, particularly legal changes that allow Japanese insurance and securities companies to offer some of the same kinds of annuities and other financial packages to consumers as their American counterparts. Also, Japanese law is now much more liberal regarding entry of foreign financial institutions into Japan.

Attempts to reform a political/legal system that promotes producer collusion at the expense of the general public have been mixed. For years, because of the pressure of hundreds of thousands of small, politically powerful, and largely inefficient "mom and pop" stores, Japan's large store opening law made it extremely difficult for large domestic or foreign multipurpose stores such as K-Mart or chains such as 7-Eleven to open. All of this forced Japanese consumers to spend millions more yen than necessary on high-priced goods. Thanks to the elimination of the large store opening law, multipurpose large stores as well as a host of chain convenience stores have opened up throughout Japan, and consumers are enjoying increased purchasing power as a result. Still, entire industries, such as construction, are protected by existing laws that reward cartels and penalize consumers.

Japan is becoming a more open economy to foreign direct investment (FDI). Although still low compared to foreign direct investment in other countries, the amount of foreign investment in Japan increased by more than 100 percent between 1997 and 2000. In 1998 Japan had 1,542 cases of FDI for a total value of $10.5 billion. The 727 foreign investments made in the first half of 1999 totaled $11.3 billion and exceeded the entire total of the previous year. This trend has continued.

Some examples of FDI growth include Renault's purchase of a strong minority share in Nissan, the New York investment firm Ripplewood Holdings's purchase of the Long Term Credit Bank of Japan, and Merrill Lynch's acquisition of the retail offices and personnel of the now-defunct Yamaichi Securities. Only a few years ago such acquisitions were impossible, but the combination of hard-pressed Japanese companies that needed infusions of foreign cash to survive and government approval of increased FDI has caused the situation to change.

Even given the improvement, a comparison of foreign investment in Japan with comparable developed economies depicts just how closed the Japanese economy has been to outside capital. FDI in other industrialized countries is almost ten times as high relative to respective gross domestic product when compared to Japan. FDI in Japan is 0.7 percent of GDP, compared to 10 percent in the United States and an average of 12 percent in the rest of the industrialized world.

Japan still needs to truly open its markets to foreign imports, however. Even though official trade barriers were abolished years ago, in market after market the large combinations of a variety of product regulations keeps the penetration of foreign manufactured goods very low compared to all other developed countries and continues to be a major reason why Japanese consumers pay such high prices for so many goods. Changing these regulations almost amounts to trench warfare in one specific market after another, since there is no possible general legislation that will affect the total problem.

There has been impressive recent progress in the deregulation of several major industries. One of the biggest successes is in communications. In 1994 portable telephones were deregulated in Japan, and that policy change led to a 22-fold rise in ownership of portable and car telephones in the ensuing six-year period—from 2.13 million phones in the beginning of fiscal year 1994 to 47.58 million at the end of November 1999. The quasi–state-owned Nippon Telephone and Telegraph (NTT) still enjoys a near monopoly, though, in communications, and levels excessive charges on long-distance and overseas telephone companies as a condition for the companies to link up with NTT's local networks. This keeps consumer telephone and Internet charges excessively high by world standards.

Real deregulation has also occurred in the airlines industry, as fares appear to be dropping and passenger air travel increasing. However, the case of airline deregulation is illustrative of both the influence of Japanese culture on the regulation process and of the danger this cultural influence might pose for the Japanese economy. After observing U.S. air deregulation efforts in the 1970s, Ministry of Transportation (MOT) officials began to consider deregulation in 1980. However, MOT officials wanted the procedure to proceed fairly for all companies, advocated giving the companies time to adapt, were reluctant to confront recalcitrant airlines, and worried about the effect of deregulation on employment. This meant that the deregulation process took twenty years, during which time those Japanese who flew were paying excessively high prices. Additionally during this time Japanese airlines were losing business to their American competitors. The nature of international competition probably makes it important that despite the great premium placed on harmony in Japanese culture, the pace of deregulation proceed more rapidly than was the case with the airlines industry.

In higher education, despite a scramble for students that has resulted in some innovative new programs in colleges and universities, there appears to be little progress yet in increasing demands upon students or in making university education and research more meet the needs of the economy. Japan cannot afford to leave its universities unreformed if it expects to continue to be a world leader in sophisticated industries throughout the twenty-first century.

The national government bureaucracy in Japan is perhaps the greatest single obstacle to widespread structural economic reform. Japan's long tradition of Confucianism means that bureaucrats have had an honored and powerful place in Japanese society. The Meiji Period reforms made national bureaucrats even more powerful, and until Japan's economic slowdown, it was a rare case indeed when Japanese would overtly challenge bureaucratic power. Also, the thousands of individuals who are in middle- and upper-level positions in important ministries such as finance and international trade and industry are, by in large, highly intelligent people who were selected from among the top graduates of Japan's most prestigious universities. It is they who actually must carry out many proposed reforms, which certainly makes a process more difficult since they have propagated much that now needs changing.

Still, over ten years of economic malaise, the scandals associated with the bureaucracy that surfaced in the 1990s, the pressure of efficient multinational Japanese companies and their foreign competitors who are hurt by economic structural defects, and the growth of new entrepreneurs in such industries as information technology all act as powerful forces that could very well overcome bureaucratic resistance and transform an already powerful Japanese economy from a high-cost system with too large of a role for government to a much more efficient economy that is more predicated on market principles. Because Japan is a democratic country, the ultimate decisionmakers who will answer this question are millions of ordinary Japanese and their elected representatives.

References
"After Japan's Election: Sunset for the Men in Suits," *The Economist* (1 July 2000): 26–28.
Alexander, Arthur J. "Prospects for the Japanese Economy: Looking Beyond the Next Quarter," *Japan Economic Institute* (25 August 2000): 1–13.
Allen, G. C. 1981. *A Short Economic History of Modern Japan.* New York: St. Martin's Press.
"Bad Loan Blues Return," *The Oriental Economist Report,* Vol. 69, No. 6 (June 2001): 4–5.
Bickers, Charles, and Ichiko Fuyuno. "Banking on the Robot Evolution," *Far Eastern Economic Review* (23 November 2000): 38–42.
"EAA Interview with Edward J. Lincoln," *Education About Asia,* Vol. 5, No. 1 (Spring 2000):22–25.
Ellington, Lucien. "Learning from the Japanese Economy," *Japan Digest* (December 1999).
———. 1992. *Education in the Japanese Life-cycle: Implications for the United States.* Lewiston, NY: Edwin Mellon Press.
Frost, Peter. "The 'Asian Contagion': A Readers Guide," *Education About Asia,* Vol. 4, No. 2 (Fall 1999): 17–22.
Halberstam, David. 1986. *The Reckoning.* New York: Avon Books.
Helwig, M. Diana. "Japan: A Rising Sun," *Foreign Affairs,* Vol. 79, No. 4 (July/August 2000): 26–39.
Ito, Takatoshi. 1992. *The Japanese Economy.* Cambridge, MA: MIT Press.
Katz, Richard. "Friendlier Territory," *The Oriental Economist Report,* Vol. 69, No. 5 (May 2001): 8–9.
———. 1998. *Japan, the System That Soured: The Rise and Fall of the Japanese Economic Miracle.* Armonk, NY: M. E. Sharpe.
———. "Structural Dualism Worsens," *The Oriental Economist Report,* Vol. 68, No. 11 (November 2000): 8–11.
"Koizomi's Dilemma," *The Oriental Economist Report,* Vol. 69, No. 6 (June 2001): 1–2.
Lincoln, Edward J. 1999. *Troubled Times: U.S.-Japan Trade Relations in the 1990s.* Washington, DC: Brookings Institute Press.

Macpherson, W. J. 1996. *The Economic Development of Japan, 1868–1941.* New York: Cambridge University Press.

Mak, James, Shyam Sunder, Shigeyuki Abe, and Kazuhiro Igawa, eds. 1998. *Japan: Why It Works, Why It Doesn't.* Honolulu: University of Hawaii Press.

Miyauchi, Yoshihiko. "Reform Is in the National Interest," *The Oriental Economist Report,* Vol. 68, No. 3 (March 2000): 16.

Mulgan, Aurelia George. "Japan: A Setting Sun," *Foreign Affairs,* Vol. 79, No. 4 (July/August 2000): 40–52.

Nakamura, Takafusa. 1985. *Economic Development of Modern Japan.* Singapore: Japanese Ministry of Foreign Affairs.

Olstrom, Douglas. "Prospects for a 'New Economy' in Japan," *Japan Economic Institute* (18 August 2000): 1–14.

Porter, Michael E., and Hirotaka Takeuchi. "Fixing What Really Ails Japan," *Foreign Affairs,* Vol. 78, No. 3 (May/June 1999): 66–81.

Reid, T. R. 2000. *Confucius Lives Next Door: What Living in the East Teaches Us about Living in the West.* New York: Vintage.

Rosenberger, Nancy. 2001. *Gambling with Virtue: Japanese Women and the Search for Self in a Changing World.* Honolulu: University of Hawaii Press.

Takahashi, Hiroyuki, and Jeanette Voss. "'Parasite Singles': A Uniquely Japanese Phenomenon?" *Japan Economic Institute* (11 August 2000): 1–12.

Tashiro, Masami, ed. 2000. *Japan 2001: An International Comparison.* Tokyo: Keizai Koho Center.

CHAPTER THREE
Japanese Institutions

People in every developed nation create complex institutions that promote particular purposes. Three of the most important institutions in any society are government, education, and organized religion. A rudimentary understanding of Japan is impossible unless these institutions are explored in some depth. As is the case in most modern nations, Japanese government and politics, education, and organized religion are dynamic rather than static institutions.

With the exception of a newly enacted national government reorganization, the *structure* of Japanese government has remained unchanged since the adoption of the present constitution following World War II. In the past few years, however, Japan's *politics* have arguably become more volatile than at any other time in the postwar period. Public opinion polls indicate an increasingly alienated electorate. The postwar political status quo characterized by one party and bureaucratic rule was successfully challenged in the 1990s and is under attack from all sides today.

Educational institutions are under almost as much scrutiny as are Japanese politics. As this book goes to press, the Ministry of Education is initiating a major national curriculum change, and Japanese universities are facing massive drops in enrollment and increasing criticism for the quality of education that students receive. Societal questioning of the structure and productivity of precollegiate and higher education is occurring along with an even deeper public concern with the substantial perceived recent increases, by Japanese standards, in youth crime, particularly violent crime.

Traditional Japanese religious institutions also face challenges that endanger the postwar status quo. The much-publicized Tokyo subway poison gas murders of the 1990s were the actions of one of the so-called new religions, many of whose members were young educated Japanese. Currently in Japan there is widespread public discussion of a spiritual/values crisis and a need to strengthen religious institutions.

One of the positive post–World War II accomplishments of the Japanese people is that serious and open discussion about institutions can occur, because after 1945 Japan made the transition from an authoritarian to a democratic form of government. What were the developments leading to democratic government in Japan? What is the current structure of Japanese government, and how is it being changed? What are the prospects for political reform in Japan?

JAPANESE GOVERNMENT AND POLITICS

The Roots of Japanese Democracy

Japan became a democratic country with the adoption of the present constitution in 1947. Still, despite the Meiji Period oligarchy and the militarist rulers of the 1930s and 1940s, in many ways the country had been moving toward more democratic governments since the late nineteenth century. Certain aspects of Japan's political heritage are vital reasons why democracy, a form of government that is very difficult to institutionalize in most countries, flourished in post–World War II Japan.

Several features in Japanese pre–World War II society provided a foundation for later democratic government. Japan had long been a politically unified country when the democratic constitution was adopted. Also, the Japanese possessed an important ingredient for building a successful democratic society: a relatively high level of literacy nationwide. Despite periods of domestic turmoil, Japanese political history has been largely evolutionary and nonviolent. This climate of stability proved to be a fertile one for the growth of mass democracy in Japan. Certain political institutions vital to the growth of democracy also evolved in the nineteenth and early twentieth centuries. The 1889 Meiji constitution provided for a two-house legislature. By the end of World War I and all through the 1920s, Japan had a parliamentary government. Also, beginning in 1925 all adult Japanese males enjoyed the right to vote. Although the military gained political dominance in the 1930s and early 1940s, by the time of the 1947 democratic reforms, the Japanese already had experience with representative government.

The 1947 constitution, written by U.S. occupation staff and imposed upon a reluctant Japanese government after Japanese authorities did not make satisfactory progress for occupation leaders, nevertheless still serves as the foundation of Japanese democracy. It provides for universal suffrage for both sexes and for an independent judicial branch. Also, much to the consternation of some conservatives to this day, the constitution limits the emperor's governmental powers and states that he is solely "a symbol of the state and of the unity of the people" (Reischauer 1981, 229). Article Nine, whereby the Japanese people forever renounce war as a sovereign right of the nation, also remains controversial, even though Japan now has substantial air, land, and sea self-defense forces.

The 1947 constitution did not change the prefectural governmental structure that has existed since the Meiji Period. Today Japan has 47 prefectures, each with its own governor and legislature. Although prefectures are roughly analogous to U.S. states, there is a significant difference: While prefectures have some control over such policy matters as public law and order and hiring teachers, they do not have nearly the autonomy from the national government as do states and the federal government. About 60 percent of local government revenues come from central government-funding sources. Prefectural governors must constantly negotiate with national government bureaucrats regarding many policy matters because numerous guidelines and directives accompany these revenues.

A major innovation of the 1947 constitution was to make the legislature, or Diet, in theory the highest organ of state power with sole law-making authority. The bicameral Diet remained with a more powerful lower House of Representatives and a less powerful upper house, the House of Councilors, which replaced the pre–World War II nonelective House of Peers. The Japanese people elect representatives to the Diet, and the party with the most seats in the House of Representatives then elects the executive or prime minister, who in turn selects cabinet ministers and other appointed officials.

National Governing Structures: Theory and Practice

Although the Japanese bureaucracy and the Liberal Democratic Party will be described more extensively later in this chapter, it is important that readers bear in mind that the postwar dominance of one political party (the LDP) and the extensive power of government bureaucrats are critical to understanding how Japan's national government functions. Even though Japan's postwar governmental parliamentary structure resembles Great Britain, because of the above factors government and politics are different in Japan than in the West. Still, despite one-party dominance and extremely powerful nonelected bureaucrats, ultimately Japan is a government of the people. The LDP has retained power for all but a short period since 1955 because voters were happy with economic prosperity, and it is in great decline now because of the economic malaise. Special interest groups, for better or worse, are free in attempting to influence both elected and nonelected officials. Even minority opposition parties can influence, because of the consensual nature of Japanese society, the final form of legislation much more than their numbers might indicate. Finally, basic freedoms of

One somewhat annoying aspect of Japanese political campaigns is noise. The man in the platform on top of this car is broadcasting loud exhortations for a political candidate in Nagasaki. (Courtesy of Lucien Ellington)

expression are guaranteed to Japanese just as is the case in Western democracies.

Electoral campaigns in Japan are much shorter than the United States, being limited by law to only forty days. Despite this, many Japanese politicians, like their counterparts elsewhere, are always unofficially campaigning. Door-to-door campaigning is prohibited during the official campaign period, but citizens in urban areas are constantly subjected to candidates' supporters blaring out platitudes on loud speakers. National elections, which were until a few years ago always held on Sundays, drew a much higher percentage of voters than in the United States until recently, when soaring cynicism about politicians resulted in a substantial drop in voter participation rates.

The major elections are those for the Diet. The 252 members of the upper house, the House of Councilors, are elected for six-year terms by two methods: One hundred fifty-two members of the upper house are elected from districts in the prefectures, with a locale's size determining how many upper-house seats are allocated to it; and the remaining upper-house members are chosen in a national election by all of Japan's eligible voters. Terms are staggered so that one-half of the upper house is replaced every three years. The power of the upper house is limited compared to Japan's lower house, or House of Representatives, which is home to the Japanese prime minister. If the upper house defeats a bill, the bill can still become a law if the lower house passes it for the second time with a two-thirds majority.

Until 1994, the House of Representatives consisted of 512 members elected from 130 districts, with each electoral district having anywhere from two to six Diet seats. Voters would only vote for one candidate, but the winners in any given district would be the two to six candidates who received the most votes among perhaps ten to twelve candidates running. This proportional system was the subject of much criticism in Japan due to perceptions that it promoted legislator overaccentuation on constituency services, factionalism, and personality. Because the LDP dominated the Diet, rival LDP candidates for seats often would be elected based upon how much money and favors could be doled out to supporters rather than based upon their stances on political issues.

In 1994 the lower-house system was significantly modified. Now there are 300 single-member districts throughout Japan, where local voters choose lower house members and 200 seats in eleven national blocks that are awarded based on proportional representation (the number of lower-house members was thus reduced from 512 to 500). Dual candidacies are legal, so a party may run a candidate for both a single member district seat and for election by proportional representation. Theoretically, lower-house terms are for four years. However, in practice, governments either call elections or opposing parties in the Diet force elections through no-confidence votes before four years have passed.

Thus far, much less has changed as a result of electoral reform than anticipated. The LDP in particular, and several other parties as well, continue to deaccentuate policy stances and rely upon personal organizations in running for office.

Once a lower-house election is concluded, the leader of the party who either has a majority in the lower house or who assembles a majority coalition of parties normally becomes prime minister. In 1994 an exception occurred when LDP leaders built a coalition government by awarding Socialist Party chair Murayama Tomiichi the prime minister-ship. The prime minister names a cabinet consisting of heads of ministries and various other government agencies.

Theoretically, Japanese prime ministers have relatively strong executive powers along British lines, but Japanese political culture has resulted in, for the most part, quite weak prime ministers throughout the postwar years. Until very recently, LDP faction leaders anointed party leaders in smoke-filled back rooms and then LDP Diet members usually approved the choice by vote. In 2000, the LDP changed its party leader selection process in reaction to negative public reaction to a perceived-mediocre candidate who was selected as party leader and, subsequently, prime minister. Under the new system each of the LDP's 47 prefectural chapters were awarded three votes for party leader while each LDP Diet member would get one vote in the selection.

In spring 2001, after the new LDP leader selection process was employed, Japan had its eleventh prime minister in almost twelve years. The new LDP selection process seemed to make a difference as the prefectural LDP chapter repre-sentatives bucked the old-guard party leadership and voted heavily for a reform candidate, Koizumi Junichiro, who became party leader and then prime minister.

Koizumi, who enjoyed initial great voter popularity because of his reform rhetoric, could be long-lived as prime minister. If this proves not to be the case, the prospects of any strong executive leadership continue to be dim in Japan. It is difficult for prime ministers to exercise policy leadership with such short tenures. Japan has a long history of nominal leaders who are actually puppets of so-called shadow shoguns. This is often the case in LDP-dominated Japan since faction leaders have normally selected noncontroversial politicians to become party leaders and later prime ministers. The power of the Japanese national bureaucracy is also still so strong that the Japanese prime minister is much more limited in his initiatives than is his British counterpart.

It has become a source of frustration for foreign policy makers and diplomats that Japan's prime ministers tend to be weak leaders, especially since the size of the Japanese economy means decisions in Japan can have major international repercussions. There appears to be a growing sense on the part of the Japanese public and foreign observers that no one person is really in charge of the Japanese government. Since 1980 only one Japanese prime minister, Nakasone Yasuhiro, has been considered a strong executive. It is no coincidence that Nakasone managed to stay in power for about five years (1982–1987), the longest tenure for any Japanese prime minister in decades.

Even though scholars disagree on how much power it actually possesses, the Diet as a legislative body exercises more relative power in Japanese politics than does the prime minister. Still, a plausible case can be made that Japan's national government is as much government by bureaucracy as government by Diet and prime minister. In the postwar years most legislation—and, until 2001, especially important legislation, including the national government budget—emanated from the bureaucracy. Even though Diet members who occupy cabinet positions are the nominal policymakers, often they reflect the views of the civil servants in the ministries who have the real expertise on the issues.

Among the national government ministries, the Ministry of

Finance (MOF) is seen as particularly important. Until recently the MOF has exercised (among other powers) unchallenged de facto control of the budget, responsibility for design of the national tax system, and regulatory authority over the banking and securities sectors. The elected politician who is the official Minister of Finance has a very tough job, to say the least, in actually shaping the direction of this vast ministry.

LDP control of the government has increased bureaucratic influence. Often bureaucrats retire and then successfully run as LDP candidates for the Diet. Approximately 25 percent of LDP Diet members are ex-bureaucrats. (Readers might recall from Chapter 2 that the relationship between LDP Diet members, national bureaucrats, and big business was addressed.) Diet members, often in return for contributions from business, act as go-betweens to the bureaucracy on behalf of their private-sector contributors. The result of such cozy interactions often means special favors for both big business and bureaucrats, with the typical Japanese consumer paying higher prices due to government-arranged cartels or monopolies.

It should be borne in mind just what a deep-rooted tradition respect for officialdom is in Japan. National government bureaucrats are the academic elite who are recruited from the top of the classes of the very best Japanese universities. Until recent scandals involving bureaucracy, employees of national government ministries were much more respected than were politicians in Japan.

Political Parties

Japan is a multiparty democracy, but familiarity with the LDP is still a major key to better understanding the nature of Japanese politics, government, and even public policy. In 1955 powerful business associations, fearing the rise of socialism in Japan, proposed and helped to implement a plan that resulted in the merger of two conservative parties, the

Liberals and the Democrats. The party quickly dominated Japanese politics and remained in power for thirty-eight years, until defeated by a seven-party coalition in 1993. Before the end of 1994 the LDP was sharing power again in a coalition government with its biggest former rival, the Socialist Party, although a member of the latter party was prime minister. By 1996 an LDP member was again prime minister, and as of the publication of this book this continues to be the case.

If readers are wondering how a party begun by business groups could coalesce with socialists, they are beginning to understand the nature of the LDP. The LDP is essentially conservative in that it is probusiness and has consistently supported the Japan-U.S. alliance in the region through the entire Cold War and afterward. Even though the LDP entered the 1996 coalition with the socialists in order to regain power, it was the socialists and not the LDP that essentially publicly repudiated most of their platform (losing a great deal of credibility with the public). Still, the LDP's 1996 action is indicative that it is much more than just a conservative party. The LDP may very well be the biggest "umbrella" party among democracies in that it has a large middle-of-the-road group of constituents and because its leaders are extremely pragmatic. For years the LDP enjoyed support from relatively heterogeneous groups.

The pragmatic lack of attention to ideology on the part of the LDP also was a product of the old multiple-member lower-house electoral system. Since LDP members found themselves running against each other in the same locales, they put more effort into developing factions based upon personality and the ability to raise money instead of stressing policy positions or ideology. Even though the electoral system has been drastically changed, factions remain in the LDP, and at any given time there are three to five national factions who all have their own preferred candidates.

Voters returned LDP politicians back to power year after year for several reasons: Until 1994, the multiple-member exclusive proportional lower-house electoral system favored LDP candidates because the party was the only one with ample enough funds to run several candidates in a single district.

Also, until the mid 1990s and reapportionment, rural areas containing farmers, whom the LDP heavily subsidized, had a disproportionately high amount of electoral clout compared to urban dwellers and agrarian interests and consistently voted LDP. Urban residents had to both pay for government subsidies to farmers and pay higher prices for food because of government-protected agricultural interests. The LDP developed a well-oiled machine throughout Japan where businesses contributed in return for influence with the bureaucracy while LDP politicians also worked in the Diet and through the national ministries to bring pork-barrel government spending projects home to their constituents, regardless of need.

Equally important, during much of Japan's postwar period a large segment of the electorate in both urban and rural areas was quite satisfied by Japan's economic rise and out of gratefulness voted LDP again and again. Also, even voters who became disenchanted with the LDP did not see viable political alternatives. One problem all opposition parties, and most notably the LDP's biggest rival, the Socialist Party, developed during the long years of LDP dominance is a lack of experience in actually holding elective office and formulating policy. Voters were quite aware of the practical-experience credibility gap of opposing parties.

For most of the postwar years the Socialist Party (now the Social Democratic Party of Japan, SDJP) was the biggest opponent of the LDP. Recently, though, the SDJP's standing with voters has dropped, partially because of its repudiation of longstanding positions during its coalition with the LDP, and also because of the recent popularity of neoconservativism in Japan, as is the case in other developed countries. Surprisingly, though few Japanese are Marxists, the Japanese Communist Party has also done well through many of the postwar years by downplaying Marxism and concentrating on popular issues such as the environment. In addition, many urban residents voted for the Communist Party as a protest vote against the LDP. Another prominent opposition party since the 1960s has been Komeito, or the "Clean Government Party." Komeito is closely aligned with the Buddhist sect Soka Gakkai and appeals primarily to followers of that sect and to poor people in urban areas. Komeito's ideology is amorphous. Since the early 1990s, as the public has become increasingly discontented with the LDP, new parties have risen and dissolved or merged with other groups. In the June 2000 lowerhouse elections, in which the LDP barely retained governmental power in a coalition with New Komeito and the New Conservative Party, perhaps the most impressive showing by an oppositional party was the votes received by the New Democratic Party, a centrist-to-conservative party.

Currently, the LDP's standing with urban voters is relatively low, and cynicism among the Japanese electorate is widespread. There is widespread concern on the part of many Japanese about the current state of the nation's politics and its government's ability to formulate and implement effective public policy.

The Political Problem of the Economic Malaise

By far the biggest short-term public policy problem Japan faces is its domestic economic malaise, which the public has endured for over a decade. Japan also has a range of other domestic issues, some of which will be discussed in other parts of this book, but they are dwarfed at present by economic problems. The most major international question is, given the end of the Cold War, what is Japan's new role in the world? This issue is addressed in detail in Chapter 5.

The Japanese economy is in no danger of collapse, but signs of recovery since 1990 have been few and far between. Enormous bank debt exists. The government has unsuccessfully attempted to prime the pump through public works spending programs and ended up incurring enormous deficits. Unemployment is higher than any time since World War II. Consumer confidence has been low, despite a deflationary situation with stable prices. The general problem is this: The economic arrangement that the Japanese used to create the postwar "miracle years" no longer works. The Japanese government can no longer protect millions of jobs in inefficient industries without seriously hurting successful companies, damaging the economic well-being of the population as a whole, making Japan less competitive economically, and, because of the size of the Japanese economy, hurting the economies of the rest of Asia and the West.

Many economic analysts are critical of Japan for the Asian "melt-down" of the late 1990s, where a number of economies in the region experienced severe recessions. Years ago, countries such as South Korea and Indonesia adopted the Japanese system of capitalism by government guidance, heavy protection of domestic industries, and politicized banking sectors. Their top-down inflexible capitalism made recovery from the crisis more difficult. Also, with its massive purchasing power the Japanese economy should have been the locomotive that helped pull Asia out of the economic doldrums. However, because of the thicket of regulations that preclude purchases of many imports, a number of economists felt the Japanese weren't buying nearly enough Asian goods and services, thereby helping to keep regional economies stagnant.

The postwar political system characterized by LDP dominance and too much government by bureaucracy is in large part a reason for the perpetuation of Japan's economic problems. Although the LDP is a pro-business party, it has remained in power by protecting extremely inefficient industries at the expense of the general public's economic well-being. For example, the Japanese construction industry is solidly behind the LDP, and in return, politicians have created many unneeded public building programs such as technical colleges in rural areas with low youth population and high-speed train stations in the countryside. Japan has 6 million construction workers, many more than are actually needed. In return, the construction industry gives enormous amounts of kickbacks and contributions to LDP politicians. These 6 million Japanese construction workers constitute a little over 10 percent of the nation's workforce. By comparison, construction workers make up only slightly over 2.5 percent of workers in the United States. Japan's farmers and "mom and pop" small storeowners also contribute vast sums to the LDP and in return are protected from more efficient foreign and domestic competition.

This protection of inefficient businesses is, in a sense, a disguised welfare program. Because government unemployment and social security payments are modest, for decades the policymakers have transferred wealth from the public and from highly successful companies such as Sony and Toyota to the least efficient industries, such as construction and food processing. The government does this by protecting the inefficient industries from competition. This policy raises costs for productive Japanese companies such as Toyota and makes many products expensive for consumers. The long-term effect of all this has been to lower productivity, enhance public and private debt, and make the public and successful large companies more and more negative about government.

It is not just the LDP that is responsible for the policy decisions that have created the economic problems that concern both Japan and foreign nations. Bureaucrats have directed and guarded the interests of industries they are supposed to regulate by creating cartels and discouraging domestic and foreign competition. Until very recently, banks continued to lend money to financially shaky construction and real estate businesses while denying capital to more worthy firms in other sectors because the insolvent firms were already heavy borrowers and if they failed, the loans would have to be written off.

The combination of one long-time party dominance and great bureaucratic influence, coupled with the political and bureaucratic incentives to protect clients, has led to a great deal of corruption that throughout the 1990s was regularly reported in the media. One LDP vice president was discovered to have about $50 million in cash and gold bullion in his office, most of which was thought to be construction industry kickbacks. One prime minister and several other top LDP members were implicated as recipients of insider trading information from a firm in return for political favors. Also, throughout the same time period the media also reported instance after instance of shady situations where bureaucrats were bribed or given special gifts by both elected officials and private-sector interests in return for favors. The level of overt public criticism of national bureaucrats in Japan is higher now, due to several of these widely reported scandals, than at any time in Japanese political history. One exposé by a former Ministry of Health bureaucrat even became a best-selling book.

Both the public and large internationally competitive Japanese industries have called more and more for reform of the old postwar political/economic system. The LDP now suffers like never before at the polls because of voter discontent. Deregulatory reform is being enacted, albeit at a slow pace, in many economic sectors. Even within the LDP there are now reform factions who seriously challenge how much longer the traditionalists can protect the weak at society's expense.

The biggest political challenge to widespread and meaningful economic reform is that so many people are protected by the old system that there are always elected officials and bureaucrats to represent their interests. Because Japan has suffered an economic malaise and not a collapse, only modest changes have occurred despite much rhetoric. Still, more and more Japanese realize that if Japan is to regain its economic viability, the nation's political leaders must make the policy decisions that result in less government protection of the inefficient and less rule by bureaucratic fiat.

The Electorate and Government Reorganization: Solutions?

As this book goes to press the LDP faces the most intense negative perceptions from voters in its history. New political parties such as the Democratic Party of Japan may offer viable alternatives for voters who want to elect candidates who will use government to reform the economic system and clean up some of the attendant political corruption. Voters might also, through their choices, strengthen the reform elements in the LDP. What will happen at the voting booth is impossible to predict, but there is an intense ongoing open political debate in Japan now that was not present a decade ago about many of the issues.

Although what happens at the voting booth is anyone's guess, as of January 2001 a major governmental reorganization (which gained Diet approval in 1997) went into effect. The two primary purposes of the reorganization are to reduce the power of bureaucrats and increase the authority of elected officials, and to reduce the number of government employees. The number of national ministries and agencies was cut from twenty-two to twelve in an attempt to promote more flexibility in policymaking and implementation. This was affected by merging several ministries and agencies and creating two gigantic cabinet ministries, the National Land and Transportation Ministry and the General Affairs Ministry. The idea is that the reduction in the number of separate bureaucratic agencies and ministries will make elected officials' jobs easier in interacting with bureaucracy.

Another objective of the reorganization is to strengthen elected officials' power by increasing the executive authority of the prime minister. A special cabinet office that reports to the prime minister was established to create and formulate fundamental domestic and foreign policies. Also, this cabinet office has four groups of advisers, including a ten-member Economic and Fiscal Advisory Council made up of cabinet ministers and three members of the private sector. This council is charged with making recommendations for the national budget and macroeconomic policy.

The objective of the creation of the cabinet and councils, in particular the Economic and Fiscal Advisory Council, is to take budget and economic leadership away from the Foreign Ministry and place it in the hands of the elected executive. The reorganization also provides for the reduction of 25 percent of national civil servants in the next ten years and a substantial reduction in the number of legal towns, cities, and municipalities. Both of these measures' intent is to reduce government expenses and influence over the public and the economy.

It is much too early to know the level of effectiveness of the reorganization. What is reasonable to predict however, is that the days of old "55" political system, so named because 1955 was the year the LDP was created, are numbered. As noted Columbia political scientist Gerald Curtis observes, "Old verities—a prestigious and competent bureaucracy, a public consensus on national goals, one party dominance, an opposition that opposes for opposition's sake and does not offer a creditable alternative to the party in power—are gone"(Curtis 1999, 241–242). The problem is, as of now, no one really can predict with certainty the specific nature of new government and political institutions that are now rising.

JAPAN'S EDUCATIONAL SYSTEM

Cultural and Historical Foundations for Learning

Riverdale, New York, a suburb of New York City, is a community with a large concentration of Japanese families who are temporarily assigned to American branches of Japanese companies. Several years ago American educators in the Riverdale school district, upon enrolling Japanese children, were puzzled as to why their parents usually requested two sets of textbooks for each child. The teachers eventually learned that the Japanese children's mothers wanted their own textbooks so they could better assist their sons and daughters with homework. The Riverdale case is only one of several examples of the serious attitude most Japanese take toward education.

Many observers regard Japan as perhaps the world's most education-conscious society, and the results the Japanese achieve often support this argument. Linguists consider the Japanese language to be one of the world's most difficult to read and write, yet estimates are that well over 95 percent of the Japanese people are literate. Almost as many books are published in Japan annually as in the United States, though Japan has only about half the population of the United States. In one comparison of twelve developed countries. Japan was first in per-capita newspaper circulation. In international tests, Japanese students are usually at or near the top in standardized test performance in mathematics and science. Recent statistics indicate that approximately 97 percent of Japanese students graduate from high school, compared to 88 percent of American students. Furthermore, experts on Japanese education, such as Thomas Rohlen, estimate that the average Japanese high school graduate has attained about the same level of education as the average American who has completed two years of college.

Historic, economic, and cultural factors have all contributed to the Japanese passion for education and success with it. Education has always been considered a highly important aspect of Confucianism, which is still very influential in Japan. Even though there has been some slippage relative to the past, teachers still enjoy a relatively high level of respect in Japan compared to educators in many other developed countries.

Japan was also educationally successful by world standards long before present times. Although the Japanese did not construct a national government school system until the Meiji Period, late Tokugawa literacy rates were comparable to those in Western Europe and the United States. One of the key elements of the 1868 Charter Oath establishing the new Meiji government was the challenge "To seek knowledge throughout the world" (Duke 1986, 15). As Japan rushed to catch up with the West in the nineteenth century and the first half of the twentieth century, education remained extremely important. The U.S. occupation of Japan created much greater access to secondary schools and universities, thus further enhancing the historical Japanese commitment to education.

Much of the Japanese attachment to learning and a seemingly constant public dialogue about education is in part due to a national survival mentality. Because Japan is a crowded country and lacks almost all natural resources, the educational level—or in economic terms, human capital—of the citizenry is considered highly important for economic well-being. Although the situation is changing as more and more women work outside the home, Japanese women are more likely to quit work than their American or European counterparts when they have school-aged children. It is still considered more important for a Japanese mother to monitor her children's education than to find fulfillment in the workplace. The Japanese are also a homogenous people by world standards, a fact that makes the task of mass education easier than is the case in countries with more heterogeneous populations. Since World War II, Japan has become one of the most middle-class countries on earth; traditionally, in any culture, members of the middle class are the most avid believers in education.

The Structure of Japanese Education

Although historic, economic, and cultural factors are important, the structure of Japanese education has also contributed greatly to both impressive student attainment and, many would argue, to critical weaknesses in Japan's schools. Japanese public and private elementary and secondary schools, as well as institutions of higher education, are part of a centralized national system under the leadership of the Ministry of Education. Although such centralization is common in most developed countries, this configuration is in sharp contrast to the United States, where education is primarily a state and local responsibility.

The Japanese government spends close to 5 percent of GDP on education, which is approximately 2 percent less than the combined U.S. local, state, and federal educational expenditures as a percent of GDP. However, studies indicate that the average family in Japan spends considerably more on the education of their children than do their counterparts in the United States. Japan has compulsory education through the ninth grade, and educational expenditures for elementary and junior high schools are divided almost equally among the local, prefectural, and national governments. Although well over 90 percent of Japanese students attend and graduate from high school, the national government funds a much lower percentage of high school costs and considers upper secondary school funding to be a prefectural responsibility. Still, one result of substantial national contributions to Japanese elementary and secondary education is that there is much less variance in per-pupil expenditures in Japan than in the United States. The tax base of a particular locale in the United States can cause drastic differences in expenditures for students depending upon where they live.

Traditionally, Japanese public and private elementary and junior and senior high schools all followed a national curriculum developed by the Ministry of Education for both required and elective subjects. However, recent reforms (to be addressed later in this chapter) are stimulating some curricular diversity. Still, by and large, Japanese students study the same topics nationwide. Japanese students spend at least

Music is no frill in Japanese elementary and junior high schools and is a required subject. Here Japanese elementary students are practicing one of two rudimentary musical instruments they are required to learn to play. (Courtesy of Lucien Ellington)

six weeks longer in school each year than their American counterparts—summer vacation in Japan lasts only about half the time of most summer breaks in the United States. All Japanese schools from kindergarten through university operate on a trisemester academic year, with the school year beginning in April and ending the following March. Japanese students have short winter and spring holidays in addition to summer break.

During the U.S. occupation the Japanese adopted the 6–3–3 elementary, junior, and senior high school model. Although there are efforts to change this structure, Japanese schools are still mostly organized according to the old American model. Japanese students study the same subjects as their American counterparts, but with some differences. The level of mathematics instruction is more advanced in Japan than in the United States, so that by the end of eighth grade, Japanese students have studied beginning algebra and plane geometry.

Experts consider the Japanese written language to be one of the most difficult in the world to learn. In order to read Japanese, one must learn two different syllabaries, *hiragana* and *katakana,* and memorize thousands of Chinese characters, or *kanji.* Almost all kanji have two or more pronunciations. The Japanese Ministry of Education has ascertained that before one can read a newspaper, a minimum of 1,945 kanji must be memorized. The latter number is required before a student can complete junior high school. Therefore, an important difference in Japanese and Western education is the greater amount of time students in Japan spend on learning the written language when compared to their counterparts elsewhere.

Beginning in junior high school, virtually all Japanese study English until they graduate from high school, and recently there have been experiments with English language study for elementary students. Japanese students tend to spend much more time learning to read and write English than speak it, largely because the examination system assesses knowledge of the written rather than spoken language.

Also, art and music in Japan are part of the course of study for all students through junior high school and are not considered to be "frills." In art class, students both study art history and engage in studio art assignments. The national curriculum provides chances for Japanese students to learn about and practice both Asian and Western art. The same is true in the case of the music curriculum. Students learn music appreciation and how to play musical instruments such as recorders in elementary school. Although in many countries music is taught by specialists, in Japanese elementary schools, classroom teachers also double as music teachers. Japanese elementary teachers are well-positioned to handle this duty because each elementary education candidate must pass a rudimentary piano-playing test in order to procure a teaching license.

Japanese students take few electives through junior high school, but beginning in high school, there are different possibilities for young people depending on their interest and abilities. Between 75–80 percent of all high school students enroll in academic courses in secondary schools designed to prepare them for university. Many academic high school graduates, however, don't go on to four-year institutions of higher learning. Although all students take many of the same courses in academic high schools, there are math/science and humanities/social science tracks that offer students some coursework options. In Japan, a few American-style comprehensive high schools offering different tracks exist, but they aren't particularly popular.

Japanese students who attend vocational high schools enter mostly commercial or industrial high schools, although a few agricultural and fisheries high schools are also available. Students in any kind of vocational high school take a combination of academic and vocational courses. Japanese commercial high school students aspire to work in offices, whereas industrial high school students hope to be considered for manufacturing jobs.

When Westerners think of Japanese education, many imagine academics to be the only goal of Japanese schools. In the case of elementary and junior high schools the assumption is clearly incorrect, and even Japanese high school students are encouraged to have nonacademic pursuits. Elementary school students spend substantial time on nonacademic work such as art, music, moral education, and sports and cultural festivals. Junior high students spend nearly one-third of in-school time on nonacademic classes such as art, music, moral education, physical education, shop, and home economics. In addition, all junior high students and high school students have access to extracurricular clubs, and there are all-school cultural and sports festivals for which students spend time preparing. Parents and teachers consider education of the whole child very important, and the amount of time Japanese students spend in nonacademic classes reflects these societal beliefs about wholesome child-rearing.

Moral education for Japanese children and young people is considered to be especially important. A value adults are particularly interested in conveying to students is the importance of effort. It is common in Japanese classrooms to see signs exhorting students to try very hard, and teachers often use the verb *gambaru,* meaning "stand firm" or "persevere." This emphasis upon trying hard reflects a significant difference between Japanese and American conceptualizations of young people. American teachers often emphasize individual differences such as I.Q. whereas Japanese educators tend to believe that everyone is roughly equal in abilities but those who try the hardest succeed. Respect for the school itself is another important value that is transmitted to the young in Japanese education. Students and teachers clean the school together on a regular basis, and there are far fewer custodial staff in Japan than in the United States.

Following the rules is considered even more important in Japan than in many other countries, and schools have numerous—and to outsiders, sometimes seemingly pointless—regulations. There is one correct backpack for elementary students and one correct way to adjust the straps. There is one correct list of school supplies. School uniforms, required of most junior and senior high school students, are to be worn in one correct manner. There are also numerous rules for parents (usually mothers) about everything from appropriate *o-bentos,* or box lunches, to exactly how the child's homework desk should be arranged at home. School rules on appropriate student behavior also exist for weekends and holidays. Although some schools are stricter than others in enforcement, in general, Japanese educators and many parents have no compunction whatsoever about providing very extensive rules of conduct and dress for students.

Educational institutions are only as effective as the people who work in them. One characteristic of Japanese schools at every level is that they have a low number of administrators. Normally, there are only two administrators, a principal and a head teacher, although some schools are beginning to hire counselors. The principal is often an educator near the end of his (a few are women) career and usually spends more time working with external influential parties such as prefectural and Ministry of Education officials than actually supervising the daily routine of the school. The latter chore falls upon the head teacher. Usually head teachers teach just one class a day and, along with the faculty, actually run the daily affairs of the school.

Japanese teachers at all levels tend to be impressive by anyone's standards. Most were academically at least slightly above average compared to their college classmates who entered other fields. One study in the 1990s indicated that 48 percent of newly qualified but not yet employed teachers had grade-point averages exceeding B+ compared to 42 percent of other bachelor degree recipients. Furthermore, teachers at all levels in Japan take more academic content courses and fewer, less demanding education courses than their American counterparts. Teacher salaries in Japan are comparable to salaries for pharmacists, middle managers, and other professionals. Once hired, a teacher has a lifetime job, as dismissal is quite rare.

Because of Confucian influences, teaching has always been a relatively high-status occupation in Japan, and there have usually been more applicants than positions. Recently, shrinking numbers of students in school because of almost two decades of declining birth rates have made it even more difficult to obtain a teaching position. Annually, more than 200,000 applicants compete for fewer than 40,000 available positions in the Japanese public school system. Prefectural and metropolitan school boards also employ rigorous selection processes, including written examinations and interviews, as well as skill and physical fitness tests.

Once teachers are hired, their workloads are quite demanding, but in different ways than is the case in U.S. schools. Japanese teachers at all levels teach fewer classes a day than their American counterparts. For example, Japanese junior high teachers usually teach four classes each day, and their high school counterparts usually teach three daily classes. By contrast, American junior and senior high teachers are responsible for five to six classes a day. However, Japanese teachers put in more hours a week at school than do U.S. teachers. Because there are few administrators in Japanese schools, teacher committees assume significant responsibilities. Japanese teachers are also expected to visit each student's home at least once in an academic year, tutor students in special summer classes, work in extracurricular activities, and even patrol neighborhoods during summer vacation to make sure students aren't frequenting the wrong kind of places.

Even though teachers and administrators believe in whole child education and devote much time to nonacademic instruction in schools, the Japanese, particularly at the junior and senior high school levels, require students to learn much more academic content than is the case in the United States. Part of the reason behind the high academic expectations for students can be attributed to Confucian respect for education and other cultural factors. Still, probably an even greater reason many Japanese junior and senior high school students work so hard is the high school and university examination system.

The Examination Race

Virtually all Japanese students take high school examinations in their ninth-grade year, administered in the prefectures. Since approximately half of Japan's high school seniors go on to some kind of postsecondary education, large numbers of students also take university entrance examinations

One of the biggest contrasts in Japanese education is illustrated in these two photos. Japanese elementary schools tend to be warm and nurturing places, while Japanese secondary schools, because of the examination race, tend to be much more businesslike. Note that the elementary students in the top photo don't wear uniforms and appear quite relaxed, while the junior high students in bottom photo have on summer uniforms and are listening to didactic instruction, which is typical after elementary school. (Courtesy of Lucien Ellington)

(both a national examination and often individual university examinations) during the last year of upper secondary school. These examinations are important rites of passage for most Japanese young people and of much interest to the nation as a whole.

The examination system has become increasingly controversial in Japan. Public and private high schools in any Japanese city are academically rated by the general public from top to bottom on the basis of the quality of universities that their graduates tend to enter.

Ninth-grade students who wish to have a good chance of passing examinations to attend a highly ranked university work very hard to pass entrance examinations for one of the better high schools. The examination system also affects the nature of instruction. Japanese elementary schools tend to have in many ways relaxed environments, and teachers use a variety of classroom activities. Because teachers in junior and senior high schools are under pressure to prepare students for entrance examinations, instruction tends to focus upon factual knowledge and to be largely didactic.

Because examination scores are the primary means for determining admission to high schools and universities, the number of private cram schools, or *juku,* in Japan has grown tremendously in recent years. Recent studies indicate that 24 percent of elementary students, 60 percent of lower secondary students, and 30 percent of high school students attend juku. In urban areas the percentages are higher than these national averages, and enrollment is growing in rural locales. Almost all elementary juku are not focused on examination preparation but enrich students' in-school experiences through supplementary lessons in piano, swimming, or conversational English. Virtually all juku at higher levels specialize in examination preparation. Although the average juku is quite small and is often run out of a private home, there are also several large corporate national juku chains that enroll thousands of students. Typically, students preparing for high school or university entrance examinations will attend juku two to three times a week after school or on Saturdays for six months to a year before the examinations. Although juku costs vary, recent average monthly tuition is over $150, excluding supplementary materials costs.

Although there are exceptions, most Japanese national and prefectural universities are more prestigious than their private counterparts because private universities are newer and easier to enter. All students who wish to enter a government university take a common examination in January on core academic subjects. Public universities and the more elite private universities use the common examination as a screening device and not as the final determinant of a candidate's entry. In late February or early March, some universities also require candidates who exceed that institution's cutoff score to take a second, one-day examination written by the university academic department they are attempting to enter. The most successful candidates on this second examination are then admitted to the university. Although the examination system is rigorous for students attempting to enter middle-level and highly-ranked universities, there is a certain equality of opportunity at work. No matter how rich or influential one's father is, if a student does not score high enough to enter Tokyo University, the top-ranked Japanese institution of higher learning, he or she won't be admitted.

Japanese high school seniors who are seeking admission to elite institutions such as Tokyo University often fail examinations on their first try and spend a year, or sometimes even two or three years, studying for and attempting the examinations again. Depending upon the year, as many as one-third of all Japanese admitted to university annually have spent at least a year after high school graduation studying for examinations.

For many Japanese young people, doing well on university entrance examinations and gaining admission to the right university is extremely important because it directly affects later employment opportunities. In Japan large companies and government institutions hire new managerial-level employees from a few universities. The university to which a student is admitted is usually far more important in determining future job offers than is academic performance while in college. Life is particularly hard for high school juniors and seniors who are seeking admission to the best universities—and often even the average ones. Required to memorize enormous amounts of information to pass the university entrance examinations, Japanese students tell each other that if one expects to pass the examinations he or she had best sleep no more than four hours a night in the crucial months before test day.

Student Life and Behavior Patterns

Although Japanese secondary schools are much more work than play for students preparing for examinations, many students still manage to participate in extracurricular activities. In junior and senior high schools, clubs are a regular part of the weekly schedule, and schools offer many of the same competitive sports that are found in American schools, including the highly popular baseball and soccer as well as basketball, increasingly American-style football, swimming, and track. Large numbers of Japanese students also participate in traditional sports including judo, kendo (a form of Japanese fencing), and sumo wrestling. There are also many nonsports extracurricular clubs, including brass band, dance, drama, flower arranging, and tea ceremony. Japanese teachers encourage extracurricular activities because they believe students learn to be good group members through participation. In contrast to their American counterparts, Japanese students will participate in only one or at most two extracurricular activities but spend many hours with the particular club or sports team.

Almost all Japanese junior and senior high school students

wear uniforms, which adults believe help to inhibit class distinctions among students and assist in promoting order. Japanese students are taught that while most people have very similar innate abilities, it is the amount of effort that determines whether a person succeeds or fails. Generally, because education is quite time consuming for many youngsters and for cultural reasons, Japanese high school students are less likely than their American counterparts to engage in alcohol and drug use, couples dating, and after-school jobs. Among Japanese young people, deviant behavior of all kinds has been much lower per capita than is the case in the United States.

In recent years though, Japanese youth misbehavior has risen relative to the past and is now a major national concern. Since the 1980s more and more Japanese young people, particularly junior high students, contract "school refusal syndrome" where they won't go to school. Also, especially at the junior high level, the number of students suffering from *ijime,* or bullying, by their peers has been increasing annually. More ominous examples of recent Japanese youth misbehavior include increases in violent crime, teenage prostitution, gang activity, and substance abuse.

Higher Education

With approximately 3 million students enrolled in 1,200 universities and junior colleges, Japan has the second-largest higher educational system in the developed world. In contrast to the prewar years and postwar decades, women are now fully participating in higher education, with roughly equal percentages of men and women enrolled in higher education. As is the case with secondary schools, public universities in Japan have higher status than most private institutions. The old prewar imperial universities, with Tokyo University at the top, are the institutions that are the most difficult to enter. A few select private universities, such as

Keio and Waseda, and some prefectural universities are considered relatively prestigious. Private universities, which constitute the majority of Japanese higher educational institutions, are considered to have low status. Only about 25 percent of Japan's university students are enrolled in public institutions. The Japanese government in the postwar years built quite a few public universities but not enough to satisfy student demand for higher education. In general, students who aren't admitted to public universities must opt for more expensive, but inferior, private universities. An important government ministry or powerful corporation will usually exclusively recruit new employees from a few prestigious universities. Higher education governance is partially the responsibility of local institutions, but the Ministry of Education also has authority in the process.

For a variety of reasons, both Japanese and foreign observers consider the nation's university system to be mediocre compared to other levels of Japanese education and to other developed nations' institutions of higher learning. Many Japanese universities are difficult to enter but are academically rather undemanding. University faculties tend to be not particularly interested in teaching and have low expectations of students. Many students, having just won the examination wars, use their college years to have fun. Subsequently, the popular press often describes Japanese universities as four-year vacations. Although some majors, such as engineering, are considered important by the private sector, most employers pay much more attention to the university that a student managed to enter than to his or her college course of study.

Japanese universities also tend to be structurally quite rigid. It is extremely difficult for a student to change majors in many universities since it would entail taking a new departmental examination. Because of the examination system, transferring from one university to another is virtually impossible. Unlike the situation in the United States where so-called nontraditional students regularly enroll in universities, it is still extremely difficult for a student who is not age 18–21 years to enter a Japanese university. Japan's graduate education also is underdeveloped compared to European countries and the United States. Although numbers are increasing, only slightly more than 7 percent of Japanese undergraduates go on to graduate school, compared to 13 percent of their U.S. counterparts. Many Japanese companies and ministries feel that the university system does not meet enough of the practical needs of society. The large numbers of private sector-university applied research ventures that take place in the United States are largely absent in Japanese universities.

Educational Reform

Despite the impressive performance of Japanese students when compared to their peers in other developed nations, as the twenty-first century begins there is widespread dissatisfaction on the part of many Japanese about the nation's educational system. Some major educational reforms will be implemented in April 2002, and a second set of reforms are being debated at the time of this book's publication. In an education-conscious society such as Japan, the state of the nation's schools is always a public policy topic, but domestic concern about Japan's schools has been particularly high since the early1980s when Prime Minister Nakasone and the Diet established an Ad-Hoc National Commission on Educational Reform. The late Prime Minister Obuchi also created a National Conference on Educational Reform in March 2000.

Those individuals and organizations that are promoting educational reform in Japan are doing so for both educational and values-related reasons. Many Japanese believe the examination system is too stressful, that the schools are too rigid and don't meet the needs of individual students, that today's students show little interest in studying, and that the educational system in general needs to produce more creative and flexible individuals for the twenty-first century. Also, large numbers of Japanese blame the schools for an increase in child misbehavior, rising rates of prolonged student absenteeism, student physical violence, student bullying, and the rise of teenage crime. The set of reforms that will be implemented in April 2002 is an attempt to make the curriculum more flexible and capable of meeting individual student needs. By the beginning of the 2002 school year all half-day Saturday classes will be eliminated in order to reduce student workload and stress. Also, nearly one-third of the curriculum in elementary and junior high schools will be eliminated, with deep cuts in all major subjects. The replacement classroom activity will be a new endeavor entitled Integrated Studies that will have few guidelines and no accompanying textbooks. The goal of Integrated Studies is to provide students and teachers the freedom to study whatever interests them, whether the topic is religion, the environment, or foreign affairs. Some elementary schools are planning to implement English-language study in the Integrated Studies time block.

The second set of proposed educational reforms, the result of the Obuchi-appointed educational advisory body, address both values and academic issues and are quite controversial. In an attempt to make higher education more flexible, there is a proposal to drop the age that a student can be admitted to university from eighteen to fifteen. One of the most hotly debated recommendations is a proposal that all elementary and junior high students be required to perform two weeks of annual community service, with the amount of time extended to one month for high school students. This suggestion reflects the notion that contemporary Japanese youth are not being taught that they have an obligation to society. Opponents of the proposal worry that such activities will detract from academic performance. There are also proposals to reduce class size, increase the amount of moral education in the schools, and initiate a system that rewards competent teachers while punishing substandard teacher performance. Also, there is much official and unofficial rhetoric about drastic reform of the examination system, but as of yet, no official proposals have been formulated.

Although it is impossible to assess the impact of both scheduled and proposed educational reforms, one thing is certain. Since the Meiji years the Japanese have placed an extremely high value on education and consistently made it a high national priority. There is absolutely no reason to expect that education will be afforded any less attention as Japan negotiates the twenty-first century.

JAPANESE RELIGION

Are Most Japanese Religious?

Japanese religious practice and public attitudes toward religion are markedly different than is the case in the West. Also, for well over a decade there has been widespread discussion of a spiritual crisis in Japan, particularly among the young. The Japanese religious landscape is dynamic. Even though dominant forms of religion have been practiced for over one thousand years, new religions have been created in the nineteenth and twentieth centuries, and some of them are quite powerful. One of the new religions, Aum Shinrikyo, shocked Japan and the world in 1995 when it was found to be responsible for gassing innocent people on the Tokyo subway.

Both historically and at present, one of the biggest differences between organized religion in Japan and the West is the syncretic nature of Japanese religious practice. Most Japanese have no problem with incorporating aspects of different religious creeds and practice into their lives. Many Japanese, for example, have family shrines where Shinto and Buddhist icons are both present. At least one study indicates that 65 percent of Japanese have small family religious home shrines. It is quite common for Japanese to marry and christen babies at Shinto shrines and gather for funerals at Buddhist temples. Even though Christians constitute less than 1 percent of the Japanese population, getting married in Christian churches recently became somewhat of a fad among Japanese young people. Often the marrying couples will have both a Christian and a Shinto wedding service.

Although proponents of Buddhism, Shinto, and Confucianism had significant doctrinal and political differences at various points in Japanese history, peaceful religious syncretism is nothing new. The tradition goes back well over one thousand years. The first historical record of the figurative transfer of a Shinto kami (divinity) in a portable shrine was in 749 C.E. when a kami was taken from Kyushu to Nara to protect the construction of the Buddhist Temple Todaiji, which contains one of Japan's two Great Buddhas.

When surveyed, most Japanese report they are not religious and don't believe in God, but part of the problem with the question lies in exactly what constitutes being "religious." Certainly religious practices and influences are widespread in Japan.

When the subjects of religious practices and the relative influence of traditional religions on contemporary Japanese life are addressed, most scholars of religion and philosophy agree that Confucianism actually exerts the most influence on how Japanese actually act. There has been a long debate over whether Confucianism is a religion or philosophy, but there is no question that it has profound influence in northeast Asian countries. The irony of Confucianism in Japan is that many Japanese don't even think of themselves as "Confucian," but the teachings are deeply integrated into Japanese life. The very terms "Confucianism" and "Confucian" are Western inventions. Northeast Asians have traditionally called the belief system "the teachings of the scholars."

Although Confucian teachings had been influential before the Tokugawa era, it was during that period of Japanese

A typical home shrine. Buddhist, Confucian, and Shinto icons might all be present in the same shrine. (Courtesy of Lucien Ellington)

Each year millions of Japanese visit religious sites such as the temple in the Horyuji complex in Nara where this statue of the Buddha of Boundless Light, Amida, is housed. This particular icon was created in 1232 C.E. (Library of Congress)

history that the government adopted so-called neo-Confucianism as part of official state ideology. As the Japanese rushed to Westernize, Confucian ideas fell out of favor during the first part of the Meiji era, but they were too much a part of the fabric of Japanese life to disappear. Confucianism is very much in evidence when Japanese action is observed today.

Most Japanese are quite secular in their metaphysical views. Confucius, while not an atheist or even overtly agnostic, focused his teaching on appropriate virtue and conduct in this world. Since the Tokugawas incorporated Confucianism into the nation's legal system over three hundred years ago, Japan has been more a secular than a religious-faith based nation.

The Japanese emphasis upon both academic and moral education, the entrance examination system, and the rewards that well-educated people accrue in Japanese society are beliefs and practices partially resulting from Confucianism. Confucius strongly emphasized education for virtue as well as knowledge, and he believed in an aristocracy based upon these characteristics instead of bloodlines. Most Japanese business and political elites positioned themselves for their current positions by working hard and succeeding in Japan's relatively meritocratic educational system.

Confucianism also directly affects Japanese attitudes toward work, society, and the group. Confucian teachings strongly stress the virtues of hard work, obligation, and reciprocity. In all northeast Asian countries a widely accepted work ethic is quite apparent. Countries like Japan and South Korea are annually at, or near, the top of developed countries in number of hours worked. As is the case with other Confucian countries, Japan is a status-conscious society. Confucius is not an egalitarian belief system, and this is reflected in the Japanese propensity to find few things equal, and to assign differing levels of status to both individuals and institutions. Within these institutions, superiors and subordinates owe each other protection, loyalty, and good team play. These Confucian propensities manifest themselves very clearly in

Japanese business practices such as superiors helping to find potential spouses for subordinates, and employees voluntarily not taking their full annual vacation time so as to put in more hours in their offices.

The Confucian notion that the family is the all-important unit in society is deeply imbedded in Japanese culture. The most obvious sign is Japan's still-low divorce rate compared to other developed countries. The Confucian notion of family is hierarchical rather than egalitarian. Although elderly people are now more and more living apart from their children, the continued relatively high levels of respect shown the elderly in Japan, and the practice of ancestor worship in many Japanese homes, is in large part Confucian-based. The still unequal treatment of women in the Japanese workplace partially reflects Confucian notions about the segregated roles of the sexes.

Confucius was very concerned about public as well as family life. Rule by virtuous leaders was a constant subject the sage addressed in his teaching. Confucius felt that rulers should lead by example and that developing a sense of shame in people was a much better tool to make them behave than specified and detailed legal codes. The Japanese propensity to first ascertain the trustworthiness of a potential business partner rather than heavily relying on contracts, the somewhat general nature of Japan's statutory laws, and the minimal role of litigation as a problem-solving method in Japan each partially reflect Confucian influences.

Like any belief system, Confucianism is an ideal conceptualization of human action; how people behave in the real world is often contradictory to cultural belief systems. Japan's political leaders have certainly engaged in corrupt practices. Still, Japanese rates of violent crime, theft, drug abuse, and divorce are among the lowest in the world. Recent U.S. and Japanese statistics indicate the United States has 519 prison inmates for every 100,000 people, while the Japanese have 37 prisoners for every 100,000 people. Japan has one-third as many police per capita as the United States,

Both of these photos have Shinto ramifications. The large edifice in the top photo is a Torii Gate, which always signifies a Shinto Shrine. The people in the bottom photo are participants in an annual matsuri, or Japanese festival. Most Japanese festivals have Shinto roots. (Courtesy of Lucien Ellington)

one-fifth as many judges per capita, and one-twentieth as many jail cells per capita.

It is also quite common throughout Japan to see government-financed signs and billboards exhorting people to do the right thing. Upon entering an urban Tokyo park, for instance, a visitor will encounter a host of messages requesting park patrons to keep things clean for others, preserve the grass, jog on designated paths and not cut corners, and not do anything that might bother other people who use the space. Although such good behavior admonitions are common in many countries, they are much more numerous in Japan than in the West. This practice reflects the Confucian notion that people will probably act virtuous if they are constantly reminded to do so. Although it is impossible to quantify the relationship between Confucian teachings and the high relative level of social stability in Japan, there is little doubt that a relationship does in fact exist.

In direct contrast to Confucianism, Buddhism and Shinto each exercise relatively little influence on the actual actions of Japanese. Although almost 90 percent of Japanese report they are Buddhists, very few people are familiar with Buddhist theology or pursue Buddhism in a serious way. Two of the largest three Japanese Buddhist sects, Pure Land and True Pure Land, focus upon worship of Amida, the Buddha of the Western Paradise. The third large sect, Nichiren, is devoted to veneration of the Lotus Sutra, a classic work of Buddhist theology. Neither of these three sects are theologically very sophisticated.

Although there are devout Buddhists and Zen meditation adherents, most Japanese limit their relationship with Buddhism to using priests for funerals and visiting culturally or historically important temples. The Tokugawa government, in an effort to discover hidden Christians, forced every Japanese family to register with a Buddhist temple. However, with the great rural to urban demographic shift of the twentieth century, many Japanese families have lost connections with their family temples and use whatever temple is available nearby for funerals.

Shinto shrines, like Buddhist temples, are everywhere in Japan, but the religion is not a significant ethical influence on Japanese except in promoting a certain reverence for nature. Millions of Japanese do observe the custom of visiting Shinto shrines on New Years Day, and some shrines do a brisk business selling good-luck charms for marriage, fertility, examination success, and even auto safety. Children are christened at shrines and taken there during special festivals during their third, fifth, and seventh years. Many couples have Shinto weddings. Important Shinto shrines hold annual festivals where revelers carry large portable shrines that figuratively transport the local kami all around the immediate area of the home shrine. It is not uncommon for large companies to have small shrines honoring particular kami. Still, Shinto, with no theology, sacred texts, or charismatic leaders, is a religion of ceremony, not a religion of belief.

In Japan, Buddhist and Shinto influences can be found in the arts and even in recreational activities. Zen Buddhism in particular was very influential in shaping Japanese arts. Even today, traditional practices such as brush painting, haiku poetry, landscape gardening, flower arranging, and noh theater, all of which accentuate the beauty of simplicity, are at least partially influenced by Zen. Popular nature-oriented activities, which derive from Shinto and to a lesser extent Zen Buddhism, have been so important in Japanese life that there are special words in the language for the acts of moon and flower viewing. Temples and shrines are quite popular sightseeing sites for Japanese tourists. Many of the larger ones, such as Sensoji Temple in the Asakusa section of Tokyo, have a festive atmosphere with attendant souvenir shops and food stands on temple and shrine grounds or in extremely close proximity.

Although most Japanese engage in the religion-related practices and activities just described, it is also true that,

Zen Buddhism, with its emphasis upon the natural, has profoundly influenced Japanese arts including gardening. This Kyoto rock and water garden appears natural but every stone has been placed. (Courtesy of Lucien Ellington)

with the exception of adherents of the so-called New Religions, most Japanese seem to lack firm religious convictions. Dominant Japanese religions lack the highly specific prescriptive codes of conduct found in such faiths as Christianity, Judaism, and Islam. Japan is characterized by more religious toleration than many societies and by a lack of clearly defined moral laws that people can violate. Although most Japanese engage in religious practices, the typical Japanese is much more secular than his or her American counterpart. The true religious believers in Japan are virtually all adherents of the so-called new religions.

The New Religions

Since roughly the 1850s there have been at least three religion booms in Japan where new and often quite unorthodox faiths have attracted large numbers of people. The first boom coincided with the end of Tokugawa rule, and the second occurred after World War II. Some observers assert that the third boom, which dates back to the 1970s, is still occurring. There are hundreds of the new religions, and several, the largest of which is Soka Gakkai, have millions of members.

Most of the new religious movements have high-profile leaders, many of whom behave in somewhat similar fashion to charismatic Christian evangelists in the United States. The new religions tend to promise happiness on earth and deliverance from suffering if members faithfully subscribe to the creeds. Other characteristics of the new religions include lavish headquarters and mass meetings attended by thousands. Until recently, the overwhelming majority of followers of the new religions were lower-middle-class or poor people, many of whom spent their youths in rural areas and moved to the city for economic reasons. Lately, there is some evidence that the socioeconomic class backgrounds of people who are attracted to the new religions are becoming somewhat more varied. The new religions also seem to be appealing to more and more of Japan's young.

Soka Gakkai merits special attention because of its large following, great wealth, and political activities. Soka Gakkai, or in English, "Value-Creation Society," was founded in 1930 but began to attract a large number of adherents after World War II. Soka Gakkai was originally affiliated with the over-700-year-old Nichiren Buddhist Sect, but the two religious organizations severed ties in the early 1990s. Soka Gakkai has about 9 million members in Japan, many of them working-class women, and over 1 million members in other countries including the United States. The sect's beliefs and practices are a combination of mantra chanting, positive thinking, and self-help strategies. Soka Gakkai makes generous donations to charities and claims to promote peace, culture, and education. Still, Soka Gakkai's claim that other religions are in error makes many Japanese quite ill at ease.

Large numbers of Japanese are also disturbed by the wealth and influence of Soka Gakkai. Estimates are that the sect has amassed approximately $82 billion through sale of burial plots, rental property, and publications. Soka Gakkai also has a political arm, the New Komeito, or "Clean Government" party, which commands about 7 million votes, approximately a tenth of Japan's voting population and an estimated fifth of voters who turn out in most elections. Because of this political strength the LDP included New Komeito in one of its recent coalition governments.

Although many Japanese continue to be uneasy about Soka Gakkai, the Japanese people were shocked by the March 20, 1995, actions of Aum Shinrikyo, a doomsday new religions cult led by Shoko Asahara, a partially blind former meditation teacher. Allegedly acting to divert police attention since authorities were already investigating previous cult activities, Aum Shinrikyo members released deadly Nazi Germany–era sarin gas inside five Tokyo subway cars during rush hour, killing twelve passengers and making more than 5,000 other passengers sick. Authorities then found weapons, poison gas, and torture chambers at the Aum Shinrikyo compound near Mount Fuji as well as clear evidence that cult members had murdered individuals who tried to leave Aum Shinrikyo. Although the cult's membership had shrunk to a little over 1,000 people by the year 2000, in its heyday Aum Shinrikyo claimed to have 10,000 Japanese members as well as 30,000 members in Russia.

Aum Shinrikyo's actions stimulated a discussion in Japan that went far beyond the specific crimes that the cult perpetrated. Many of the cult's leaders were young well-educated Japanese with university degrees. A number of social commentators as well as some young people feel the country is experiencing a spiritual malaise. Those concerned about what is perceived as a spiritual vacuum believe that since the end of World War II the most highly valued goals of most Japanese have been economic development and materialism.

There is certainly evidence that more and more young people want something more from life than simply affluence. Whether the traditional religions will rise to the occasion and fill the spiritual needs of the Japanese or if more and more people will turn to the new religions are questions that will probably be answered as the new century unfolds.

References

"Aum Followers Down by 10." *The Japan Times Online.* 16 August 2000. http://www.japantimes.com.

Buckley, Roger. 1998. *Japan Today.* New York: Cambridge University Press.

Curtis, Gerald. 1999. *The Logic of Japanese Politics: Leaders, Institutions, and the Limits of Change.* New York: Columbia University Press.

Dawkins, William. "New Religions Have Been a Feature of Japan's Modern History." *Financial Times* (London). 3 April 1995. Available online at http://www.lexis-nexis.com.

Dawson, Chester. "In God's Country." *Far Eastern Economic Review* (22 June 2000): 26–27.

"Demand for Educational Reform Met: Ministry Launches 41 Pilot Projects in an Effort to Improve Curricula." *The Japan Times Online.* 8 April 2000. http://www.japantimes.com.

Duke, Benjamin. 1986. *The Japanese School: Lessons for Industrial America.* Westport, CT: Greenwood Press.

"Education Law in Need of Drastic Review: Report." *The Japan Times Online.* 23 December 2000. http://www.japantimes.com.

"Educational Reform, Not Regression." *The Japan Times Online.* 1 August 2000. http://www.japantimes.com.

Ellington, Lucien. 1992. *Education in the Japanese Life-cycle: Implications for the United States.* Lewiston, NY: Edwin Mellen Press.

———. 1990. *Japan: Tradition and Change.* White Plains, NY: Longman.

French, Howard W. "A Sect's Political Rise Creates Uneasiness in Japan." *New York Times.* 4 November 1999, Late Edition-Final. Available online at http://www.lexis-nexis.com.

Fukuzawa, Rebecca Erwin, and Gerald K. Letendre. 2000. *Intense Years: How Japanese Adolescents Balance School, Family, and Friends.* New York: Routledge Falmer.

"Group Urges State to Aid Survivors of Sarin Gassing." *The Japan Times Online.* 21 March 2001. http://www.japantimes.com.

Hani, Yoko. "Teacher Upbeat on Proposals of Education Reform Panel." *The Japan Times Online.* 4 January 2001. http://www.japantimes.com.

———. "Cabinet Interview: Better Education System Hinges on Revision of Law, Machimura." *The Japan Times Online.* 9 December 2000. http://www.japantimes.com.

Hosakawa, Ryuichiro. "Only Education Reform Can Save Japan." *The Japan*

Times Online. 6 April 2000. http://www.japantimes.com.

Hurst, G. Cameron, III. "The Enigmatic Japanese Spirit." *Orbis,* Vol. 42, No. 2 (Spring 1998).

"Japanese Universities Need to Teach New Skills." *The Asian Wall Street Journal,* Weekly Edition, 11 June 2001.

LeTendre, Gerald K. 2000. *Learning to Be Adolescent: Growing up in U.S. and Japanese Middle Schools.* New Haven, CT: Yale University Press.

Marshall, Andrew. "It Gassed the Tokyo Subway, Microwaved Its Enemies, and Tortured Its Members. So Why Is the Aum Cult Thriving?" *The Guardian* (London). 15 July 1999. Available online at http://www.lexis-nexis.com.

Masuzoe, Yoichi, ed. 2000. *Years of Trial: Japan in the 1990s.* Tokyo: Japan Echo, Inc.

McCargo, Duncan. 2000. *Contemporary Japan.* New York: St. Martin's Press.

Millard, Mike. 2000. *Leaving Japan: Observations on the Dysfunctional U.S.-Japan Relationship.* Armonk, NY: M. E. Sharpe.

"Ministry Shakeup Just a Beginning." *The Japan Times Online.* 9 January 2001. http://www.japantimes.com.

Nabeshima, Keizo. "Still Waiting for Real Reform." *The Japan Times Online.* 12 January 2001. http://www.japantimes.com.

————. "Reorganization Isn't Reform." *The Japan Times Online.* 16 October 2000. http://www.japantimes.com.

"New Religions Rivaling Old Traditions in Japan." *The Los Angeles Times.* 13 May 1995, Home Edition. Available online at http://www.lexis-nexis.com.

Ohmori, Fujio. "The Flawed Consensus on Education Reform." *Japan Echo,* Vol. 27, No. 6 (December 2000): 14–16.

Parry, Richard Lloyd. "Japan Braced for the Party of Mantra and Machiavelli." *The Independent* (London). 25 June 2000. Available online at http://www.lexis-nexis.com.

"Popularity of Cults Reflects Japan's Gaping Spiritual Void." *The Japan Times.* 22 December 1999. Available online at http://www.lexis-nexis.com.

Radin, Charles A. "Young Adults in Japan Find Spirituality in New Forms." *The Boston Globe.* 21 May 1995, City Edition. Available online at http://www.lexis-nexis.com.

Reader, Ian. 2000. *Religious Violence in Contemporary Japan: The Case of Aum Shinrikyo.* Honolulu: University of Hawaii Press.

"The Rebuilding Starts Now." *The Japan Times Online.* 1 January 2001. http://www.japantimes.com.

"Reforming Education." *Mainchi Daily News.* 2 March 2001. Available online at http://www.lexis-nexis.com/uni . . .e20aa1162cbcbd76977 aa56f87dbc8.

Reid, T. R. 2000. *Confucius Lives Next Door: What Living in the East Teaches Us about Living in the West.* New York: Vintage.

Reischauer, Edwin O. 1981. *Japan: The Story of a Nation.* Third Edition. New York: Alfred Knopf.

"Revamping Education." *Mainichi Daily News.* 25 December 2000. Available online at http://www.lexis-nexis.com/uni . . .5816eeab4d4ec 0be0dac72f11cd4be.

Rohlen, Thomas P. 1997. "Differences That Make a Difference: Explaining Japan's Success." In William K. Cummings and Philip G. Altbach, eds., *The Challenge of East Asian Education: Implications for America.* Albany: State University of New York Press.

Sadao, Asami. "New Religions Tend to Thrive Amid Social Malaise." *The Daily Yomiuri.* 24 May 1995. Available online at http://www.lexis-nexis.com.

"School Reform Goals Outlined; Panel Head to Aim for Custom-made Educational System." *The Japan Times Online.* 11 March 2000. http://www.japantimes.com.

Sprague, Jonathan, and Murakami Mutsuko. "Japan's Dilemma." *Asiaweek.* 16 March 2001. Available online at http://www.asiaweek.com/ asiaweek/magazine/nations/0,8782,101784,00.html.

"State Secretaries to Establish Own Policy Body." *The Japan Times Online.* 8 January 2001. http://www.japantimes.com.

"Support, at a Price." *The Economist* (U.S. Edition). 3 July 1999. Available online at http://www.lexis-nexis.com.

Takenaka, Heizo. "Real Reform Is Just Beginning." *The Japan Times Online.* 26 December 2000. http://www.japantimes.com.

Tashiro, Masami, ed. 2000. *Japan 2001: An International Comparison.* Tokyo: Keizai Koho Center.

Tsuneyoshi, Ryoko. 2001. *The Japanese Model of Schooling: Comparisons with The United States.* New York: Routledge Falmer.

Wanner, Barbara. "Lower House Elections Portend More Muddling Through in Japan." *Japan Economic Institute Report,* No. 28A, Parts A and B (21 July 2000).

Webster, Fiona. "The Wellspring of Pacifism in Japan." Review of *Prophets of Peace: Pacifism and Cultural Identity in Japan's New Religions,* by Robert Kisala. *The Japan Times Online.* 12 April 2000. http://www.japantimes.com.jp.

Wray, Harry. 1999. *Japanese and American Education: Attitudes and Practices.* Westport, CT: Bergin and Garvey.

Yamamoto, Shinichi. "Making the Grade: Japanese Universities Aim to 'Outshine the Competition.'" *Look Japan.* May 2000. Available online at http://www.lookjapan.com/May00/May00_cover.html.

Yamazaki, Masakazu. "Clarify Two Categories of Education" *The Daily Yomiuri.* 27 November 2000. Available online at http://www.lexis-nexis.com/uni . . .ce7b50050f642848703a21ea24fae.

Yamamoto, Tadashi, ed. 1999. *Deciding the Public Good: Governance and Civil Society in Japan.* New York: Japan Center for International Exchange.

CHAPTER FOUR

Japanese Society and Contemporary Issues

The purpose of this chapter is to assist readers in better understanding Japanese society and contemporary issues. The group orientation of most Japanese is the major characteristic that makes them different from Americans and people in other Western countries. Although all cultural stereotypes have limitations, any exploration of contemporary Japanese society must address the dominant role of the group in shaping individual Japanese actions.

After exploration of the general role of groups in Japanese life, one of the primary societal units, the family, is examined. In contemporary Japan, the role of women within families is changing more dramatically at present than at perhaps any time in history. Japanese children learn how to be good group members at school and practice many of those human relations skills in the workplace. How does the groupism of Japanese society influence what children are taught and how they work as adults?

Even recreation in Japan is influenced by groupism. Japanese are more prone than other people to spend leisure time as part of school or work groups. Japan is an extremely affluent nation, and its people have disposable income to enjoy a rich variety of leisure pursuits. What are the favorite hobbies of Japanese? What sports do ordinary people like to play and watch? Do fads interest the Japanese? Do the Japanese borrow recreational activities from other cultures or prefer traditional forms? What do Japanese proclivities for recreation tell us about the culture in general?

A visitor to virtually any small, medium, or large city in

the United States can easily find an establishment, usually a nightclub, that features a tape machine, microphones, and a TV monitor with accompanying song lyrics. On many television channels throughout the United States viewers can also find full-length relatively sophisticated cartoon science fiction or historical dramas. Many American children love to play with Power Rangers. Although most Americans don't know it, these activities emanate from Japanese popular culture, which is extremely vibrant although often somewhat unusual, to say the least, to foreigners. Although many Americans know that haiku, the tea ceremony, and Zen Buddhism are Japanese, they know nothing of popular culture in Japan. Even many knowledgeable Japan experts largely ignore the impact of popular culture on modern Japanese life.

Although Japan's group-oriented culture has been a positive factor in both the high level of social stability and economic affluence the Japanese enjoy, it has also caused Japanese society to at times be a very inhospitable place for any category of "outsider." How are the Japanese hurt because of too much groupism? Who has suffered because of this label in Japan? Is the situation for the outsider in group-oriented Japan getting better or worse?

An examination of significant domestic contemporary issues in many of the world's countries could very likely include the problem of rapid population growth, but in Japan the exact opposite is the case. Fewer and fewer Japanese women are having babies than at any time in history. In one United Nations survey of twelve developed nations in the late 1990s, Japan was eleventh out of twelve in the number of births per 1,000 people. The same survey revealed that by 2000 Japan was expected to be third in the percentage (17.4 percent) of the total population 65 years of age or older. By 2050 the projection is that Japan will have the highest or almost highest percentage (32.3 percent) of senior citizens in the world. What trends in Japanese society have stimulated these new demographic developments?

How will a dearth of young Japanese and many senior citizens affect Japanese life?

As an island nation, Japan historically has long had an ambivalent relationship with the rest of the world. How has Japan's relationship with other countries changed with the end of World War II, and now, the end of the Cold War? How might changing relationships with foreign countries affect the life of everyday Japanese? At least some of the answers to these questions are possible through a rudimentary understanding of the people who collectively constitute "Japanese Society." It behooves any reader who is curious about Japanese society to think first about the role of the group in various aspects of Japanese life.

THE GROUP AND THE INDIVIDUAL IN JAPAN

Learning about families and how ordinary people relate to each other in school, the workplace, and recreationally is much easier to understand if we begin with a basic generalization. Japan has been historically, and remains without doubt, one of the most group-oriented societies on earth. In the words of the late Harvard professor and famous Japanologist Edwin Reischauer, "Certainly no difference is more significant between Japanese and Americans, or Westerners in general, than the greater Japanese tendency to emphasize the group, somewhat at the expense of the individual" (Reischauer 1977, 127). Most professional Japan observers would argue that, if anything, Reischauer understated the importance of the group!

Usually Japanese do not view the American myth of the Lone Ranger as positive. Despite increasing signs of individualism among the young, more often than not the socially condoned Japanese hero is the good team player who subordinates his or her desires to group interests. It is important to keep in mind that Japan is a free society and individuals enjoy political liberties. In Japan group norms are occasionally defied. Still, such occurrences are rare compared with Western countries, including the United States. Group loyalty is taught early and reinforced in almost every aspect of Japanese life.

If you consider what you have already learned about Japan in this book, the reasons for the famed Japanese devotion to the group become more apparent. Japan for much of its history was relatively isolated from the rest of the world, and people learned to live together peacefully while being spared the traumas of outside invasion or war. Wet paddy rice cultivation, one of the earliest and most vital economic activities of the Japanese, demanded group cooperation. Also, since Japan is a relatively homogeneous society with little ethnic diversity, it is much easier for group cooperation to be nurtured than in many other countries. Geographically, Japan is also a somewhat hazardous place—and the earthquakes, typhoons and fires historically forced people to work together to survive.

In addition to history and geography, several of Japan's most influential religious and philosophical systems celebrate group spirit and harmony. Whereas Christianity teaches that every person has a separate soul from the rest of the universe, a fundamental tenet of Buddhism is that all animate and even inanimate beings are one. Confucianism, with its major objective of societal harmony, greatly influenced Japanese thinking about the importance of the group over individual interest. Samurai also emphasized such group-oriented values as loyalty and responsibility to others.

As a result, Japan is not only a society in which many different kinds of groups often fiercely compete with each other, but one in which groups, regardless of whether they are school classes, companies, tea ceremony clubs, or even the underworld, demand and receive great loyalty from its members. Japanese are not only loyal to particular groups to which they belong, but within the typical group, a clear hierarchy exists with different members having different amounts of status. Also, at times, many Japanese tend to be distant, and often rather unfriendly, to people who are not members of their group.

With the passage of time, however, the roles of certain groups and the members within them have changed considerably. Since World War II this has certainly been true of families and in the role of women.

FAMILIES AND THE ROLE OF WOMEN

Until the mid-twentieth century Japan was primarily a rural nation and extended families were the norm. In traditional Japanese families several generations lived under one roof, wives were clearly subservient to husbands and mothers-in-law, and the large majority of marriages were arranged. It was also quite common for families to have more than two children. In traditional Japan, husbands and wives as well as older relatives, children, and siblings usually worked together as farmers or proprietors of small enterprises. When a younger son or a daughter in one family married, often he or she moved away, joined another family, and was no longer considered a member of the original family. Similarly in a family with only daughters, when the oldest married, her husband would often become part of her family and sometimes would even adopt his wife's family name.

As Japan urbanized and industrialized after World War II, family structure has become much more like the United States and Western Europe. A larger percentage of retired adults in Japan than in the United States still live with or near their children, but the nuclear family is now the norm. Also, Japanese families are having fewer and fewer children than ever before; the statistical average is less than two per household.

Despite slight rises in recent years, Japan's divorce rate is only about one-third that of the United States. Still, it would be a great mistake to assume that, typically, Japanese husbands and wives are emotionally closer than their American or Western European counterparts. In fact, due to long-held differences in Japanese and Western conceptualizations of the family, strong evidence indicates that many Japanese husbands and wives are not particularly close. Confucianism and other influences cause many Japanese to view marriage in decidedly nonromantic terms.

Although there are many exceptions, many Japanese still view marriage as an economic arrangement that helps to perpetuate family lines and contributes stability to life. Although the practice has declined in recent decades, some marriages are still arranged by the respective families.

One important difference in Japanese and Western fathers is, on average, that Japanese males spend much less time at home than do their American or European counterparts. Although there seems to be some evidence of change among younger men, typically, Japanese fathers are seldom involved in child rearing or with household chores. According to surveys, less than half of Japanese *salarimen* (a Japanese adaptation of the English words "salary men," referring to office workers) eat dinner with their families most nights, and at least a third spend less than three waking hours a day with their families. In the private sector and in many government institutions, Saturdays are workdays whether officially counted as such or not. Sundays tend to be the only day that fathers will be involved in any kind of family activities. Japanese women tell a revealing joke about the nature of husband-wife relations: a good husband makes much money and is never home.

Westerners have often had the most mistaken stereotypes imaginable about Japanese women. In the United States, there has been a recent *geisha* "boom," which does nothing to dispel the notion that Japanese women's sole mission in life is to please men. Even the popular Western notion of geisha often omits or minimizes the fact that the several thousand true geisha that still ply their trade in Japan go through years of training in classical Japanese music and dancing before attaining that status. The average Japanese woman, while certainly not primarily a passive pleaser of men, is still prone to more discrimination, particularly in the workplace, than is the case in most Western developed countries.

Like women historically in most cultures, Japanese women did not work out of the house. In fact, *kanai,* the Japanese term that husbands use for their wives, literally means "inside the house." Before World War II women were legally second-class citizens in many ways; they attained equal rights with the adoption of Japan's present constitution. Still, as late as the 1970s most of the Japanese women who worked outside the home did so out of economic necessity. During that decade women were still supposed to marry by age twenty-five and have two or perhaps three children. Women reported feeling "strange" if they didn't have their first child within a year or two of marriage and the second a couple of years later.

In the 1970s practicing traditional arts such as playing *koto,* a stringed instrument; doing *ikebana,* or flower arranging; or practicing the tea ceremony was the most acceptable way for a middle-class woman to spend her leisure time. By the 1980s Japanese attitudes had changed to the point that it was socially acceptable if middle-class women worked part time.

By the 1990s massive numbers of women were entering the Japanese workplace, changing their own lives and the Japanese family as well. According to government estimates for 1990–1999, about half of all women aged fifteen or older had jobs or were looking for work. Even so, a large number of married women still stop working when they have young children. Recent employment rates of married women whose youngest child is below the age of three is 28.2 percent. The rate goes up as the age of the youngest child increases, reaching 72.7 percent among married women whose youngest child is age 12–14.

Even though almost half of all Japanese women work out of the home, a higher percentage of women have part-time jobs than in the West, and the ratio of part-time to full-time workers is highest among women with children. On average, women only earn about 60 percent of the money than men get for the same type and amount of work. It is also, with some exceptions including education and fashion, still difficult for female graduates of universities to obtain jobs commensurate with their educational levels. The majority of large Japanese companies do not make managerial positions available to women university graduates because of a belief that upon becoming mothers, women will devote more time to child-rearing than work. There does seem to be some progress, however, in the earning power relative to men of women under thirty, as recent statistics indicate women in this age cohort now earn 86 percent the hourly wages of their male peers.

Although small, the number of women in the workforce with managerial and professional responsibilities is definitely increasing. This is partially due to the implementation of the Equal Employment Opportunity Law in 1986, which established a two-track system for female job applicants. Women seeking a general-track job are treated separately from men. General-track jobs are normally less demanding and have limited opportunities for overtime pay and promotion, but women in this track need not worry about being transferred to a different area. Integrated track jobs for women place them in the same category as men, meaning they are subject to transfers, promotion, and overtime pay. Although progress can be attributed to the categorization portion of the law, the statute also reflects the still deeply held Japanese view that women in the workplace are special cases. Only women are given two tracks from which to choose. Men are expected, because they are male, to be in the integrated track.

Still, many working females are typically young unmarried women, for whom the Japanese have a nickname that may be translated as "office ladies." These young women work for a corporation for five to six years after they graduate from high school, or junior college, and upon marrying are expected to leave the company. Japanese view these work years for a woman as a time she can learn about the world before settling down.

Office ladies are never given meaningful work but instead are expected to create a pleasant environment for the permanent, mostly male employees by making and serving tea and running errands. Many executives in Japanese companies feel obligated to help their young male employees find wives. Management often view the pool of office ladies as a good source of brides for these young men.

Until quite recently, the almost universal expectation of a married Japanese woman was that her important role was not marketplace work but child rearing and home management. Although women in most cultures play the leading role in raising children, the bond between mother and child in Japan is particularly strong. Mothers sleep with their young for a longer period of time after the child is born than in the West and generally give young children more attention than do Western mothers. Often Japanese children develop a stronger sense of dependence on their mothers than children in other cultures do.

Young children are treated quite leniently in Japan and are rarely spanked when they misbehave. Instead, the Japanese mother is more likely to forgive the child and make the child feel guilty for not conforming to her wishes. Many sociologists argue that this early development of a sense of shame when one fails to conform to others' expectations helps to create the feeling shared by many adult Japanese of not wanting to let other group members down.

Traditionally Japanese housewives have done virtually all household chores, and despite some societal rhetoric, this largely still seems to be the case today. Although husbands can be major actors in deciding big-ticket household expenditures such as automobile purchases, wives have traditionally controlled family budgets, and it is not uncommon for wives to give their husbands an allowance! In addition to the added pressure of often having a part-time or full-time job and no real help at home, many married women today have a new burden: the care of a fast-growing elderly population.

There are clear signs in contemporary Japan that many young women look at married life and have ambiguous feelings about its respective costs and benefits. The average age for a first marriage for Japanese women is now slightly below twenty-eight, and as of the late 1990s, almost 50 percent of Japanese women in their twenties were not married. By comparison, in the 1980s, only 30 percent of the same female cohort were unmarried. Young Japanese women seem to be enjoying the freedom afforded by income from the workplace and foregoing the tremendous responsibility Japanese society has placed upon married women.

Though the increase in the average age Japanese women marry and the drop in fertility are clear signs that attitudes about women's lifestyles are changing, it is too extreme a position at this time to imagine that all young Japanese women are unhappy with traditional female roles. Many Japanese women still enjoy the housewife role that brings power over family finances, and after the children are old enough for school, leisure and recreation time. Also, women who do work often don't encounter the pressure that their male counterparts confront in Japanese companies, including the de facto requirement to spend evening leisure time with work mates.

Japanese attitudes about gender, the family, and the workplace, despite changes, remain different in many ways than dominant Western positions. Even though there are neutral alternatives, one of the most common words Japanese wives use when referring to their husband is *shujin,* or master (of the house). One recent survey of almost 200 white-collar and educated women from three different Japanese urban areas found that 89 percent used either the term shujin (my/our master)or *uchi no shujin* (master of the house) when addressing their husbands.

LEARNING GROUP SKILLS: THE SCHOOL

In order to better understand the Japanese people, and particularly their strong group orientation, it is important to look again at schools. In addition to being places where subject matter knowledge is taught, schools also serve the extremely important function of teaching Japanese to be good group members.

The process begins in Japanese kindergartens, where, unlike in the United States, more emphasis is placed upon getting along with others than on academics. When a child enters first grade, his or her unofficial course in group loyalty continues. Students usually remain together as a class with the same teachers through the first and second grades. Classes, or *kumi*, as the Japanese call them, constantly learn, play, and even eat together for two years, and children often

Japanese learn early to work on behalf of the group. In this photo, a small group (han) of Japanese students are serving the rest of the class (the kumi) lunch in the classroom. (Courtesy of Lucien Ellington)

develop a strong attachment to the kumi. Japanese teachers often work hard to foster this attachment by focusing their attention on the kumi as a whole at the expense of individualized instruction.

Most Japanese elementary schools do not have cafeterias, and kumi eat together in the classroom along with the teacher. Within each kumi, smaller groups of students, called *han,* are responsible on a rotating basis for bringing the food to and from the school kitchen to the classroom. The hans also take turns cleaning the classroom.

Each kumi and han in elementary school also incorporates student leaders, often in the case of han on a rotational basis, who assist the larger classroom group and the smaller groups within it to operate effectively. Teachers sometimes give classroom assignments to the han, and group loyalty is fostered as children work together to complete tasks. Almost all Japanese sixth- and ninth-graders take field trips lasting several days to important cultural and historical sites. Children are often assigned bus or train seats on the basis of the particular kumi and han to which they belong, and teachers check attendance by consulting the kumi and han leaders.

As described earlier, extracurricular activities are important in junior and senior high. These activities teach young Japanese appropriate group behavior. When a Japanese student joins a club—for example, a tennis, flower arranging, or dramatics group—he or she is expected to exhibit complete group commitment. This means the individual not only will engage in the utmost effort to make his or her club successful but will also show the appropriate amount of respect to club members, usually older students, who have higher status. For example, it is quite common in high school baseball practice for sophomores to play very little, sometimes regardless of their abilities. Instead younger team members spend most of their time retrieving bats and balls and keeping the playing field in good shape for the juniors and seniors.

Young people who attend university and join clubs

encounter the same expectation of total group loyalty and respect for senior members. By the time a Japanese person reaches adulthood, much of his or her socialization has emphasized teamwork, and group hierarchies and expectations. This pattern of personal interaction often continues in the workplace.

THE WORKPLACE GROUP

Certainly since World War II, the workplace has replaced the traditional extended family of earlier times as the primary group for many Japanese males. Although the so-called lifetime employment system only applies to approximately one-quarter of private-sector workers, Japanese workers in general change jobs less often than do their Western counterparts. In many companies and government ministries, new employees are treated, at least superficially if not in actuality, like new family members (this was illustrated by the new members welcoming ceremony discussed in Chapter 2). Some companies even have special training programs for new workers that focus exclusively on building loyalty.

Many more Japanese males than Westerners still tend to define themselves by their workplace. Typically, when a white-collar employee of a large firm introduces himself he will say something like, "I am Yamato and I work for Toyota," rather than identify whether he is an accountant, an engineer, or an attorney. Japanese workers are also much more likely than their Western counterparts to passively accept transfers to undesirable locations rather than find a job with a competitor. It is quite common in Japan for male office workers and managers to be transferred to another part of the country, and, because their children are in positive school situations, leave their family behind and visit on weekends.

As mentioned earlier in this book, Japanese employees, particularly in large companies, tend to put in long hours on the job together, much of which is unpaid overtime. Japanese have a different attitude, in part because of group expectations, than Westerners do about what actually constitutes "working." Although Japanese employees can and do work extremely hard, it is a cultural expectation that employees demonstrate group loyalty by being at work at various times of the day, particularly late in the afternoon if the boss has not left, whether they are actually working or not. It is common in many companies and government ministries to find employees at their desk drinking coffee or reading the newspaper and obviously not working.

It is also common practice in Japanese companies for white-collar employees at various levels, especially males, to socialize together after work on a regular basis. This often entails drinking and dinner and is one of the reasons many Japanese men spend so little time at home. Company employees will even take "vacations" together at spas or other recreational facilities owned by their firm where they hear motivational speeches and otherwise exclusively associate with fellow employees.

Companies, in turn, tend to be much more paternalistic toward employees than is the case in the West. It is common for a work associate, particularly an eligible bachelor's superior, to match-make an employee by introducing him to suitable single women. Although layoffs have increased during recent economic hard times, they are still much more rare in Japan than in Western countries. Also, promotion and pay increases in Japanese companies are still much more primarily based upon seniority than elsewhere. The rationale for the latter practices is that individuals should be rewarded as the amount of time they are loyal to the group increases.

Decisionmaking in the workplace often reflects the group orientation of the Japanese. Traditionally, Japanese organizations often employ a group decisionmaking process called *nemawashi*, or root binding, taken from the gardening procedures used by growers of miniature bonsai trees. As trees are repotted, roots are carefully pruned and positioned to determine future shape. Many times before a decision is made in a Japanese company, leaders will carefully check with many people who could be affected by the decisions, starting with the junior employees. If too many employees have objections, leaders might drop an idea altogether or modify a proposed decision. Even if top management makes a decision contrary to subordinates' decisions, most Japanese consider it important that prior consultation has occurred.

Although Japan is a group-oriented society it is also a vertical culture in which one's relative status is quite important. Usually, personal workplace status is based on the overall reputation of the organization for whom one works, one's educational level attained including particular institutions from which one matriculated, and how long a person has been with the organization. Except for employees who have equal educational status and joined the company at the same time, most Japanese have very few equals on the job. One's associates usually have either higher or lower status.

Even if a person is better at a job than an associate who happens to have been with the company longer, the former, because of his lower status, is expected to be deferential to the senior worker. Hierarchy and status are important not only within, but also between, Japanese groups. It is common for many Japanese, when meeting strangers, to immediately exchange cards containing the person's name, company, and title. These card exchanges help Japanese know a stranger's status so that they can react accordingly.

Groups in any society obviously require leaders, but Japan's strong group-oriented culture often causes even high-ranking officials or managers to exhibit quite different behaviors toward their subordinates than is true in more individualistic cultures such as the United States. As is true with Japanese politicians, workplace leaders are expected to keep a relatively low profile and certainly not appear to be overly aggressive and autocratic in workplace interpersonal relations.

Japanese often attain leadership positions in an organization not because they are dynamic or flamboyant—in fact these are viewed as negative personality traits—but because they are good listeners and consensus builders. Top Japanese executives are expected to be the first to sacrifice when hard times arrive. For example, Japanese management takes pay cuts when companies do badly, and sometimes seniors will even resign for a subordinate's misdeed if it is considered serious enough.

Although the workplace mores and practices described above are very much in evidence in twenty-first century Japan, readers should keep two caveats in mind: First, the most cohesive groups tend to be larger companies and government institutions with the greatest benefits going to permanent employees, who in the private sector are mostly male. Temporary employees in large Japanese companies often lose their jobs when economic hard times occur. Second, though there is little doubt most Japanese enjoy the security afforded by their workplace practices, the changing nature of global competition and Japan's continuing economic malaise may very well force companies to radically change their approach to employees in order to remain financially solvent.

RECREATION AND POPULAR CULTURE

Groups of Japanese sightseers not only visit famous places in their own country but travel abroad together as well. Readers might recall seeing Japanese groups at tourist spots in the United States such as the Grand Canyon. Although such group travel is also common practice for citizens of other developed countries, it is much more frequent with Japanese. It is normal for club, school, or work groups to travel together, and reportedly many Japanese feel miserable if forced to travel by themselves. Just as the group is important in school and work, it also plays a vital role in travel and other leisure activities. Although Japanese have individual interests—two solitary pursuits, reading and watching television, are quite popular—Japanese also show a strong tendency toward group forms of recreation.

Adult clubs play a large role in the lives of many Japanese, and the range of these clubs varies tremendously. Foreign-language (particularly English) literature, poetry, and flower arranging clubs are just a few examples of organizations in which group members pursue mutual hobbies. In large and medium-sized cities, newspapers sponsor cultural centers where, particularly on Saturdays but other times as well, people of all ages gather for classes on everything from haiku to underwater photography. Festivals are quite popular all over Japan, and various club, school, and work groups participate.

Even though crowded conditions sometimes make sports participation problematic, both traditional and Western sports are popular. Sumo, which is approximately two thousand years old, is a duel between two gigantic, scantily clad men; the loser is the first wrestler who touches the ground with any part of his body or is forced out of the ring. Every year there are six major professional tournaments, each lasting fifteen days. These tournaments are attended by thousands of people and watched by millions on national television.

Among businessmen, golf is much more popular than is the case in the United States. In Japan's group-oriented society, the sport is so associated with corporate white-collar males that in some companies it is an expectation that this category of employee will at least appear interested in the sport. Golf is tremendously expensive in Japan but provides a source of conversation as well as recreation for the legions of salarimen who claim to be adherents. There are also organized karate, kendo, archery, mountaineering, soccer, and tennis clubs throughout the country.

Baseball is now so popular in Japan that it is considered part of the culture and not viewed primarily as an American import. In the early 1870s, Horace Wilson, an American teaching in Japan, introduced the sport to the Japanese. By the 1930s American all-stars were visiting the country and

Baseball is popular in Japan as in the United States, and crowds are typically more lively at a professional Japanese game. There are always organized cheering sections. See photo on opposite page. (Courtesy of Lucien Ellington)

playing against Japanese teams. Although baseball was suppressed during World War II, it returned during the U.S. occupation. Every spring the national high school playoffs held in Koshien Stadium near Osaka are broadcast on television and followed by millions. Japan has two professional major leagues as well as minor league teams, and a World Series occurs each fall. Although the game is played essentially the same way in Japan as in the United States, one need only watch Japanese baseball on television or attend a game to see visible evidence of the group orientation in the culture. Fans of respective teams engage in extremely synchronized cheers. In fact, some fans of Japanese major league teams belong to organized cheering sections and sit together in the outfield.

A number of Japanese major league players have been successful in the United States. Because of the group solidarity the Japanese feel about home-grown stars such as Suzuki Ichiro and Nomo Hideo becoming popular in the United States, American games in which these stars participate are broadcast in Japan. Recently, however, another sports import, soccer, has become more popular—some say at baseball's expense.

Although baseball—along with Halloween and TV, also immensely popular in Japan—are clearly foreign imports, much of Japanese popular culture is largely native. Four of the most pervasive and money-making phenomena in contemporary Japanese culture are *animae, karaoke, manga,* and *pachinko.* Three out of four of these massively popular pastimes originated outside of Japan, but the Japanese transformed them so dramatically that often nobody even knows other cultures had a hand in any aspect of their development.

Animae is the Japanized version of the word *animation,* and it refers to Japanese movie and TV animation. The Japanese were wild about Walt Disney animation from the time it first appeared in the country, but animae is a much more extensive popular cultural trend in Japan than Disney cartoons are in the United States. Although animae is popular with children, there is also a large adult market for Japanese animation. The variety of subjects that end up as animae far surpasses the range of animated cartoons produced in the United States. Fantasy, history, mythology, religion, and science fiction intended for adult audiences end up as animae in Japan. Retellings of Japan's ancient myths, a four-hour epic about a demon terrorizing Tokyo in the 1920s, and a science-fiction film about an archeologist searching for God's last message to humanity constitute just a smattering of the wide-ranging subjects included in this genre. Japanese animae has developed a cult following, particularly among teenagers and college students, in a number of foreign countries.

The very literate Japanese people can claim the highest or second-highest per-capita book and magazine consumption in the world. Manga, or comic books, account for nearly one-third of all the books and magazines published in Japan. As is the case with animae, even though there are comic books in the United States, the length, scope, and variety of Japanese comic books makes the whole medium almost incomparable with its American variant.

Japanese manga are very thick, often running to hundreds

of pages, and are available in a wide variety of places including bookstores, train kiosks, and coffee houses. Like animae, manga cover many different topics. Some manga are written for children, while subjects ranging from economic history to pornography are obviously for adults. It is quite common to see salarimen on trains and subways wearing Brooks Brothers suits and reading manga. Famous serialized manga characters and plot have included *Ashita No Joe* (Tomorrow's Joe), a young Tokyo working-class boxer who battles his way to the top; *Doraemon,* a robot cat from the future who befriends a ten-year-old (also the subject of very popular movies and a TV show); and *Fireball,* a science-fiction story in which a super-psychic battles a megacomputer. The artists who draw and write manga are now becoming cult heroes in many countries. Probably the most famous manga artist of all is the late Tezuka Osamu, a physician who in his forty-four-year career produced everything from a twelve-volume series of karma and reincarnation to an examination of the Nazi era.

Karaoke, or "empty orchestra," originated in Japan in the early 1970s, is now an indispensable part of the nightlife of Japan, and is becoming increasingly popular in other parts of Asia and the West. In karaoke, patrons sing their favorite songs (lyrics are available on video prompters) while an automated machine plays the accompanying music. Karaoke started as a feature in nightclubs but has increased in popularity such that parties of five to ten Japanese will rent a karaoke box in a dedicated karaoke establishment, bring food and refreshments inside, and sing to their heart's content in relative privacy. Annual revenues from karaoke bars in Japan now equal about $11 billion, and there are an estimated half-million karaoke establishments throughout the country.

The most controversial—and to many foreigners and Japanese nonaficionados, incomprehensible—Japanese popular cultural phenomenon of all may be pachinko. Pachinko began in the United States in the 1920s as a children's toy called the Corinthian Game. A primitive form of pinball, and played horizontally as with the latter game, it was played by shooting little balls through a slot on the right side of the board with the goal of getting the balls past barriers and into little holes. The game was introduced to Japan in the 1920s and became popular in candy stores. Because adults liked it too and there were crowds in the little shops containing the machines, someone had the bright idea of placing the game machine in a vertical position.

In the years after World War II, pachinko parlors began to sprout up like mushrooms on the Japanese landscape. Today one can find colorful and somewhat garish pachinko establishments in rural villages that don't even have movie theaters. There are an estimated 18,000 pachinko parlors and approximately 50 million players throughout Japan. In a recent year the industry earned revenues equal to approximately $305 billion. This figure represents about one-quarter of all earnings in the entire service sector of the economy. Clearly pachinko is big.

A first visit to a brightly adorned neon-covered pachinko parlor is truly a bizarre experience. There are rows and rows of electronic machines emitting incredible levels of noise. People sit transfixed for hours in front of the machines, feeding little silver balls into them. If some of the balls end up in the right holes, the machines make noise and spit out numbers of additional silver balls. Gambling is not legal in pachinko parlors, so winners who collect large numbers of balls can trade the balls in for small gifts, such as ash trays, lighters, perfume, golf balls, and coffee beans. Successful players can then take their booty right outside to a small shop and sell their prizes for cash while the authorities ignore the process.

Pachinko was once patronized for the most part by middle-aged men, but the industry has successfully expanded its consumer markets, and Japanese of all ages and both genders now play the game. Japanese critics of pachinko are numerous, vocal, and constantly berate players for the hours they spend in front of the machines, but the industry continues to become more popular and more high-tech. Pachinko cable TV stations and hand-held personal digital assistants are now available, and both provide up-to-the-minute reports for addicts on the locations of machines that are yielding the most balls. Although more famous outside Japan than pachinko, Zen meditation has never even begun to attract the number of adherents as this most peculiar Japanese pastime.

GROUPISM: A CRITIQUE

The strong orientation of Japanese society toward the group can result in many benefits for individual Japanese, including a great sense of belonging and security. However, the great pressure placed on the individual by the group in Japan also has a negative side. There are *kata,* or appropriate procedures, for almost any act Japanese perform if one wants to be correct in his or her action. This applies to everything imaginable, including the appropriate language, depending upon another's age or status; the appropriate placement of shoes by an entrance; and the correct way to wrap a gift. Japanese often find that close attention must be paid to almost every word and gesture in order not to offend others. Japanese individuals often report that they much admire the American trait of direct and open use of language. Both of these kinds of group-induced pressures, the endless number of kata and constant vigilance with speech, can be extremely stressful to Japanese.

Many Japanese also indicate they respect the freedom Americans enjoy to be different without fear of being ostracized. Japan has not been a society where individuals who dare to be different have traditionally fared well. The old Japanese proverb that the nail that sticks up too much gets hammered down has often meant difficult times for, among others, young people and workers who do not fit in with the group.

The rigidity of Japanese schools is, in part, a direct result of the pressure for conformity. Students who have special learning needs, or who have been abroad and out of the educational system for a time, are often either ignored or bullied. This kind of ostracism and bullying directed at individuals who don't conform to the group also applies to adults. Miyamoto Masao, a Western-trained medical doctor and psychologist with the Ministry of Health, wrote periodical articles and a book exposing the bureaucracies' foibles. Miyamoto reported being told by coworkers in private that even though they admired what he was doing, because he was the target of bullying they could not afford to be seen with him or known to be his friend.

Miyamoto's troubles began earlier with his work group when he requested two weeks of vacation—time to which he was legally entitled. Although his superior expressed shock, Miyamoto took the holiday anyway. He then became a pariah among those with whom he worked because Japanese government bureaucrats don't do such unconventional individualistic things as take full vacations. Miyamoto argues that Japan's societally pervasive pressure to conform to group mores is a kind of totalitarianism without an identifiable center. There is no individual, legislative body, judiciary, or committee who specifies these group pressures, but group members usually know full well what is expected of them and most behave accordingly, despite their personal feelings.

Whether deserved or not, Japan has a reputation for not being a particularly creative society. Many Westerners and Japanese contend that the pressure to conform to group norms in Japanese schools inhibits individual creativity.

The victims of ijime, or school bullying, usually have either physical characteristics or mannerisms that set them apart from other student groups. An example is found in the children of Japanese workers stationed overseas. As Japanese companies established foreign branches, the children of the transferred employees attended foreign schools, particularly in the United States, home to the most amount of Japanese investment. Upon their return home to Japan, many of these

People in all cultures enjoy eating, but the Japanese are known for their particular affinity to the aesthetics and the ritual of daily meals. (Courtesy of Lucien Ellington)

children were subject to criticism and, sometimes, harassment from fellow students for their perceived strange foreign ways. There were even cases where Japanese teachers criticized students for being too good in conversational English. Gifted students and slow learners in Japanese schools also have traditionally had a very tough time in school. In the past few years there has been progress in establishing school-based special education programs. Still, despite an easing of the rigid requirements that prevented accelerated students from skipping grades, few accommodations are made for very bright high school students. Japanese educators, government officials, and members of the public are now experimenting with various ideas, including the recent educational reforms that were addressed in Chapter 3, to create a better climate for students who are perceived as different from the norm.

As world economic competition becomes more intense,

there is mounting evidence that group-oriented business thinking hurts many Japanese companies. Traditionally, Japanese companies have formed keiretsu, or business groups, and purchased materials and products from member companies, regardless of price. As Japanese manufacturing costs have increased, this strategy is less and less economically defensible. Companies can also lose business opportunities because of the slow decisionmaking process fostered by a great concern for group consultation. Many times, top Japanese managers or government officials might not be the most competent people in a given organization but have attained their position because of a talent for offending the least number of people. Increasing numbers of young people are also seriously questioning the previously largely unchallenged value that an individual should sacrifice his private life for the welfare of the company.

In large part because of their sense of uniqueness from other cultures, racial homogeneity, and group solidarity, the Japanese have not particularly related well to minorities in Japan or foreigners in general. The largest ethnic minority group in Japan are the approximately 700,000 Koreans who live mainly in the Kansai district around, or in, Osaka, Kyoto, and Kobe. There are also over 230,000 Chinese who live in several Japanese cities including Kobe, Nagasaki, and Yokohama, all of which also have Chinatowns. During the economic boom times of the 1980s, hundreds of thousands of legal and illegal immigrants found their way to Japan and were employed doing dirty and low-status jobs that Japanese were reluctant to perform. These workers came from a variety of places, including Southeast Asia and Iran. It is estimated that 700,000 of these workers remain in Japan. About 300,000 of these foreign workers are illegally in the country.

In addition to ethnic minorities who have come from elsewhere to Japan, there are four other groups of residents who most Japanese consider separate from the majority Japanese "group." One is the Ainu, an indigenous people who are comparable to Native Americans in their physical features and culture. Around 24,000 people in Hokkaido identify themselves as Ainu, and an undetermined number of Ainu live in other parts of Japan. Another is the approximately 3 million ethnic Japanese called *burakumin,* who are treated like a minority group. The burakumin, who now live primarily in the Osaka area, became outcastes because of the jobs their ancestors held during the Tokugawa era—butchers, workers in slaughterhouses and tanneries, and garbage collectors. A third group is the 200, 000 or so descendents of Japanese families that settled in Brazil during the nineteenth century and have since returned to Japan. Finally, although Okinawa is now a Japanese prefecture, the original residents of this island have a distinctive culture and language that separates them from the majority group.

Each of these minority groups has experienced discrimination at some level because they don't fit in with larger societal notions of being Japanese. Although there were Koreans who found their way to Japan in earlier times, many of today's Koreans who reside in Japan can trace their ancestry back to 1910, when Korea became a Japanese colony. Japanese ill-treatment of Koreans has a long history. During the 1923 Tokyo earthquake, angry mobs murdered entire families of ethnic Koreans because of a rumor that they were the cause of the catastrophe. Even though most of the 700,000 Koreans in Japan are second-, third-, or fourth-generation residents and speak Japanese as a first language, only approximately 200,000 are Japanese citizens. Most Koreans in Japan have foreigner status, cannot vote or become civil servants, and have limited access to other employment such as teaching. Until recently, Koreans who were not citizens were also subjected to fingerprinting, but discrimination is lessening toward this group since most of them now intermarry with Japanese. It is still common for a young woman's parents when she is about to get married to hire a private investigator to make sure the groom doesn't have either Korean or Chinese blood.

Elements of the Japanese public often blame Chinese in Japan who are guests or illegal workers, along with other foreign workers from other non-Western countries, for crime increases, even though many times there is no evidence of wrongdoing. In one case in the mid-1990s a number of Iranians were arrested near Yoyogi Park in Tokyo for selling illegally produced telephone cards. However, evidence revealed that the *yakuza,* or Japanese mafia, had produced the cards and were using the Iranians as fronts to distribute them.

In the past, Japanese treated the Ainu much like how whites treated Native Americans in the United States: by robbing them of land and pushing them further and further north. Although today Japanese tourists visit Ainu settlements in Hokkaido to learn about their traditional culture, the fact that people of Ainu descent living in other parts of Japan are reluctant to identify themselves is an indicator of at least some continuing Japanese prejudice. Burakumin have traditionally encountered employment discrimination as well as discrimination from some Japanese when they attempt to marry non-burakumin. Because of recent burakumin political activism, the Japanese government has begun to provide significant funds to improve burakumin neighborhoods, but it still has not passed legislation outlawing burakumin discrimination. Brazilians of Japanese descent report assorted problems in interacting with Japanese as they attempt to fit into the larger society.

Even though Okinawa is today a prefecture of Japan, most Japanese do not consider the 1.2 million people who live on Okinawa to actually be Japanese, and the Okinawans are very much aware of their "minority" status. Although a great deal of contemporary Okinawan resentment focuses on the large number of U.S. military bases on the islands, Okinawans also resent much about Japan. In one mid-1990s poll, over 46 percent of Okinawan respondents saw themselves as not Japanese, 31 percent saw themselves as both Okinawan and Japanese, and only 12 percent of the sample considered themselves exclusively Japanese.

For over 150 years Japanese have admired many aspects of Western culture, and Japan is arguably the most Western of Asian nations; however, Americans, Australians, and Europeans often encounter what they consider to be Japanese racial insensibility or insensitivity. For example, it is quite common for Westerners to hear themselves referred to as *gaijin* within earshot. The exact Japanese meaning for gaijin is "outside person," which is not the most hospitable of inferences for a visitor. Any foreigner, regardless of origin, will often be described not as an American, Chinese, German, or Australian, but as a gaijin.

Despite all this, the Japanese do appear to be becoming more accommodating to diversity. The plight of minorities has received more and more media and political attention. As recounted, in part due to media attention, burakumin have won concessions from the national government. The practice of fingerprinting Japanese of Korean ethnicity who are not citizens has ended.

Although some critics claim the decision was an entirely pragmatic one to boost Japanese business with foreigners, the government of Japan since the mid-1980s has contended that the Japanese people are too insular and has promoted internationalization initiatives. For over a decade the national government has imported several thousand English-speaking recent college graduates to work in schools and local governments with the aim of promoting better understanding of spoken English and to assist with exchange programs.

In the spring 2000 meeting of G–8 nations (the Group of Eight, an organized group of nations with developed economies, consisting of the United States, Japan, Italy, Britain, Germany, France, Canada, and Russia) held in Tokyo, the Japanese government also announced that in an effort to further internationalize Japanese young people, it was taking steps to almost double the number of foreign university students in Japan over the next decade. At the time of the announcement there were 56,000 foreign university students in Japan. Japanese government officials hope to increase that number to 100,000 by 2010.

The policy both demonstrates the good intentions of Japan's leaders and illustrates the problems that must be surmounted to make Japan a more hospitable place for foreign students. When Japan is compared with other developed countries, it hosts significantly lower percentages of foreign students. The current number of foreign students in Japan represent only about 1.5 percent of all university students. In Britain, foreign students constitute almost 17 percent of all university students, in Germany almost 9 percent of the total, in France 8 percent, and in the United States about 6 percent of all students.

Until the policy change, if a foreign student wanted to enter a Japanese university, he or she was required to pass both a content and Japanese-language test and had to take those tests in Japan. The new policy combines the two tests and, in addition to provision of the examination in Japan, establishes ten overseas locations where aspiring students may instead take the examination.

In a recent trip to Japan, I personally witnessed perhaps one of the most impressive and poignant signs that there is a true Japanese rethinking of attitudes toward those who are different from the greater population. Traditionally, the mentally handicapped have been marginalized in Japan to a greater extent than in other developed countries. Families who had mentally disabled or other special-needs children often developed a sense of shame and secluded their offspring. Mentally challenged people were often treated by the larger society as if they didn't exist.

In June 2001 a small town in Nagasaki prefecture hosted a party for a group of American teachers who were doing home stays in the area. The feature entertainment at the party was a rousing performance by a group of taiko drummers. Taiko, featuring large drums, riveting rhythms, and colorfully attired enthusiastic drummers, has a long and honored role in Japanese festivals and other social events. This group of drummers, who gave a great performance and were extremely well-received by both Japanese and foreigners, was unique in one sense. They were all teenagers who had I.Q.s of between 50 and 75. Before they performed, it was announced that these drummers, who perform throughout the prefecture, were students in a special school. Certainly in this case, the celebration, instead of suppression of diversity, was quite real and serves as encouraging evidence that in some cases, an overly group-oriented society is becoming more tolerant.

FEW BABIES AND MANY OLD PEOPLE

Although in earlier chapters declining fertility and the graying of Japan were briefly addressed, these profound demographic trends deserve extended attention since they also loom large in the minds of policymakers and the general public. They are quite interrelated: Fewer births mean fewer full-time workers called upon to support larger numbers of retirees.

Probably the most profound probable effect of fewer births is the strain of supporting increasing numbers of old people with fewer workers, but there are other ramifications for Japanese society and the economy as well. If the trend continues it could very well make Japan's considerable budget deficit even larger due to declining tax revenues. Educational institutions have been feeling the effects of this trend for about a decade—each year there are fewer elementary and secondary students and subsequent declines in demand for teachers. There is also evidence that the Japanese housing market is contracting because singles are much less likely to buy homes than are married couples.

As described earlier, Japan now has one of the very lowest birth rates in the developed world. Throughout the decades after World War II the average number of children in Japanese families decreased. During the 1980s and 1990s, the average was approximately 2.2 children per married couple. The problem lay in the fact that the percentage of Japanese in their twenties who are marrying has radically dropped. In 1970 approximately 70 percent of men and 45 percent of women between the ages of twenty and twenty-nine were not married. By 1995, the percentages of unmarried people in this age bracket had grown to 85 percent for men and 65 percent for women. Note that the percentage of nonmarried women grew even faster than the percentage for men; preliminary recent statistics indicate the percentages of unmarried women in this age group are still rising.

There is much debate about why young Japanese of both sexes don't appear to want to marry nearly as much as in the past. Some observers argue it is for selfish reasons. Approximately 10 million singles in their twenties live at home with parents and enjoy income from jobs but few household or child-rearing responsibilities. Some pundits and social scientists even use the English loan words *parasaito shingurus,* parasite singles, in reference to the childless unmarried young Japanese. Some economists point out that lack of job opportunities and an unemployment rate for people in their twenties of approximately 10 percent, because of the economic malaise and the Japanese reluctance to lay off older workers, are the real reasons young people are staying single and childless.

Still other social critics argue that in the case of women, today's well-educated Japanese women do not want to endure the enormous responsibility with little help that has been the lot of most Japanese wives. Certainly, when conventional Japanese expectations of how wives should behave are considered, it is understandable that many educated young women might prefer to delay marriage, or perhaps avoid it entirely. The wife of a typical Japanese salariman is at home many nights without the companionship of a husband, who is socializing with work mates. Meanwhile, since virtually all Japanese married couples have children, the conventional housewife is expected to sacrifice much of her personal life, with no spousal help, in the interest of childrearing. If housewives with children work, it usually has been in part-time jobs, doing very dull repetitive tasks for low pay for six to seven hours daily. One international study indicated that Japanese married women who work had it much worse than married women in other developed countries because of the shortage of domestic help in Japan.

Currently, rising numbers of young women who formerly married in their twenties are continuing to work and using their disposable income to travel abroad, buy stylish clothes, and have extremely active social lives. They now constitute a major consumer market. There is even a magazine that targets these "single aristocrats" who live with their parents and whose earnings become almost pocket change. The motto of the magazine, roughly translated, is that a young woman should expect more from life than a career and a Prince Charming. The situation of young women delaying marriage has become so widespread in Japan that apparently growing numbers of men with no prospects want to marry, but cannot find Japanese wives.

This has been the situation in many rural areas for about ten years, where a number of villages, in an effort to stave off plummeting fertility rates because of a dearth of Japanese women, have organized trips to Southeast Asia for rural men in search of wives. Village officials have subsequently arranged group marriages for Japanese farmers and their Filipino brides. There are also marriage agencies in urban areas like Tokyo, some of which have offices abroad, that specialize in finding Chinese and Korean wives for Japanese men.

Whether the rising number of Japanese women who are delaying marriage and childbirth is a truly long-term trend is unknown at this time. However, the subject of Japan's growing number of singles in their twenties, particularly single women in that age cohort, is a major topic for discussion in contemporary Japanese electronic and print media.

Japan still has a relatively high proportion of young people compared to citizens over age sixty-five, but the situation is rapidly changing. Japan is first in the world in both male (almost seventy-seven years) and female (almost eighty-three years) average life expectancy, and demographers predict by 2025 Japan will have the highest proportion of old people in the world. The rapid graying of Japan will almost certainly have widespread effects on the economy and public policy, families, and the overall quality of life.

Until 1993 Japanese were eligible for national pensions at age sixty, but in December of that year the government changed the law so that by 2013 the minimum age for eligibility is age sixty-five. Although many Japanese have supplementary pensions, those old people who depend entirely upon the national pension are already not adequately funded for basic needs. One estimate is that even with the 1993 changes the national pension and other major employee pensions will not, beginning sometime between 2020 and 2030, be able to meet obligations. The graying of Japan also puts new stresses upon the nation's health-care insurance system as well. The question of how to pay for expected services is a major economic and political issue that is made even more serious by low Japanese birth rates.

Currently, about 15 percent of Japanese age sixty-five and older live alone, which is a considerably smaller figure than that for the United States (40 percent). However, the Japanese figure is expected to rise to at least 20 percent relatively early in the twenty-first century. This is a more profound change in Japan than might be expected because of the Japanese cultural tradition of adult children caring for their elderly parents and allowing the latter to live in their homes (this is a more common occurrence than in the West). As of this book's publication, just under 2 percent of all Japanese elderly live in nursing homes, but the percentage of institutionalized elderly will almost certainly increase in the near future.

Because women end up with a disproportionate share of the burden of caring for elderly relatives who live with their adult children, the graying of Japan places more stress on Japanese wives at a time when more and more women tend to be entering the workplace. Demographic research indicates that in 1997 one out of fifteen Japanese women in their forties cared for elderly relations at home. However, by 2025 the projection is that 46 percent of middle-aged women will provide home care for elderly family members. Over two-thirds of these women will be caring for an elderly person who is bedridden or suffering from senile dementia. Given the decline in marriage rates, it is also questioned whether the number of families in the future with which old people can live will be sufficient to meet the demand for elderly care. In April 2000 the government passed a new public long-term care insurance system offering coverage for both outside paid home helpers who go to private homes and for more services at care facilities.

Japan is only the second country in the world to adopt a long-term care insurance program. Every Japanese citizen age forty and over is covered by the program and is required to pay insurance premiums. If care is needed it is provided in place of monetary payments. The service is based upon level of care needed, and municipal governments are responsible for long-term care program management. Long-term care is a social insurance plan in that one-half of the funding comes from premiums and one-half from government funds. The greater an individual's need for care, the bigger the maximum limit on the cost of his or her service. People who use the service are expected to pay 10 percent of total care expenses, however. The long-term care initiative was a daring proactive step on the part of the Japanese government as it attempts to deal with one issue relating to the graying of Japan.

There is also the quality of life question for the elderly. Some Japanese companies, particularly small firms, have never provided large pension benefits, so it is common for retirees to work part or even full time. Also, because many Japanese husbands and wives are not particularly close, male retirement often heightens tensions as couples who have never spent much time together are suddenly in a new and not particularly pleasant situation.

The Japanese have long had a reputation as one of the world's most adept people at meeting challenges. The twin demographic problems of scarce numbers of young people and many elderly will almost certainly test that reputation as the new century unfolds.

JAPAN AND THE WORLD

Japan's rise as an economic superpower and the end of the Cold War make the Japanese quite uncertain as to what their place is now on the world stage. When Japan was rebuilding its economy in the 1950s and 1960s the world expected rather little of it in terms of leadership. As mentioned earlier, American occupation officials successfully inserted a no-war clause in the 1947 constitution prohibiting Japan from having a military. Although this clause was modified later in practice, Japan still has only 236,000 military personnel, and the Self-Defense Forces are limited to a defensive role. When the Cold War began the United States, realizing the strategic importance of Japan made it a de facto military protectorate. Throughout the Cold War the Japanese were free to pursue economic development and released from the burden of having to make decisions of international import or exercise world leadership.

The situation is vastly different in the twenty-first century. As the second-largest economic power on earth, Japan is expected by much of the rest of the world to exercise global leadership congruent with its financial clout. Yet this expectation troubles many Japanese as well as some of their immediate neighbors. The United States, while continuing to recognize Japan's strategic importance in a volatile region, now places much more emphasis on Japan becoming more of an active partner in security, and on economic and political reform, than it ever did during the Cold War. Japan's new international role in view of these recent developments has not been defined. There is also the unfinished international business that now goes back almost sixty years: The issue of

Japan's role in World War II is still a critical one and shows little sign of disappearing.

Unlike Germany in Europe, Japan avoided publicly accepting clear responsibility for aggression in World War II. In addition to clear public statements of remorse, the Germans went to great lengths to atone for war guilt and during the immediate postwar years removed former Nazis from various government positions. The Germans also held their own war crime trials in addition to the Allied trials. The Japanese engaged in none of these actions. Although American occupation officials removed Japanese militarists from many positions during the early part of the occupation, a number of these individuals were able to regain influence once the Cold War began and the United States became more focused on other nations' potential aggression than past Japanese actions.

The Japanese language includes two words, *tatamae* and *honne,* that represent important feelings-related concepts. Tatamae means the public feelings one expresses to others, while honne is how a person really feels about an issue. Although there is scant public opinion data on the issue, numerous other kinds of evidence lead a number of scholars to the conclusion that a large number of Japanese still hold feelings of racial superiority toward other Asians.

Many scholars believe Japanese negative attitudes toward the rest of Asia began in the latter part of the nineteenth century. Before the 1894 Sino-Japanese war, Japan had great respect in general for China; however, its easy victory over China markedly changed Japanese public opinion toward the Chinese. Japan's colonization of Korea and its early victories in World War II in Asia apparently reinforced Japanese notions of superiority, as did Japan's later economic miracle. A related feeling that many Japanese seem to hold is that Japan is not really an Asian country. Today's proponents of this view cite Japan's level of economic development and status as the only G–8 country in the region as support for their position. However, this conceptualization of Japan not really being part of Asia, but more advanced, goes back to the Meiji era.

Although many Japanese decidedly don't hold condescending attitudes toward other Asians, a strong case remains that some Japanese feelings of racial superiority toward other Asians is behind the insensitivity on the part of many government officials and the public to the issue of Japanese action in Asia.

In Southeast Asia, Japan is viewed with quite a bit of admiration but some trepidation because of its past. Anti-Japanese feelings among Chinese and Koreans are still quite pronounced and they extend far beyond those now-elderly people who witnessed, or were the victims of, Japanese aggression. In a recent Chinese newspaper survey of young people's attitudes toward the Japanese only 14.5 percent of respondents had a good impression of Japan. Almost 50 percent of respondents had an average impression and 41.5 percent had a bad impression. Asked what famous person first came to mind when Japan was mentioned, the young respondents' most frequent reply was Tojo, the Japanese wartime prime minister. The event most associated with Japanese in the survey was the Nanking massacre.

South Korea, though allied with Japan, continues to be bitter over the Japanese government's forced prostitution of Korean women during World War II. Elderly Koreans, who were taught Japanese when they were part of the empire, often get quite angry if anyone attempts to speak Japanese to them. Although the twentieth-century Japanese colonization and World War II are the most recent wounds, Korean resentment of the Japanese goes back centuries. The case of the Ear Mound in Kyoto is illustrative. Virtually every Korean knows about the hill that contains the ears and noses of approximately 100,000 Koreans killed by Japanese warriors in the late-sixteenth century. That few Japanese even know of the mound's existence reinforces a widespread Korean belief that the Japanese don't consider people of the Korean Peninsula worthy of much attention.

Even though two Japanese prime ministers recently have apologized for Japan's wartime actions, many Chinese and Koreans don't think the apologies were sincere enough. Although the issue of Japan's wartime role appear to be dormant for periods of time, incidents emanating from Japan occur that cause it to resurface on a regular basis.

For example, in the 1980s and 1990s several high-level Japanese politicians made public statements that appeared to exonerate Japan's role in World War II. In 1994 Sakurai Shin, Japan's minister of the environment, stated that World War II was not a war of Japanese aggression. The statement caused a media outcry in other Asian nations, and Sakurai was forced to resign from the cabinet; even so, he remained in the Diet as a member of the House of Representatives. All together, there have been eight examples in recent years of Japanese government officials making statements either defending Japan in World War II or misinterpreting history. Two of the most egregious examples of these pronouncements were that Japan did not exercise colonial rule in Korea and that the Rape of Nanking didn't occur. Although several cabinet officials, like Sakurai, ended up resigning, the voters reelected them to Diet seats.

There also are continual controversies over how Japanese school textbooks treat the issue of Japan's role in World War II. The longest-running controversy revolves around Professor Inega Saburo of Tokyo University of Education. Inega brought three separate lawsuits against the Ministry of Education, beginning in 1965, for their censorship of his depiction of the Nanking incident and other Japanese wartime actions in his high school text. Inega argued such government action was a violation of academic freedom and unconstitutional. In 1997 the Japanese Supreme Court finally ruled in favor of Inega.

In 2001 yet another textbook controversy erupted when the Ministry of Education approved a new middle school textbook written and edited by a group of nationalist academics. The book omits the most important and traumatic aspects of

Japan's wartime actions, including the use of Korean women as prostitutes for the Japanese Army. The South Korean government initially protested the book by temporarily recalling its ambassador, and President Kim Dae Jung brought the textbook issue up in meetings with Japanese business leaders. South Korean officials also alleged there had been clear errors in twenty-five areas in the book. After protests from China as well, the Japanese government had the book reviewed and revised prior to its publication in summer 2001.

Immediately the Chinese government issued a statement expressing strong indignation. There were street protests in South Korea over the book, and President Kim Dae Jung refused to receive a delegation of Japanese politicians who had traveled to Seoul to discuss the text. Furthermore, the South Korean government, which had only recently began to lift restrictions on Japanese popular cultural imports such as cartoons, films, and music, threatened to reverse its position because of the text.

Although there are Japanese, particularly on the political left, who have urged that the nation take more responsibility for its actions in World War II, there are also apparently large numbers of Japanese who feel little or no remorse for Japan's actions in Asia during the Pacific War.

What are Japanese attitudes toward the West, and especially the United States? The most accurate answer is ambivalence. For well over 100 years the Japanese tried very hard to catch the West in economic development. At the same time, elements of the Japanese population have feared that Western culture and values were a threat to Japan's social stability. In the 1980s when Japan's economy was doing well and the United States was experiencing problems, some Japanese business and government officials began to exhibit attitudes of superiority toward the United States. In several cases, prominent private and public-sector figures criticized American companies for being too profit-oriented and speculated whether the United States was too racially heterogeneous to have a successful society any longer. However, such comments have ceased with the economic malaise the Japanese experienced in the 1990s and beyond.

Many ordinary Japanese, though, are still critical today of American high crime rates, problematic race relations, and dysfunctional families. Still, Japanese at times seem to have an inferiority complex about elements of Western and American culture. American and other Western models are used for many Japanese television commercials and print advertisements. English-language loan words have replaced perfectly good Japanese terms. The most popular elective surgery in Japan is eye surgery, mainly among females, in order to make the eyes look Western. American popular culture inundates Japan. When asked why Western instead of Japanese models were used, one advertising executive made the inaccurate comment that all Japanese tend to look alike and Westerners were more glamorous.

The seeming ambivalence the Japanese people exhibit about cultural aspects of the United States is also reflected in surveys indicating how people in each nation feel about each other, and in the positions the two nations take toward each other regarding economic and strategic issues.

If public opinion polls in both nations are to be believed, Japanese and Americans basically have friendly feelings toward each other. In recent polls, about three-quarters of the Japanese public who were sampled liked the United States, with one-quarter claiming to dislike or have negative feelings toward the United States. These results in Japan have been stable for the past few decades. As a point of comparison, in a similar poll of a national sample of Japanese adults on attitudes toward Russia, only 10 percent of Japanese respondents claimed to be positive toward that country, even though the poll was taken after Soviet communism collapsed. Large numbers of Japanese poll respondents do criticize the United States for pushing Japan too hard on trade issues, however, although the percentages who make this criticism vary considerably depending upon how visible the issue is at a given point in time.

Even higher percentages of Americans, over 80 percent in many polls, claim to admire Japan. American responses often cite Japanese industriousness, superior products, and stable educational system and families as admirable qualities. At the same time, large numbers of Americans have the erroneous notion that Japanese only live to work and are not interested in other aspects of life. Often, American public opinion respondents have the not-so-erroneous notion as well that Japan deliberately keeps out foreign goods.

If opinion polls are to be believed, Japanese always view the United States as an important country. American public opinion, by contrast, tends to vary more about Japan's global impact. In the 1980s and well into the 1990s—even though Japan was experiencing a recession in the latter decade—substantial numbers of Americans incorrectly thought that Japan was an economic enemy and could "take over" the U.S. economy. Now that most of the American public is aware that Japan's economy has been experiencing problems for some time, there is the just as incorrect a notion afoot in the United States that Japan—the second-largest economy in the world—is no longer important as an object of study or significant to American interests.

The longstanding U.S. trade deficit with Japan has been a source of intermittent friction since the 1970s. Because the U.S. economy is so much larger than Japan's, at no time has its trade deficit with Japan threatened overall U.S. economic well-being. However, if the U.S. economy is not doing well in a given period, for example, during the last year of George Bush's presidency and the initial months of the first Clinton administration, then the U.S.-Japan trade deficit almost always becomes a serious political issue. The U.S. media reports the merchandise trade deficit, and many Americans invariably and incorrectly look upon Japan as being partially responsible for the nation's recession.

Even though Japan has never caused a U.S. recession, because the Japanese do practice more protectionism than other major developed countries, they are vulnerable to increased American criticism any time the United States experiences a protracted economic slowdown. The overall U.S.-Japan relationship then becomes at risk due to heightened trade friction. Although the American economic successes of the past few years diverted U.S. attention from the trade deficit, it is not only in Japan's best economic interest to buy more foreign, including U.S., goods and services, it probably is astute politics since it helps the Japanese stabilize relations with the world's only superpower.

Future U.S.-Japan economic relations will be extremely important and, from time to time, very high profile, but in some ways U.S.-Japan security issues are much more complex. Japan has enjoyed a situation for over fifty years where it could be free from having a substantial military force, largely follow the American lead on foreign policy issues during the Cold War, and concentrate on the economy. This unusual period of time when Japan was free from decision-making on security issues is over. Although both nations have regularly renewed the original U.S.-Japan Mutual Security Treaty that was first signed in 1951, it is clear the United States wants Japan to take much more of an active role in its own defense. Recently, in response to U.S. pressure, the Japanese have increased the amount of their contributions toward the costs of U.S. military bases and the 47,000 U.S. troops in Japan. However, the United States is looking for more than money. Regardless of what party is in the White House, the United States wants Japan to be an active partner in the defense of the archipelago and the region. This means a substantially larger Japanese military.

Shortly before the November 2000 U.S. presidential elections, a bipartisan commission headed by Richard Armitage and Joseph Nye released a report that reflects the thinking of most American political elites on U.S.-Japan security questions. The report's authors expressed concern that regional security questions had been on the back burner for too long and that the whole question of what to do about the defense of Japan and regional security needed to be addressed in a systematic and focused manner. Significantly, the report calls for a future U.S.-Japan strategic relationship to be modeled after the U.S.-British alliance: As is the case with Britain, Japan would become a full partner with the United States in defense and security issues. This would entail more collective decisionmaking between the two countries and larger and more active Japanese armed forces.

Given the current defense arrangement, the potential volatility of northeast Asia, and the relative strength and mutuality of interest of the U.S.-Japan friendship, the report makes sense. Right now, estimates are that if Japan were attacked, even though the Japanese Self-Defense Forces are quite "high tech," a serious attack could be held off for only two days. The conclusions of the report are quite logical. The problem is that the whole question of expansion of the Japanese military and even of retention of U.S. forces in Japan is an extremely controversial Japanese domestic political question that evokes strong emotional reactions.

It is important to recall that the reason Japan does not have a military force anywhere commensurate with the needs of a country its size is because of U.S.-imposed constitutional restrictions. Any expansion of the size and role of Japan's military will only be accomplished after constitutional revision, something that has never been done on any aspect of the document since it was adopted during the U.S. occupation.

Both the actions of the electorate and political parties through the years and opinion polls indicate that the majority of the Japanese public are quite happy with the status quo of essentially possessing little military power. The Japanese government has for many years pursued a policy of limiting defense expenditures to less than 1 percent of gross national product (GNP), and no political party has ever had the strength to break that ceiling. There are political leaders, including several former prime ministers and the current prime minister, who have recognized Japan's need to expand its military capability. As of the early part of the twenty-first century, however, about the only groups calling for military expansion other than mainstream Japanese political elites are right-wing nationalists.

Large numbers of Japanese, particularly educators, seem to be quite proud of Japan's status as the only major nation without a significant military. Also, two generations of Japanese have come of age experiencing nothing remotely resembling armed conflict. Membership in the Self-Defense Forces is not considered to be high-status work. In general, many Japanese would prefer to forget that nations, including theirs, might have a need for a military. For example, I participated in a recent organized small group discussion on Japan-U.S. security issues in Tokyo with American and Japanese teachers and university students. All Japanese participants were firmly against any military expansion, and several strongly asserted that there was no possibility under any circumstances that Japanese mothers would ever consent to having their sons forced to become soldiers.

The Japanese public's attitude about the U.S. role in Japanese and regional security is ambivalent, somewhat divided, contradictory, and complicated by the Okinawa controversy. Recent surveys indicate that while two-thirds of the Japanese public support the U.S.-Japan military alliance, two-thirds of the public also would like to see the number of U.S. military bases reduced. Although Okinawans make up less than 1 percent of Japan's population, the issue of U.S. military in Japan is most controversial in that prefecture.

U.S. bases on Okinawa constitute 75 percent of all U.S. military facilities in Japan and cover about 20 percent of Okinawan territory. Okinawans have long held divided opinions about the American presence. Okinawa has the lowest average income of any Japanese prefecture, and the bases bring in over $1 billion annually. In a prefecture with nearly double Japan's unemployment rate, 8,000 Okinawans work on the U.S. bases, and many others in entertainment and services also owe their livelihood to the American presence. Still, many Okinawans are bitter that the bases are located on some of the best land in the prefecture, and they worry about the environmental consequences of the installations. Also, Okinawa was the site of one of World War II's most horrendous Pacific Theater land battles. It is not lost on Okinawans that their islands might again be targeted for military destruction if U.S. forces are drawn into war somewhere in the region.

The Okinawan situation became even more controversial in 1995 when three American servicemen raped a twelve-year-old Japanese girl. The incident was heavily publicized, and the trial of the Americans in a Japanese court caused many Okinawans to demand that American forces be removed. Even though the three Americans were convicted in March 1996 and received prison sentences (one for six and one-half years and two for seven years) this caused even more controversy since many Japanese believed the sentences were too short.

The situation is even more complex because the people, formerly subjects of an independent kingdom until Japan acquired the islands in 1879, have always felt mistreated by the Japanese. Prevailing Okinawan opinion is that Japan deliberately plays a role in helping to keep the U.S. bases in Okinawa because the rest of Japan wants the bases, but not on Japan's main islands.

Japanese political elites, top bureaucrats, prime ministers, and cabinet officials are not nearly as apparently confused about security issues as is the public. Government and political leaders disagree about to what extent Japan should expand its military, and on what level of presence U.S. forces should have in Japan. What the political elites understand, though, is that regardless of who provides it, Japan must have a coherent and viable national defense. The problem is that the Japan's leaders are more astute than the public on the issue, and in a democracy, this means education and incremental change must first occur.

Despite much controversy in Japan, progress has been made. In response to U.S. calls for a more active Japanese defense and security role, the United States obtained commitments from Japan in 1997 that the Japanese will take primary responsibility for defense of the home islands upon the event of an attack. This commitment remains symbolic—the small size of Japan's military forces would require that U.S. forces be quickly drawn into a conflict. Still, in the same negotiations, the Japanese agreed to provide greater logistical support for U.S. forces and engage in sea and air reconnaissance, mine sweeping, and search and rescue. The Japanese have also launched a spy satellite into orbit. In 1999, Japan and the United States agreed to engage in joint research into a possible ballistic missile defense program, despite Chinese protests. In the same year, Japan and South Korea conducted their first joint military exercises at sea. Prime Minister Koizumi also announced in 2001 a desire to move toward constitutional revision so as to build a stronger Japanese military.

In 2001 there were visible signs that the new U.S. administration was determined to elevate the importance of the Japan-U.S. security relationship. Although the Clinton administration paid ample attention to joint security matters during President Clinton's first term, priorities changed in the late 1990s as the administration seemed to court China, calling it a "strategic partner," while ignoring Japan. Subsequent U.S. friction with Beijing, doubts about China's long-term ambitions in the region, and the sheer unpredictability of North Korea motivated the new Bush administration to cultivate Japanese political leaders and to appoint knowledgeable Japan specialists in high-level U.S. government positions. The new U.S. policy is that a strong U.S.-Japan partnership might gain both countries more, rather than less, leverage over China and motivate China to be less strident in some of its foreign relations.

The search for answers about Japan's new postwar security role and the future of the U.S.-Japan security partnership occur in a region that is rivaled only by the Middle East as a source for potential geopolitical crises, and, if any occur, it is rather difficult to imagine Japan remaining completely neutral. In 2000 the Chinese government increased military expenditures by at least 10 percent annually for the eleventh year in a row. Beijing has made it quite clear that it considers the Republic of Taiwan Chinese territory. The United States does not have a written obligation to defend Taiwan. It is, however, in writing in the Taiwan Relations Act, the congressional legislation that sets official U.S. policy toward Taiwan, that the United States has the option to defend Taiwan in case of attack. If the Chinese engage in military action against Taiwan, there would be significant pressure in the U.S. Congress for military involvement. If U.S. military involvement occurred it is quite possible the Japanese could become enmeshed in the crisis.

Despite some recent thaws in North-South Korean relations, more than a million troops from opposing sides remain deployed within miles of each other on the Korean Peninsula. North Korea, with one of the most unpredictable governments on earth, managed in August 1998 to fire a test missile over Japan. Although contemporary Russia does not pose the same threat to Japan as did the old Soviet Union, Russian territory is less than 100 miles from northern Hokkaido. Given that the Russians possess the second-largest number of nuclear weapons on earth and have significant political and economic problems, the Japanese must carefully monitor developments.

As Japan gropes for new security policies, northeast Asia and the global community have mixed reactions about future directions for Japanese policy. Many of Japan's Asian neighbors worry that twentieth-century history could repeat itself if Japan expands its military capability. Yet in 1990 Japan, because of its postwar history of not employing military power in any circumstance abroad, was severely criticized by the coalition of nations that fought Iraq because it limited its contribution to a $13 billion donation instead of personnel. Thus far, Japanese Self-Defense Forces have only been in a foreign war zone as noncombatants.

In both national security and economic policy, as one scholar so aptly put it, "Japan is in the midst of the daunting task of redefining its national identity to fit its international status" (Itoh 2000, 185). Japan is a conservative society where change is gradual. It has a history of an island-nation mentality and is for the most part racially homogeneous, and large numbers of Japanese are still uncomfortable with foreigners. Many Japanese still remember the disaster that ensued less than sixty years ago when Japan was last a major actor in world geopolitics. These factors certainly make forging new directions in international relations and new conceptualizations of internationalization anything but easy. Still, the Japanese are among the world's most educated people, mostly affluent, and highly resourceful in many ways. Given these attributes it is quite logical to be optimistic about Japan rising to meet external and internal challenges in very effective, though still unseen ways, as the future unfolds.

References

Buckley, Roger. 1998. *Japan Today.* New York: Cambridge University Press.

"Bush's Japan Team Lineup." *The Oriental Economist Report* Vol. 69, No. 7 (July 2001): 6–8.

Campbell, Kurt M. "The Challenges Ahead for U.S. Policy in Asia." 31 March 2001. Distributed by Foreign Policy Research Institute.

Carpenter, William N., and David G. Wiencek, eds. 2000. *Asian Security Handbook 2000.* Armonk, NY: M. E. Sharpe.

Collcutt, Martin, Marius Jansen, and Isao Kumakura. 1988. *Cultural Atlas of Japan.* New York: Facts on File.

Ellington, Lucien. 1990. *Japan: Tradition and Change.* White Plains, NY: Longman.

French, Howard W. "Japan's Refusal to Revise Textbooks Angers Neighbors." *The Japan Times Online.* 10 July 2001. http://www.nytimes.com/2001/07/10/world/10JAPA.html.

Itoh, Mayumi. 2000. *Globalization of Japan: Japanese* Sakoku *Mentality and U.S. Efforts to Open Japan.* Armonk, NY: M. E. Sharpe.

Japan Now. Washington, DC: Japan Information and Culture Center/Embassy of Japan. November/December 2000: 6.

Johnson, Chalmers. "Japan's Woes Are Political, and U.S. Is not Helping." *International Herald Tribune.* 29 March 2001. Available online at http://www.iht.com/articles/14705.html.

Jolivet, Muriel. 1997. *Japan the Childless Society? The Crisis of Motherhood.* London: Routledge.

Kristof, Nicholas D. "The Problem of Memory." *Foreign Affairs,* Vol. 77, No. 6 (November/December 98): 37–49.

Levi, Antonia. "The Animated Shrine: Using Japanese Animation to Teach Japanese Religion." *Education About Asia,* Vol. 2, No. 1 (Spring 1997): 26–29.

Masahiro, Yamada. "The Growing Crop of Spoiled Singles." *Japan Echo,* Vol. 27, No. 3 (June 2000): 49–53.

McCargo, Duncan. 2000. *Contemporary Japan.* New York: St. Martin's Press.

Millard, Mike. 2000. *Leaving Japan: Observations on the Dysfunctional U.S.-Japan Relationship.* Armonk, NY: M. E. Sharpe.

Miyamoto, Masao. 1995. *The Strait Jacket Society.* Tokyo: Kodansha.

Naoki, Ikegami. "The Launch of Long-Term Care Insurance." *Japan Echo,* Vol. 27, No. 3 (June 2000): 28–33.

Ogawa, Naohiro. "Demographic Trends and Their Implications for Japan's Future." *The Ministry of Foreign Affairs of Japan* (speech presented at the Japan Information Center, San Francisco, 7 March 1997). Available online at http://www.mofa.go.jp/j_info/japan/socsec/ogawa.html.

Reischauer, Edwin O. 1977. *The Japanese.* Cambridge, MA: Harvard University Press.

Ryosei, Kokubun. "Japan-China Relations After the Cold War: Switching from the '1972 Framework.'" *Japan Echo,* Vol. 28, No. 2 (April 2001): 9–14.

Schilling, Mark. 1997. *The Encyclopedia of Japanese Pop Culture.* New York: Weatherhill.

Sumiko, Iwao. "Working Women and Housewives." *Japan Echo,* Vol. 28, No. 2 (April 2001): 51–53.

Tashiro, Masami, ed. 2000. *Japan 2001: An International Comparison.* Tokyo: Keizai Koho Center.

Wilkerson, Kyoko. "Reference Terms for Husbands in Japanese: Sociolinguistic Perspectives." *Southeast Review of Asian Studies,* Vol. 19 (1997): 103–120.

PART TWO
REFERENCE MATERIALS

Key Events in Japanese History

11,000–300 B.C.E.	**Jomon Culture**
300 B.C.E.–250 C.E.	**Yayoi Culture**
250 C.E.–552	**Tomb Period** (Kofun)
552–710	**Late Yamato Period**
552	Buddhism is transported from Korea to Japan
604	Japan's seventeen-point "constitution" is ascribed to Prince Shotoku
645	So-called Taika Reforms enacted
710–794	**Nara Period**
710	Establishment of Japan's first permanent capital at Nara
794–1156	**Heian Period**
794	Capital is moved to Heian (Kyoto)
ca. 1010	Murasaki Shikibu authors *The Tale of Genji*
1156–1185	**Taira Clan in Control of Government**
1180–1185	Gempei War between Taira and Minamoto
1185–1333	**Kamakura Period**
1192	The emperor appoints Minamoto Yoritomo Japan's first shogun
1274, 1281	Two Mongol attempts to conquer Japan fail
1333–1336	Kemmu Restoration attempt to increase imperial power fails

1336–1573	**Ashikaga Period**
1338	Ashikaga Takauji is formally appointed shogun and rules from Kyoto
1467–1477	Onin War marks the beginning of Japanese disunification and civil strife
1543	Portuguese are the first Europeans to reach Japan
1573–1600	**Unification Period**
1600	Tokugawa Ieyasu defeats rivals for political power at the Battle of Sekigahara
1600–1868	**Tokugawa Period**
1603	Tokugawa Iyeasu assumes the title of shogun ruling from Edo (modern-day Tokyo)
1615	The Unification of Japan is completed with the defeat of the Tokugawa's opponents at Osaka Castle
1630	Japan is closed to almost all foreigners
1630–1853	Tokugawa period is marked by peace and prosperity
1853	Commodore Matthew C. Perry "opens" Japan to foreign countries
1868–1912	**Meiji Period**
1868	A group of disaffected samurai overthrow the Tokugawas and establish an oligarchy ruling in the emperor's name
1890	Japan becomes the first Asian country to adopt a Western-style constitution
1904–1905	Japan defeats Russia and gains control of Korea
1910	Korea is formally annexed

1912–1926	**Taisho Period**
1919	Japan, having fought with the Allies in World War I, fails to get a racial equality clause in the Versailles Treaty
1926–1989	**Showa Period**
1931	Japan seizes Manchuria
1937	Start of the Chinese-Japanese War
1941	The Japanese bomb Pearl Harbor, starting World War II in the Pacific
1945	Atomic bombings of Hiroshima (August 6) and Nagasaki (August 9); Japan surrenders
1952	End of the U.S. occupation of Japan
1980	Japanese automobile production exceeds that of U.S. for the first time
1989–present	**Heisei Period**
1990	Japanese economic bubble bursts, bringing over a decade of economic stagnation

Significant People, Places, and Events

Ainu The Ainu are an indigenous people to Japan who are similar to Native Americans and ethnically and culturally different from Japanese. Historically, they inhabited northern Honshu and Hokkaido as well as southern Sakhalin and the Kuril Islands. They hunted deer and seal and fished for salmon. The Japanese launched successful military campaigns against the Ainu that were similar to U.S. government efforts against Native Americans. There are now approximately 24,000 official Ainu in Hokkaido and a small but undetermined number of Ainu in other parts of the country. Many Ainu have been assimilated into mainstream Japanese culture, but there is preservation of Ainu customs, festivals, and crafts in Hokkaido, which draws Japanese tourists much like Native American tourist attractions do in the United States.

American Occupation of Japan (1945–1952) The occupation is generally considered to be a positive development in Japanese history. Partially as a result of American policy, Japan became a democracy with a vibrant economy. Although formally an "Allied" occupation, virtually all power lay with the Americans, and in particular, General Douglas MacArthur, supreme commander for the Allied Powers. The occupation had two distinct phases, political and economic, that occurred chronologically. The Americans were initially interested in demilitarizing and democratizing Japan. The first two years of the occupation included land reform, the imposition of a constitution that was in some respects more liberal than the U.S. Constitution, and the democratization of education. However, by 1948 with the Japanese economy still in shambles and American political leaders concerned about Japan following China's lead and turning to communism, occupation policymakers began to take actions to restore Japan's economic health. These included, most notably, returning conservative business leaders to power and initiating tight monetary policies to end inflation. By the occupation's end in 1952 these policies, along with infusions of American money to purchase supplies for the Korean War, were having a positive effect on the Japanese economy.

Basho, Matsuo (1644–1694) Recognized as the Tokugawa Period's finest poet and master of the seventeen-syllable, three-line haiku, Basho was born a samurai but gave up his rank to live as a commoner. He earned his living as a poet and master teacher, working with students from all walks of life. Basho began the study of Zen later in his life, and his best-known haiku was written in the last decade of his life. Much of it is Zen-influenced. English language translations of Basho's works are widely available.

Burakumin The term translates as "hamlet people" and is the term today for a Japanese minority. In earlier times burakumin were known as *eta*. Although burakumin are apparently ethnic Japanese, since probably premodern times they have been long been regarded as outcasts because of their occupations. Burakumin were considered unclean, because of both negative Buddhist and Shinto connotations, because they engaged in such occupations as butchery, tanning, garbage collecting, and disposal of the dead. By the Tokugawa Period, burakumin were in some ways parallel to untouchables in India in that they were outcastes. Today there are an estimated 3 million burakumin, with the large majority living in the Osaka area in the Kansai District. It is still common practice for some Japanese parents to investigate the family backgrounds of prospective marriage partners to guard against possible burakumin connections. It is alleged that companies also discriminate against burakumin in hiring. Although the Japanese government has provided monies to improve the quality of life in burakumin neighborhoods, the argument can be made that it has not pursued antidiscrimination policies in an aggressive fashion.

Constitution of Japan The present constitution was drafted by Americans during the occupation of Japan and took effect on May 3, 1947. It was the second in modern times for Japan, preceded by the 1890 Meiji Period constitution. Sovereignty was given to the people in the present constitution; in the earlier 1890 document, it rested with the emperor. Most of the important political powers were assigned to the Diet, or national legislature, with that body retaining a parliamentary-style governing structure. The constitution also provided for universal suffrage and guaranteed fundamental human rights for all of Japan's citizens. The constitution contains the famous and unusual Article Nine, which both outlaws war as a sovereign right of the Japanese nation and goes on to outlaw the existence of land, sea, and air forces. The Americans, who were responsible for Article Nine, actually encouraged the Japanese after the beginning of the Cold War to become responsible for aspects of national defense. Today, Japan has substantial Self-Defense Forces that are a military but still does not have bases anywhere other than Japan and has not deployed these troops in any military operations other than as noncombatant elements. The 1947 constitution has always been unpopular with Japanese conservatives because the United States imposed it, and there have been serious discussions of amendments and revisions. However, the political left in Japan has usually strongly supported the constitution, so there have been no changes.

Dogen (1200–1253) Also known as Dogen Kigen, Dogen is considered to be one of Japan's greatest religious figures. Dogen is the father of the Japanese Soto school of Zen

Buddhism, which places great emphasis upon meditation and gradual enlightenment. Born an aristocrat and the recipient of an excellent education, Dogen, upon deciding to take up the religious life as a vocation, first searched unsatisfactorily for appropriate religious instruction in Japan. Dogen then went to China to study Buddhism and, after several unfulfilling experiences, found what he was looking for in the Chinese Caodao school of Buddhism, which emphasized silent meditation with no goal in mind and gradual rather than sudden enlightenment. Upon returning to Japan, Dogen refused to compromise with established Zen sects in Kyoto and moved to the remote Echizen area rather than give in to authorities. Today, Soto and Rinzai are the two major Zen sects in Japan.

Fukuzawa Yukichi (1835–1901) Fukuzawa was the Meiji Period's most famous educator, writer, and, above all, proponent of Western knowledge. Fukuzawa, of low-ranking samurai origins, escaped his rural conservative locale in Kyushu by going to Nagasaki, the island's most important city, to study Western gunnery. He then gravitated to Osaka where he studied in a special school of Dutch studies. Fukuzawa learned first Dutch and later English to better understand the West. He was part of the first Japanese mission to the United States in 1860 and two years later visited several European countries as part of a similar mission. In 1866, 1868, and 1870 he published one each of a three-volume series entitled *Conditions in the West*. In this, his most famous work, Fukuzawa provided readers with clear accounts of specific Western institutions as well as customs.

Fukuzawa viewed his major role throughout much of the Meiji Period as that of helping the Japanese people better understand two very positive aspects of Western civilization: science and an independent spirit. Although he was critical of much about traditional Japan, Fukuzawa saw Western learning as a way to make Japan strong and independent of foreign domination. Fuzuzawa never entered government service but championed a number of political causes, including women's rights. He also controlled a newspaper and founded Keio University, which remains today one of Japan's most prestigious private institutions of higher learning.

Great Buddhas. There are two giant Buddhas in Japan. The first was built in 746 and is located in Nara, which was Japan's first permanent capital. According to historians the Emperor Shomu commissioned the construction of the statue as protection against possible smallpox epidemics and as a symbol of imperial power. The Buddha depicted in the bronze statue is Variocana, the cosmic Buddha. The Buddha, which is over 53 feet in length, is the largest bronze statue in the world. It is housed in Todai-ji Temple, which is the largest wooden building in the world. The present building that houses the great Buddha was rebuilt in 1708, having suffered from fire at least two times. The statue has also been restored several times. The great Buddha at Kamakura, while smaller than the Nara statue, is of much superior artistic quality. The Kamakura Buddha is a depiction of Amida, the Buddha of Eternal Light. It was completed in 1252 and was allegedly constructed by the Minamoto family after their victory over the Taira family. The statue, which is over 37 feet tall, was once housed in a wooden building also. However, a 1495 tidal wave destroyed the building, and today the Buddha sits in the open.

Hiroshima Atomic Bombing. On August 6, 1945, the United States dropped an atomic bomb on the Japanese city of Hiroshima in southwestern Honshu, making it the first target for such a weapon in history. Over 80 percent of Hiroshima's buildings were destroyed, and some 200,000 people were left dead or injured by the blast. On August 9 the United States dropped a second bomb—on Nagasaki in Kyushu—doing considerable damage but less than at Hiroshima. Generally, historians consider the atomic bombings and the entry of the then Soviet Union into the war against Japan on August 8,

1945, to be the key reasons why the Japanese surrendered on August 15, with the emperor informing the nation in a radio broadcast. Some revisionist historians have argued that the atomic bombings were unnecessary because Japan was on the verge of surrender. Today both cities maintain atomic bomb museums and peace parks, but Hiroshima, in part because it was the first city to experience an atomic holocaust, is by far the most visited site.

Ise Shrine. Located in the city of Ise in Mie Prefecture, Ise is one of the two or three most important, if not the most important, Shinto shrines in Japan. It is now less a place of worship than a historically significant tourist site, but it has been venerated by famous and ordinary Japanese throughout history and was the site of popular pilgrimages, particularly during the Tokugawa era. There are both inner and outer as well as affiliated shrines. One of the reasons Ise Shrine is so important is that it enshrines the ancestral gods of the imperial family, including Amaterasu Omikami, the mythical ancestor of the imperial family who is represented by the sacred mirror icon. The shrine is first mentioned in an eighth-century Japanese poem. The main building is elegant in its simplicity and is constructed of unpainted Japanese cypress wood. Its simple design may possibly be traced to prehistoric Japanese grain storehouses. The shrine is usually torn down and rebuilt on a regular interval of, at present, every twenty-one years.

Kamakura Period (1185–1333) This period of Japanese history, when the de facto capital of Japan was moved to the seaside town of Kamakura, near Tokyo, is considered to be the height of Japan's medieval age. The beginning of the period is marked by the awarding of the title *shogun* to Minamoto Yoritomo. Shogun, which formerly was a temporary honor awarded to imperial princes who led punitive military campaigns for the imperial court, took on a different meaning during the Kamakura Period. The shoguns of that era were at least nominally the legitimate military rulers of the country, representing imperial sovereignty, although often shoguns were puppets for powerful families who exercised covert rule. The Kamakura government was called *bakufu,* or "tent government," reflecting the military orientation of the political leadership. The Kamakura Period is also famous in Japanese religious history since it was during this era that Buddhism became a popular religion for the first time. The period ended with a brief restoration of actual imperial rule.

Kawabata, Yasunari (1899–1972) Kawabata is considered one of the very finest Japanese novelists, and he was the first Japanese to win the Nobel Prize for Literature, in 1968. Kawabata was born in Osaka, orphaned at an early age, and also lost his sister and grandmother, with whom he lived, before he reached adulthood. Much of Kawabata's work certainly has overtones of melancholy. Kawabata studied both Western and Japanese literature but was ultimately more Japanese in his perspective and themes. Although he has been called a traditional Japanese novelist, his writings contain both vivid descriptions of the cultural beauty of Japan and more complex treatments of themes such as decay and death. Throughout his long career Kawabata was influenced by a number of literary schools of thought. Some of his most famous works include *Snow Country, The Master of Go, Thousand Cranes,* and *The Sound of the Mountain.* Kawabata died in somewhat mysterious circumstances some three years after receiving the Nobel Prize, in a gas-filled apartment he rented near his Kamakura home. Although his death was probably suicide, there was no note and some close to him argue his death was an accident.

Kiyomizudera Temple Located in Kyoto, Kiyomizudera, or Temple of Clear Water, was founded in 798 by the monk Enchin with the patronage of a general, Tamuramaro (758–811), who had fought to bring eastern Japan under central government control. The temple is part of the Hoso Buddhist sect. Over the centuries the temple has been the object of military attack as well as fires and earthquakes. The last major fire was in 1629, and the present buildings date from 1633. The main hall is built over a cliff and has a large open-air veranda that on a clear day provides viewers with one of the most impressive views of Kyoto possible.

Kurosawa, Akira (1910–1998) Kurosawa is considered to be one of the greatest film directors in the world. Part of his genius was that Kurosawa, while remaining Japanese in his choice of topics, addressed universal human questions. Some of his most famous films include *Rashomon,* in which the relativity of truth is examined through the medium of a story from Japan's medieval period; *Ikiru,* where a bureaucrat dying of cancer searches for fulfillment through a small social action; and *Ran,* a version of William Shakespeare's play *King Lear* in which the leading characters are Japanese feudal lords.

Hiroshige Ando (1797–1858) Along with Hokusai, Hiroshige is considered one of the two greatest masters of the woodblock print, or *ukiyo-e.* Hiroshige was the son of an Edo fireman and a fireman himself until he left his father's vocation to devote himself full time to art. Before Hiroshige, most Japanese woodblock prints had been either of women or actors. Hiroshige utilized new techniques in engraving and printing and also focused on new subjects. He was a prolific artist, producing thousands of prints. Perhaps his most famous set of works, *The Fifty-Three Stages of the Tokaido,* grew out of his first trip down the Tokaido Highway in August 1832 as part of an official procession sent by the Tokugawa shogun to present a gift of horses to the emperor in Kyoto. Hiroshige is also famous for a second series of works, *One Hundred Views of Famous Places in Edo.* While working on the latter, Hiroshige contracted cholera and died in 1858.

Meiji Period (1868–1912) This eventful period of Japanese history began when a small group of disaffected samurai, acting in the name of the then–thirteen-year-old Emperor Mutsuhito, overthrew the Tokugawa shogunate, ending over two and one-half centuries of Tokugawa rule. The name Meiji, meaning "Enlightened Rule," was adopted by the young emperor as the name for the years of his reign. However, the emperor was a figurehead, for an oligarchy constituted the political power in Japan during these years.

The Meiji Period is most important because during these years Japan developed a modern economy and a powerful military and was recognized by the rest of the world as a force with which to be reckoned. Japan fought and won two wars, first with the Chinese and then with Imperial Russia, during the Meiji years. By the end of the period Japan had freed itself from the unequal treaties earlier imposed by the West, and, with the acquisition of what is now Taiwan and Korea, Japan also became a colonial power.

Mishima, Yukio (1925–1970) Perhaps Japan's best-known postwar writer, Mishima (a pen name) was born Hiraoka Kimitake in a family who was often associated with Japan's ruling bureaucratic elite. Mishima was brilliant, erratic, and productive, with definite ideas about such enduring themes as the relationship between art and life, the nature of beauty, and the relevance of warrior values in modern society. A critic and dramatist as well as a novelist, Mishima also engaged in extensive self-promotion. Some of his best-known works include *The Temple of the Golden Pavilion,* a psychological novel based on the actual burning of Kyoto's Golden Pavilion; the four-volume *The Sea of Fertility;* and his short story, *Patriotism.* Mishima garnered worldwide attention by committing ritual suicide in 1970. This act was in large part Mishima's protest against what he perceived as Japanese abandonment of traditional values.

Mount Fuji Located on the border between Shizuoka and Yamanashi Prefectures, this 12,385-foot dormant volcano is a universal symbol of Japan. The climbing of Fujisan—Fuji is so highly regarded that it is given the honorific *san*—began as a religious practice. One religious sect with both Buddhist and Shinto elements, Fujiko, considers the mountain sacred. The Shinto shrine Fujisan Hongu Sengen Jinja, located in Fujinomiya City south of the mountain, maintains a smaller shrine on the summit. Many Japanese and foreigners alike with no religious connections climb Fuji annually for pleasure. Thousands of climbers scale Fuji during the climbing season, July 1–August 26. There are ten stations along the way. Fuji is deeply embedded in the consciousness of the Japanese people. Local mountains that resemble Fujisan are often admired simply for that reason.

Murasaki Shikibu (late tenth century–early eleventh century) A Heian Period aristocrat, Murasaki is the most famous woman novelist in Japanese history and one of the most famous novelists in world history. Her masterpiece, *The Tale of Genji,* is considered to be the world's first psychological novel. Murasaki was from a minor branch of the extremely powerful Fujiwara family. Relatively little about her life is known, but it is documented that her father served as provincial governor and Murasaki became a lady in waiting for the empress in the imperial court in 1006 or 1007. Murasaki is also famous for the *Murasaki Shikibu Diary,* which is believed to have been authored when she was in imperial service. *The Tale of Genji* was probably finished sometime in the first decade of the eleventh century. The work is episodic and has many characters. The protagonist, Prince Genji, is the ideal aristocrat: a good painter, poet, musician, and athlete. However, the book's major focus is upon Genji's talent in the art of love and chronicles his many affairs of the heart. Murasaki does a masterful job in depicting complex aspects of many of the characters in the novel and of articulating important Japanese cultural values. The Buddhist theme of transience of the world is certainly present in *Genji* as is the Japanese focus on the special beauty of highly ephemeral phenomena.

Nishida, Kitaro (1870–1945) The most important philosopher in modern Japan, Nishida was the founder of a school of philosophy that is named after the institution, Kyoto University, where he taught and achieved fame. Nishida was from a prominent family near Kanazawa, graduated from Tokyo University in 1894, and taught in several educational institutions before going to Kyoto University in 1910. Among his major works are *A Study of Good, Intuition and Reflection in Self-consciousness,* and *Art and Morality.* Nishida was inspired by foreign philosophers such as William James and Henri Bergson, but he was unique in that his thinking transcended traditional Eastern and Western thought yet retained an essentially Buddhist perspective. Nishida had a life-long association with the world-famous popularizer of Zen Buddhism, D. T. Suzuki, and his early adult years, in particular, included Zen practice. One of Nishida's seminal contributions to philosophy was his conceptualization of the idea of pure experience. Nishida saw pure experience as prior to and foundational to all subsequent mental notions, including subject and object, body and mind, and spirit and manner. His work is studied both in the West and Japan today.

Oe Kenzaburo (1935–) Oe, who won the Nobel Prize for Literature in 1994, was born in a very remote Kyushu mountain village and was a child during World War II. While a young boy and after his father's death during the war, Oe's literary imagination was stimulated by his mother, who provided him with a wide variety of Western and Japanese books. Oe entered Tokyo University in 1954 and won his first literary prize four years later for a short World War II story about a downed black airman and a small Japanese village. Oe studied French literature and did his major undergraduate work on Jean Sartre's novels. He published his first novel, *Nip the Buds, Shoot the Kids,* in 1958. The novel ensured Oe's reputation as a novelist, and he also became a relatively high-profile left-wing intellectual. In 1963, Oe fathered a mentally disabled son, who has been an influence on his writing and thinking. He was also significantly influenced by a visit to Hiroshima. Oe won the Shincho Literary Prize for his novel *A Personal Matter,* published in 1964. Oe's masterpiece is considered to be *The Silent Cry,* which was first published in 1974 and won the Tanizaki Prize. Oe addresses a variety of themes in his writing, including postwar Japanese alienation, issues of cultural identity, the dangers of nuclear weapons, the developing world, and environmental issues. He has written a wide range of essays, short stories, and novels. Other well known-works include *An Echo of Heaven, The Treatment Tower,* and *A Quiet Life.*

Pearl Harbor, Hawaii The Japanese attacked the U.S. naval fleet at Pearl Harbor on the morning of Sunday, December 7 (December 8 Japanese time), 1941. Four battleships and two other ships were sunk, and twelve other ships were damaged. American killed and wounded numbered approximately 3,700; the Japanese lost sixty-four men, twenty-nine aircraft, and five small submarines. The event is significant in Japanese, U.S., and world history because the next day the United States declared war on Japan, thereby extending World War II to the Pacific arena.

In summer 1941, the Japanese military had moved into southern Indochina in search of much-needed raw materials for its war effort in China and to strengthen its strategic position in southeast Asia. The United States, Great Britain, and Holland retaliated by freezing Japanese assets and cutting off oil sales. Furthermore, the United States was increasingly determined that Japan not only withdraw from Indochina but China as well. The Japanese were in no position for protracted negotiations with the United States, and the army in particular felt the only choice was to fight or retreat. When last-minute negotiations with U.S. diplomats proved unsuccessful, the Japanese government made the decision for the surprise Pearl Harbor attack. The U.S. Pacific Fleet was crippled but not destroyed, and the United States would gain victory over Japan in August 1945.

Ryoanji Zen Temple and Rock Garden Ryoanji Temple was built in Kyoto in1450 by General Hosokawa Katsumoto. The temple is part of the Rinzai Zen sect. The rock garden, which is one of Japan' most famous cultural sights, is said to be the work of the artist Soami, although this is not documented. The garden consists of a simple combination of raked white gravel and 15 rocks, which are set in three groups. The garden is bordered by the temple buildings and a wall. Some have speculated the stones represent islands in the ocean, while others have contended the rocks are mountains. However, the garden was designed to aid contemplation and realization through intuitive and not literal understanding. In addition to the temple and rock garden, Ryoanji also features a beautiful duck pond.

Shotoku Taishi (574–622) Prince Shotoku was appointed regent when he was twenty years old by Empress Suiko, who delegated all power to him. Shotoku was a major proponent of Buddhism and worked very hard to propagate that foreign faith in Japan. Shotoku also introduced Chinese beliefs, governmental procedures, and science and technology in an attempt to modernize and strengthen the Japanese state. Shotoku is most famous for the promulgation of the famous seventeen-point "constitution," which appeared in 604. The very first point in the document is a Confucian call for harmony. The second point, or article, is an injunction of reverence for Buddhism. Other articles call for subordinates to obey superiors and confirm that only government has the right to collect taxes. The purpose of the "constitution" was not to provide a plan of government but to describe moral notions that should be characteristic of appropriate government.

Showa Period (1926–1989) This is the name that the late Emperor Hirohito selected as his reign title. The translation is "Enlightened Peace." Events, however, would make Hirohito's choice rather ironic. This period of Japanese history included the militarists' rise to power, the war with China, World War II in the Pacific, and the atomic bombing of Japan. Conversely, Japan rose with seemingly lightening speed in a few decades after World War II to a position of world economic importance and unparalleled domestic affluence. The Showa Period also witnessed the democratization of Japan. Emperor Hirohito remains a very controversial figure in Japanese history, primarily because it is not known to what degree he was responsible for Japan's actions in World War II. Very fine scholars seriously disagree as to whether Hirohito was a political pawn or played a more active role in encouraging Japanese military aggression.

Tojo Hideki (1884–1948) Tojo was born in Tokyo and graduated from military academy and then the Army Staff College at the top of his class. Tojo's abilities earned him the nickname "razor-sharp Tojo" with peers. He has been described as a typical Japanese military bureaucrat and as a hard, decisive, and efficient officer. Serving in Manchuria in the 1930s, Tojo was an advocate of full-scale war with China. In May 1938 he returned to Tokyo and served as army vice minister and chief of the Manchuria bureau in Prime Minister Konoe's cabinet. Tojo continued to advocate expansion of the China war while serving in the government and also strongly supported the Tripartite Pact with Germany and Italy and the invasion of French Indochina. Tojo became army minister in July 1941 and opposed Konoe's goal of rapprochement with the United States. He took over as prime minister in October 1941 and allowed the Japanese government to continue negotiations with the United States while preparing to attack the U.S. naval station at Pearl Harbor, Hawaii. Tojo temporarily managed to suppress all opposition to the ensuing war, but as Japan began to do poorly in the war his position became more and more vulnerable. In July 1944 a group led by former Prime Minister Konoe and top navy officers ousted Tojo from the prime ministership. After the conclusion of World War II, Tojo was indicted and convicted as a war criminal by the International Military Tribunal and was hanged on December 23, 1948.

Tokugawa Ieyasu (1542–1616) Tokugawa Ieyasu was the third powerful military leader, following Oda Nobunaga and Toyotomi Hideyoshi, who worked to gain control over Japan. He was considered the most patient and pragmatic of the three great warlords. He utilized alliances with the first two unifiers to build his own power base in eastern Japan and three years after his victory at Sekigahara was appointed shogun, a title the Tokugawa family would retain for over 250 years. Ieyasu made an obscure fishing village, Edo (now Tokyo), his political base. Through his control of over 260 daimyo, he succeeded in unifying Japan. The date of his victory at Sekigahara, 1600, is generally considered the beginning of the Tokugawa Period of Japanese history. This period ranks as a time of unparalleled peace in Japanese history. It was also unique in that Japan was isolated from most of the rest of the world. Much of the groundwork for Japan's later economic success in the Meiji Period had its roots in Tokugawa Japan.

Japanese Language, Food, and Etiquette

The origin of the Japanese language is still debated. It has strong similarities to Korean in grammatical structure and also has some resemblance to Altaic languages such as Mongolian and Turkish. Although Japanese is grammatically unrelated to Chinese, the original Japanese written language was adopted from China over 1,500 years ago. Written Japanese is considered one of the world's most very difficult languages to learn, but spoken Japanese is relatively easy for an English-speaking person to learn to pronounce and speak.

WRITTEN JAPANESE

Written Japanese consists of Chinese characters, or *kanji*, and two kana or syllabaries, *hiragana* and *katakana*. Kanji, which means "Chinese characters," are ideograms or pictorial representations of ideas as well as sounds. Kanji are used in writing the main parts of a sentence such as verbs and nouns, as well as Japanese names. Kanji was imported into Japan sometime during the fourth century A.D. from China via Korea. Although there are said to be some 48,000 kanji in existence, roughly 4,000 characters are commonly used. The Ministry of Education has identified essential kanji for everyday life, and these are taught to all students in elementary and secondary school. Students must learn 881 kanji in elementary school and a total of 1,945 by the time they graduate from high school.

Kanji are, by far, the most difficult written Japanese characters, requiring in some cases as many as 23 strokes. Most kanji also have more than one meaning, and combinations of

233

kanji are used to create even more meanings. Kanji occasionally look like what they mean but usually do not. The following are examples of kanji, along with the most common English meanings and Romanized Japanese terms.

Single Kanji

日	川	人
sun, *hi*	river, *kawa*	person, *hito*
大	本	
big, *okii*	root/origin, *hon*	

Compound Kanji

日本	三月
Japan, *Nihon*	March, *San Gatsu*

Kana (hiragana and katakana) developed in response to problems the Japanese encountered after they started to use Chinese characters for their own language. Chinese words are only one or two syllables, and the Chinese can use a character for each syllable, but Japanese words often have many syllables, especially inflected words. The Japanese developed symbols from Chinese characters called kana to indicate a sound without meaning, as is the case with the English alphabet. However, each symbol indicates the sound of a whole Japanese syllable instead of each separate part. For example, す is *su* and つ is *tsu*. Kana usually are much easier to write than kanji because they require fewer strokes.

Hiragana and katakana each contain forty-six basic symbols representing specific sounds as well as additional modified symbols. Hiragana is used for inflected endings, grammatical particles, and other Japanese words while katakana is used for foreign loan words. For example "ice cream" is written in katakana as アイス クリーム.

The typical Japanese written sentence contains combinations of kanji, hiragana, and katakana. Written Japanese is usually written vertically with columns running from right to left. This means books and magazines begin at what would be the back of their English equivalents. Sometimes, as is the case with the English language, Japanese is written horizontally from left to right.

Both hiragana and katakana and corresponding sounds are illustrated in the charts beginning on page 236.

SPOKEN JAPANESE

Japanese pronunciation is relatively easy for most English speakers. Japanese has no tones, unlike Chinese, and many of its sounds are also found in English. A number of excellent conversational instructional materials using the Roman alphabet are now available for foreigners who want to pick up basic phrases quickly.

Japanese vowels have the following pronunciations:

a . . . . as the *a* in *father*

i . . . . as the *e* in *we*

u . . . . as the *oo* in *soon*

e . . . . as the *e* in *get*

o . . . . as the *o* in *old*

Long vowels are indicated by diacritical marks or a repeated vowel, and a long vowel must be pronounced twice as long as a short vowel. Unlike in English, long vowels retain the same basic pronunciation as the short version but are just

The Hiragana

Below each character is its name, followed by the pronunciation.
Note: The pronunciations given are not the only possible correct ones.

あ	い	う	え	お
a ah	i ee	u uu	e eh	o oh
か	き	く	け	こ
ka kah	ki kee	ku kuu	ke kay	ko koe
が	ぎ	ぐ	げ	ご
ga gah	gi gee	gu goo	ge gay	go go
さ	し	す	せ	そ
sa sah	shi she	su sue	se say	so soe
ざ	じ	ず	ぜ	ぞ
za zah	ji jee	zu zoo	ze zay	zo zoe
た	ち	つ	て	と
ta tah	chi chee	tsu t'sue	te tay	to toe
だ	ぢ	づ	で	ど
da dah	ji jee	zu zoo	de day	do doe
な	に	ぬ	ね	の
na nah	ni nee	nu nuu	ne nay	no noe

は ha hah	ひ hi he	ふ fu fuu	へ he hay	ほ ho hoe
ば ba bah	び bi bee	ぶ bu boo	べ be bay	ぼ bo boe
ぱ pa pah	ぴ pi pee	ぷ pu puu	ぺ pe pay	ぽ po poe
ま ma mah	み mi me	む mu moo	め me may	も mo moe
や ya yah		ゆ yu yuu		よ yo yoe
ら ra rah	り ri ree	る ru rue	れ re ray	ろ ro roe
わ wa wah		ん n n		を o oh

きゃ kya q'yah	きゅ kyu que	きょ kyo q-yoe
ぎゃ gya g'yah	ぎゅ gyu g'yuu	ぎょ gyo g'yoe

しゃ sha yah	しゅ shu yuu	しょ sho yoe
じゃ ja jah	じゅ ju juu	じょ jo joe
ちゃ cha chah	ちゅ chu chuu	ちょ cho choe
ぢゃ ja jah	ぢゅ ju juu	ぢょ jo joe
にゃ nya ne-yah	にゅ nyu ne-yuu	にょ nyo ne-yoe
ひゃ hya he-yah	ひゅ hyu he-yuu	ひょ hyo he-yoe
びゃ bya b'yah	びゅ byu b'yuu	びょ byo b'yoe
ぴゃ pya p'yah	ぴゅ pyu p'yuu	ぴょ pyo p'yoe
みゃ mya me-yah	みゅ myu me-yuu	みょ myo me-yoe
りゃ rya re-yah	りゅ ryu re-yuu	りょ ryo re-yoe

Source: Reprinted courtesy of Chris Rijk from his Web site: The West of Tokyo Club,
www.wot-club.org.uk

The Katakana

Below each character is its name, followed by the pronunciation.
Note: The pronunciations given are not the only possible correct ones.

ア	イ	ウ	エ	オ
a ah	i ee	u uu	e eh	o oh
カ	キ	ク	ケ	コ
ka kah	ki kee	ku kuu	ke kay	ko koe
ガ	ギ	グ	ゲ	ゴ
ga gah	gi gee	gu goo	ge gay	go go
サ	シ	ス	セ	ソ
sa sah	shi she	su sue	se say	so soe
ザ	ジ	ズ	ゼ	ゾ
za zah	ji jee	zu zoo	ze zay	zo zoe
タ	チ	ツ	テ	ト
ta tah	chi chee	tsu t'sue	te tay	to toe
ダ	ヂ	ヅ	デ	ド
da dah	ji jee	zu zoo	de day	do doe
ナ	ニ	ヌ	ネ	ノ
na nah	ni nee	nu nuu	ne nay	no noe

ハ	ヒ	フ	ヘ	ホ
ha hah	hi he	fu fuu	he hay	ho hoe

バ	ビ	ブ	ベ	ボ
ba bah	bi bee	bu boo	be bay	bo boe

パ	ピ	プ	ペ	ポ
pa pah	pi pee	pu puu	pe pay	po poe

マ	ミ	ム	メ	モ
ma mah	mi me	mu moo	me may	mo moe

ヤ		ユ		ヨ
ya yah		yu yuu		yo yoe

ラ	リ	ル	レ	ロ
ra rah	ri ree	ru rue	re ray	ro roe

ワ		ン		ヲ
wa wah		n n		o oh

キャ	キュ	キョ
kya q'yah	kyu que	kyo q-yoe

ギャ	ギュ	ギョ
gya g'yah	gyu g'yuu	gyo g'yoe

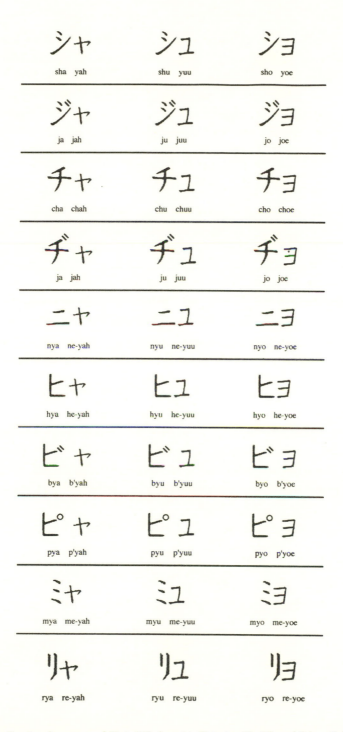

Source: Reprinted courtesy of Chris Rijk from his Web site: The West of Tokyo Club,
www.wot-club.org.uk

extended—as in *obaasan* (mother). Most consonant sounds are similar to English, with the following exceptions:

> r—made with a single flap of the tip of the tongue against the ridge behind your front teeth. The sound is almost a cross between the English *r* and *l*.

> f—before *u*, *fu* is pronounced by releasing the vowel *u* while the lips are held as if you were about to whistle.

> g—always hard, as in *good*, never soft as in *gentle*.

> ts—as the *ts* in *cats*.

Unlike English, where the word order is subject-verb-object, Japanese sentence order is subject-object-verb. Rather than saying "I bought this car," a Japanese person would say something like "I this car bought," or, in Japanese, *watashi ga kono kuruma o kaimashita*. Often, Japanese will also omit the subject of a sentence if it is obvious or not considered important. Most Japanese would probably say *kono kuruma o kaimashita*, leaving out the pronoun "I." Finally, asking questions in Japanese is even easier than in English. Asking questions that require *yes* or *no* is easy since all that is required is the word *ka* at the end of the sentence.

The following are some useful survival Japanese expressions.

> Ohayo gozaimasu!   Good morning!

> Konnichi wa.   Hello! (used from about 10 A.M. until sunddown)

> Sayonara.   Good-bye.

> O-genki desu ka?   How are you?

> Arigato gozaimasu, genki desu.   Fine, thank you.

> Domo arigato gozaimasu.   Thank you very much.

Do itashimashite.   You are welcome.

Chotto matte, o-kudasai.   Wait just a moment, please.

Mo ichido, onegaishimasu.   Once more, please.

Hajime mashite?   How do you do?

Hai.   Yes.

Sumimasen.   Excuse me.

As is the case with any national language, the Japanese language both shapes and reflects cultural values. The Japanese people in some ways take a different view than Americans do about the purpose of the spoken language. In the United States the ability to communicate ideas clearly is considered a desirable trait in an individual. Often this is not true with the Japanese. Japanese believe in preserving group harmony, and in order to do this it is important that a person often speak indirectly so as not to offend. For example, if a Japanese finds a request by an associate impossible to fulfill, he or she often uses a phrase that could be translated into English as "it's very difficult." Most Japanese would consider an out and out "no" far too direct!

One of the greatest differences in Japanese and English is the importance of levels of politeness in Japanese. A person will speak quite differently depending upon the person they are speaking to or about. Both forms and words, including verbs, nouns, pronouns, and adjectives, often change depending on the status of the person to whom one is talking. A person will use a particular word for *mother* or *father* when speaking to one's parents and a different word when speaking about one's parents to someone else. One reason business cards are much more common in Japan than in the United States is that they are a quick way for someone who meets another person to obtain an idea of the person's status and adjust language accordingly.

FOOD

Although eating is both a life-sustaining and a social activity in any culture, the Japanese are particularly well-known for going to great lengths in preparing and sharing meals. Eating in restaurants is even more popular in Japan than in the United States. A few years ago, the results of one study indicated that although Japan has only half the population of the United States, the country contains almost as many restaurants. Because Japanese homes are substantially smaller than their U.S. counterparts, it is much more common for social events such as birthday and anniversary parties to occur in restaurants in Japan.

The Japanese, who have the reputation of effectively borrowing from many other cultures, have certainly done this with food. One may find a large variety of Western and Asian cuisine in any Japanese city, and even small towns have a variety of American fast-food restaurants such as Baskin Robbins, Dunkin' Donuts, McDonalds (a favorite hang out for the young), and Wendy's. The Japanese also have their own varieties of fast-food chains. Even if the Western traveler is not inclined toward fast food, it is an interesting intercultural experience to visit at least once a Japanese Kentucky Fried Chicken or McDonalds to observe the similarities and differences in the Japanese versions of these eateries.

Though the Japanese enjoy the cuisine of other nations they are quite proud of their indigenous cuisine. Traditional Japanese food is extremely healthy, with a low amount of red meat and fat. It also tastes quite different than American and Western cuisine. Foreigners tend not to be neutral about Japanese food; they either like it very much or prefer to avoid many dishes.

Japanese restaurants often specialize in particular dishes, and it is quite common for people who go out to eat to have one dish at a particular restaurant and then go to several more and enjoy other specialties. There are restaurants where a variety of dishes may be obtained as well. The most common kind is the *shokudo,* which may be found around train stations and in shopping areas. Shokudo serve both Western and Japanese dishes, and they often have set lunches that are available at good prices. Japanese pubs, or *izakaya,* usually specialize in tasty snacks such as grilled fish, soy beans, and meat kabobs called *yakitori.* More formal traditional Japanese restaurants also serve a variety of dishes. The typical traditional Japanese restaurant will serve a large meal of many courses including both cooked and raw fish; a variety of vegetables, often served cold; some meat, egg or tofu; a variety of sauces and condiments; soup; and rice. Beer, *sake,* and tea are the usual beverage accompaniments.

In upscale establishments, as well as when eating in a Japanese home, it is wise for the visitor to carefully examine how the food is arranged. The Japanese place as much emphasis upon form as function and often take an artist's approach to food as a visual display. Although appropriate conduct at meals is discussed in the etiquette section of this book, visitors should be aware that tipping is simply not done in any restaurant in Japan. If one leaves money on the table, there is a good chance it will be returned. It is a good idea to practice with *hashi,* or chopsticks, before going to Japan. Although many restaurants and homes have Western cutlery, visitors to Japan may also often find themselves in situations where only chopsticks are available.

Common Japanese Dishes

Rice. Any discussion of Japanese dishes must begin with rice, which is not only a staple in the Japanese diet but an intregal part of national culture. Wet rice paddy cultivation was introduced to Japan very early in the nation's history. Some anthropologists even assert that the Japanese propensity to seek harmony, or *wa,* and group consensus in most endeavors originated out of necessity. Groups of families had to effectively work together to grow rice. Shinto rituals also have focused upon rice growing, and rice wine, *sake,* is used in religious ceremonies. *Gohan,* the Japanese word for steamed rice, is also the word for "meal" in Japan. In order to differentiate between meals, the prefixes *asa* (morning), *hiru* (noon), and *ban* (evening) are added to *gohan.* Since World War II rice consumption has declined, but the food is still quite popular with the Japanese. Rice cookers are a vital appliance in any Japanese home. The Japanese eat sticky short-grain rice, which has a different texture than Western varieties. It is quite normal for rice to be served with all three meals in a Japanese home, though most Japanese now also eat *pan,* or bread, with some meals, especially at breakfast. Japanese also enjoy *mochi* (rice cakes) and a variety of *senbei,* rice cracker snacks.

Sashimi and Sushi. *Sashimi* is sliced raw fish that is dipped into a small bowl of *shoyu* (soy sauce) and *wasabi,* a type of hot horseradish. Standard accompaniments are steamed rice and *gari,* pickled ginger. It is an extremely healthy food and is always served very fresh. Tuna, salmon, carp, squid, octopus, shrimp, and a variety of other seafood is used for sashimi. In order to make *sushi,* the chef cuts a small piece of raw fish into a strip and serves it on a little rice canape. The rice served with sushi has a bit of rice wine vinegar mixed into it, and a smidgen of wasabi paste often is nestled between the fish and rice. Sashimi and sushi are considered delicacies in Japan and may be obtained in sushi bars but also in other restaurants and through catering services.

Tempura. The Portuguese originally introduced *tempura,* but the Japanese call it their own. Tempura consists of vegetables, fish, or shrimp lightly coated with batter and fried. It is eaten with special sauce and tends to be a favorite Japanese food for many Westerners.

Sukiyaki. Although *sukiyaki* was also not originally indigenous, the Japanese now claim it. The dish consists of a broth with various vegetables, clear noodles, and thinly sliced beef. Individual bites of sukiyaki are usually dipped into raw beaten egg, then eaten with rice.

Ramen. These are big bowls of wheat noodles in a meat broth. *Ramen* is served with a variety of toppings including sliced pork.

Soba and Udon. *Soba* is a thin, brown buckwheat noodle. *Udon* are thick, white, wheat noodles. Both are served in a broth in cold and hot versions.

Curried Beef/Pork. The ubiquitous "curry rice" found at every train station in Japan is also not originally Japanese but has come to be regarded as almost indigenous. This stew of meat, potatoes, carrots, and other vegetables in an Indian-style curry gravy is served hot over rice. Foreigners tend to particularly enjoy this dish.

Tonkatsu. *Tonkatsu* is a deep-fried breaded pork cutlet served with a tangy brown sauce and raw shredded cabbage. It is now sometimes available made with chicken. Although the dish might not sound exceptional, it tends to be quite tasty.

Shabu shabu. This dish consists of thin beef slices and vegetables that are cooked by dipping in a light broth and sauces and then prepared in a pot over a fire at the table. A seafood version is also available. Many restaurants in Japan specialize in *shabu shabu*.

Yakitori. These are kebabs of chicken or pork, sometimes with vegetables. They are eaten with a special sauce. *Yakitori* tends to be a favorite Japanese snack food.

Okonomiyaki. This has been described as a Japanese pancake, but forget the Western taste connotations—it's actually more akin to an omelette or frittata. Usually available at restaurants by the same name, *oknomiyaki* consists of meat or seafood and vegetables cooked in a cabbage and vegetable batter.

O-bento. *O-bento* is not a food, but any visitor to Japan should know the term. O-bento are box lunches that are widely available, particularly at train stations. They normally consist of rice, chicken or seafood, and pickled vegetables. O-bento are usually tasty and nutritious. They can be simple or quite elaborate.

Confections. Japanese confections tend to be beautiful but rarely appeal to Western tastes. Many, such as *manju* and the gelatinous *yokan,* are made with a sweet bean paste. They should be tried at least once though, if possible accompanied by hot tea, and certainly admired for their visual beauty.

Common Beverages

Alcoholic. Many Westerners are surprised to find that beer is the preferred alcoholic drink of the Japanese. During the Meiji Restoration the Japanese learned beer brewing techniques from the Germans, and Japanese beer is quite good. Recently the variety of brews available has expanded. Sake, or rice wine, is the traditional Japanese alcoholic beverage and is also quite popular. Sake is part of traditional Japanese culture and is often served as part of celebrations and festivals. There are several types of sake, which is served hot in small cups or, increasingly during hot months, cold. *Shochu* is a quite potent distilled spirit made of sweet potatoes and has become more popular in recent years. Domestic and imported liquors are also available in Japan, and in recent years wine has become more popular.

Nonalcoholic. Japanese green tea, *o-cha,* is the most pervasive nonalcoholic drink in Japan and comes in several varieties, including roasted versions. Although it contains caffeine, several studies have indicated that green tea may be a quite healthy beverage. It contains Vitamin C and may have properties that inhibit certain cancers. The Japanese drink it hot and cold. Chinese dark tea (oolong) is also widely available in Japan. Coffee is extremely popular in Japan, and the country is dotted with coffee houses that often serve as de facto offices for many office workers. The Japanese also love iced coffee, which is available both in coffee houses and restaurants and in vending machines. The Japanese enjoy a variety of soft drinks, and visitors are particularly encouraged to try some of the fruit-based soft drinks available in vending machines and convenience stores.

For further information on Japanese food, consult the "Annotated Bibliography of Recommended Works on Japan."

ETIQUETTE

Japan is a very structured and conservative society compared to the United States and many other Western countries. There is a much-repeated saying about the difference in rules of conduct in the United States and Japan: In the United States anything is permitted unless it is explicitly forbidden, while in Japan anything is forbidden unless it is explicitly permitted. Although there are many exceptions to this generalization, when etiquette and manners are concerned there is much truth in the adage. Japanese are bound by many etiquette expectations. However, foreigners can take much solace in the fact that except for a few notable exceptions, the Japanese are quite forgiving of outsiders. Educated Japanese recognize how complicated etiquette can be in their culture and are truly tolerant of foreigners' mistakes.

Although the influence of the group was extensively addressed in Chapter 4 of this book, it is useful for readers to be reminded that many, if not most, of the rules of conduct that Japanese learn are based on the importance of the group in Japanese life and the need for group *wa,* or harmony. Like humans everywhere, Japanese are individuals and have varying interests and tastes. It is just that when deciding how to behave, the typical Japanese is less likely to base his or her decisions upon individual desires than is the case with Westerners. What follows is a rudimentary introduction to basic Japanese etiquette and manners, organized by topic.

Taking Shoes Off. Perhaps the worst breach of etiquette foreigners can make is to not take off their shoes when entering a Japanese home or certain public buildings such as schools or temples. This practice goes back centuries and is connected with Shinto notions of purity. Incidentally, Japanese have a much easier time keeping their houses clean as a result of this practice, and a few Westerners are so impressed they adopt the custom as well. Virtually all Japanese homes have a *genkan,* or entranceway, with a space where visitors take off their shoes and step up on to the actual floor of the house. It is important to arrange your shoes neatly by the step up as well. Normally, one wears slippers inside the house except when they enter a *tatami* (bamboo mat) room, and then they leave their slippers outside the room. Also, special slippers for Japanese toilets are right outside those structures, so when using the toilet, change from regular to WC (water closet, or restroom) slippers and change again upon leaving the toilet.

Bowing. Although some Japanese now shake hands, they typically bow when meeting each other or parting. It is polite to bow from the waist rather than just nod the head. The more high status the person one is greeting, the deeper they are expected to bow. Bows also occur simultaneously. The polite thing to do in Japan is to bow. Bowing is, to a certain extent, an art form, and it is difficult for foreigners to get it exactly right. However, Japanese appreciate the gesture.

Business Cards. Business cards, or *meishi* in Japanese, are highly important, and anyone but the most casual tourist or student is strongly advised to have some printed before visiting Japan. Typically, business cards have a person's position, organization, and various addresses. In most Western cities one can find a company that will print a business card in English on one side and Japanese on the other. Business cards have multiple uses in Japan and their own set of attendant rules. First and foremost, they are a quick way for people to judge each other's status, thereby allowing both parties to act accordingly. Business cards also serve as invaluable sources of business and professional information. In a society where personal connections are everything, recipients of an important person's business card may very well find many new opportunities. When presenting a business card to someone, the polite way to do it is to use both hands and present the card so that the person to whom you are giving it can read it. Never deal a meishi as if it was a playing card. It is also considered extremely impolite to stuff a business card in one's pocket or to take a personal business card from one's pocket and then present it to someone else. Most Japanese will have card holders for their own, and other people's, meishi.

Sitting. Although Western furniture is now used throughout Japan, there are still situations, particularly in tatami rooms with no chairs, where people sit on the floor. The correct way to sit is with one's legs underneath them. However, this can be particularly painful for large foreigners or anyone, including younger Japanese, who is unaccustomed to the posture. The Japanese often appreciate it when Westerners try the correct sitting position, but are quite easy-going about our need to stretch out our legs. If this is the case and the legs must be extended, be sure and not point the feet directly at another person.

Clothes. Although notions of what is considered to be appropriate clothing seem to be changing, Japan is more of a traditional society than most Western countries and certainly the United States. Shorts on adult men and women are not nearly as common in Japan. Loud, garish clothing among adults is still the exception rather than the rule. Most women do not wear open-toed sandals in public.

Gift Giving. Japan is very much a gift-giving society, and when visiting a Japanese home, a workplace, or office on business or pleasure, it is very much in order to bring a gift. The appearance of the gift is quite important, so while gifts need not be expensive, they should be neatly wrapped. It is also considered bad form, unless one grants you permission, to open the gift in the presence of the giver. Japanese particularly appreciate gifts that are representative of one's region or specific locale. It is important to keep in mind that Japan is a developed country and consumers can buy many of the same mass-produced products that are available in other countries. Local art objects, drinks, or books of photographs are good examples of appropriate gifts.

Distrust of Overly Verbal People. Japan, for a variety of reasons, is a country that has never particularly valued the silver-tongued orator or the incessant chatterbox. Japanese can often be quite comfortable with silences in conversation. This doesn't mean that one should be silent and withdrawn, but overly talkative people are frowned upon and considered egotistical. Overly loud people are also considered rude. This can be a real problem for Americans, who unintentionally many times are the loudest people on a Japanese train or commercial establishment.

Compliments. In group-oriented Japan it is considered good manners to be self-effacing while very complimentary of the other person. Foreigners who know a very few Japanese phrases are often told, sometimes in flawless English, that they speak such good Japanese. Expect to be complimented on a variety of attributes. Your Japanese friend or acquaintance is not being duplicitous but is only attempting to be polite.

Directness and Opinions. Because they are taught to preserve group harmony, most Japanese are somewhat indirect when asked questions and often shy away from giving opinions. For example, if asked whether one likes a particular food, it is considered rude to simply answer "yes" or "no." Especially if in a home, the hosts might very well have gone to some trouble to procure the food. The polite alternative to "no" would be the equivalent of "I like it a little," which lets the host know, in a polite manner, that one really does not care for the dish.

Japanese have, because of their socialization to be indirect, a very hard time telling another person "no" in response to a request. If, upon making a request, one hears the phrase "it is very difficult," it is best to interpret the answer as "it is impossible." Also, again out of a desire to preserve harmony, Japanese will avoid asserting direct opinions, particularly if the subject is controversial. It is probably best to avoid extensive discussion on politics or international relations unless one knows his or her Japanese conversant quite well. One rule of thumb is to ask an opinion on controversial topics if the Japanese with whom one is talking brings up the subject. It should be noted that while the above are correct generalizations, there are many Japanese who can be quite direct and opinionated.

Patience. One problem many foreigners encounter in Japan is that when making requests, they expect an immediate answer. Always keep in mind that Japan is a group-oriented society and that when a request by an outside party is made, consensus among several people must be first sought. The best strategy is simply to expect more time for any answer to a request. The positive side of this cultural trait is that once Japanese make decisions, because there is consensus, they tend to carry out the decision very expeditiously.

Hierarchy. Japan is a Confucian society that places great emphasis on age and status. When dealing with several Japanese it is important to show the most deference to the oldest or most high-ranking people. Many foreigners who don't speak Japanese have a tendency in meetings to pay more attention to the interpreter (a job that doesn't carry particularly high status) than to the person who is in charge or who is older.

Forms of Address. When addressing adults, one should normally use the honorific *san* after the person's family name, for example, Yamato-san or Yamane-san, regardless of whether the person is male or female. *Never* ever refer to yourself as "san"! When addressing a person who has higher status because of wisdom or knowledge, the Japanese term for teacher, *sensei,* is quite polite, again, after the person's family name: Suzuki-sensei, for example. Almost all Japanese address each other by family names; given names are rarely used. Children are an exception. *San* should not be used with them, and it is appropriate to use a given name. Relatives and close friends often add *chan* after a child's name as an endearing alternative to the more formal *san;* for example, Junko-chan.

Bathing. Japanese baths also have their own etiquette rules. The typical bath has a partitioned area with a shower and other washing implements such as soap and shampoo and a deep tub. If one is a guest in a home, the hosts will have already filled the tub. Japanese wash *before* they get in the tub. It is imperative that one follow this custom, using soap and shampoo and rinsing off before getting into the tub. The experience of a Japanese bath is similar in many ways to hot tubs in the United States. The purpose is to relax in the water, which is usually very hot. Never let the water out of the tub when you are done if you are a guest in a Japanese home. Most likely, other people will be using the water after you.

Public Displays of Affection. Although exceptions may be found, particularly among youth, hugging and kissing in public are not Japanese propensities. When one says good-bye to a Japanese host family, for example, it is probably best not to initiate public displays of affection; of course, it is quite appropriate to respond if the Japanese take the initiative.

Blowing One's Nose and Related Matters. It is considered extremely rude to blow one's nose in public, and this should be avoided. Also, Japanese restrooms often don't provide paper towels or tissue paper, and many restaurants don't have paper napkins (instead, a hot towel often is provided at the beginning of the meal), so it is a good idea to bring disposable tissues and/or a handkerchief with you while visiting Japan.

Eating Etiquette. In direct contrast to the United States, it is considered perfectly normal to make noise, for example to slurp noodles, while one eats. Never start eating or drinking until all diners are seated. When eating with Japanese one should utter *Itadakimasu* before beginning. Itadakimasu is a blessing of sorts. The translation is "I gratefully partake," and it is the polite equivalent of "I eat" and "I receive." After eating, the appropriate phrase spoken by all is *Gochiso sama deshita*. The literal translation is "It was indeed a feast," so what one in effect is saying is, "Thank you for the lovely meal." Chopsticks have their own special rules. One should not pass food using chopsticks to another person. Nor should chopsticks be stuck upright in any food. It is fine to pick up a small dish (many Japanese foods are served in small dishes) and hold it under one's chin in order to avoid spillage. Most Japanese eat soup by using chopsticks for the food in the soup and then drinking the broth. It is important to try and eat everything one is served if having a meal in a private home. It is considered impolite to fill one's own glass and good manners to fill other diner's glasses. If one has had enough to drink, it is best to leave the glass full and indicate by a polite refusal or a hand gesture.

Japan-Related Organizations

BUSINESS AND ECONOMIC

Japan External Trade Organization (JETRO)—United States
Atlanta Office:
245 Peachtree Center Avenue
Marquis One Tower, Suite 2208
Atlanta, GA 30303
Telephone: (404) 681-0600
Fax: (404) 681-0713
E-mail: info@jetroatlanta.org

Chicago Office:
401 N. Michigan Avenue, Suite 660
Chicago, IL 60611
Telephone: (312) 832-6000
Fax: (312) 832-6066
Web site: www.jetrocgo.org

Houston Office:
1221 McKinney, Suite 2360
Houston, TX 77010
Telephone: (713) 759-9595
Fax: (713) 759-9210
Web site: www.jetro.org/houston

Los Angeles Office:
777 S. Figueroa Street, Suite 4900
Los Angeles, CA 90017
Telephone: (213) 624-8855
Fax: (213) 629-8127

New York Office:
42nd Floor, McGraw Hill Building
1221 Avenue of the Americas
New York, NY 10020-1079
Telephone: (212) 997-0414
Fax: (212) 944-8808
E-mail: marilynwashington@jetro.go.jp

San Francisco Office:
235 Pine Street, Suite 1700
San Francisco, CA 94104
Telephone: (415) 392-1333
Fax: (415) 788-6927

Established in 1958, Japan External Trade Organization (JETRO) is a nonprofit, Japanese government-supported organization dedicated to promoting mutually beneficial trade and economic relationships between Japan and other nations. Its focus is to help American companies do business with Japan. Promotion of U.S.-Japan industrial cooperation, technology exchange, and direct investment in Japan are also areas of significant activity. In addition to directly assisting private companies, JETRO cooperates closely with national, state, and local economic development agencies as well as with industrial and trade organizations seeking to do business in Japan. Web site: www.jetro.go.jp

**Keidanren—The Japan Federation
of Economic Organizations**
1-9-4 Otemachi, Chiyoda-ku
Tokyo 100-8188 Japan
Telephone: 81-3-3279-1411
Fax: 81-3-5255-6255

The Japan Federation of Economic Organizations—abbreviated in Japanese as Keidanren—was established in 1946 as a nationwide business association. Its purpose is twofold: to work for a resolution of the major problems facing the business community in Japan and abroad, and to contribute to sound development of the Japanese and world economies. Keidanren also engages in a wide range of public relations activities at home and abroad to foster a clearer understanding of the Japanese business community.

Keizai Koho Center (KKC)
Headquarters:
Otemachi Building
6-1 Otemachi 1-chome, Chiyoda-ku
Tokyo 100-0004 Japan
Telephone: 81-3-3201-1415
Fax: 81-3-3201-1418

U.S. Office:
1900 K Street, N.W., Suite 1075
Washington, D.C. 20006
Telephone: (202) 293-8430
Fax: (202) 293-8438

The Keizai Koho Center is an independent, nonprofit organization supported by companies and major industrial organizations in Japan. It is affiliated with the Keidenran and derives its financial resources entirely from the private sector. Its purpose is to promote an understanding of Japan's economy and society at home and abroad via media, think tanks, and business, political, and educational institutions. The KKC sponsors U.S. teacher study tours of Japan.

Japan Economic Federation
11th Floor, Fukoku Seimei Building
2-2, 2 chome, Uchisaiwai-cho, Chiyoda-ku
Tokyo 100-0011, Japan
Telephone: 81-3-3580-9291
Fax: 81-3-3501-6674
E-mail: info@jef.or.jp

The Japan Economic Foundation promotes worldwide communication of the actual state of Japan's economy, industry, and trade in machine goods, and explains Japanese trade policies

CULTURE/EDUCATION/EXCHANGE

American Field Services–U.S.A. (AFS-USA)
AFS Central States:
2356 University Avenue, West Suite # 424
St. Paul, MN 55114
Telephone: (651) 647-6337
Fax: (651) 647-6628

AFS Northeastern States:
32 Hampden Street
Springfield, MA 01103-1263
Telephone: (413) 733-4242
Fax: (413) 732-3317

AFS Southeastern States:
1610 West Street, Suite 202
Annapolis, MD 21401-4054
Telephone: (410) 280-3000
Fax: (410) 280-3001

AFS Western States:
310 SW 4th Avenue, Suite 630
Portland, OR 97204-2608
Telephone: (503) 241-1578
Fax: (503) 241-1653

American Field Services–U.S.A has provided international and intercultural learning experiences to individuals, families, schools, and communities through a global volunteer partnership for more than fifty years. AFS is a worldwide leader in international exchange programs and a recognized advocate for world peace. Each year, AFS-USA makes it possible for more than 1,700 American students to live, study, and volunteer in one of forty-four countries as part of an AFS worldwide exchange of more than 10,000 students internationally. Web site: www.usa.afs.org

Asia Network Freeman Foundation Program
Professor Madeline Chu
Asia Network Freeman Programs Director
Kalamazoo College
1200 Academy Street
Kalamazoo, Michigan 49006
Telephone: (616) 337-7325
E-mail: chu@kzoo.edu

Made possible by a grant provided by the Freeman Foundation, the Asia Network promotes study in fifteen colleges and universities located throughout East Asia.

Asia Society
725 Park Avenue
New York, NY 10021
Telephone: (212) 288-6400
Fax: (212) 517-8315
Web site: www.asiasociety.org

The Asia Society is a national, nonprofit, nonpartisan educational organization that is dedicated to fostering understanding of Asia and communication between Americans and the peoples of Asia and the Pacific. The society sponsors art exhibitions, performances, films, lectures, seminars and conferences, publications and assistance to the media, and materials and programs for students and teachers to build awareness of the countries and peoples of Asia.

Fulbright Memorial Fund Teacher Program
Institute of International Education
1400 K Street, NW, Suite 650
Washington, DC 20005-2403

Telephone: (1-888) JAPAN-FMF (toll-free)
Fax: (202) 326-7698
E-mail: fmf@iie.org
Web site: www.iie.org/pgms/fmf/

The Fulbright Memorial Fund Teacher Program is designed to provide U.S. primary and secondary teachers and administrators with opportunities to participate in fully-funded short-term study programs in Japan. The program provides opportunity for professional development while strengthening curricula by increasing the level of understanding between Japanese and Americans.

Ikebana International
C.P.O. Box 1262
Tokyo 100-91, Japan
Telephone: 81-3-3293-8188
Fax: 81-3-3294-2272
E-mail address: ikebana@mta.biglobe.ne.jp

Ikebana International is a nonprofit cultural organization dedicated to the promotion and appreciation of all styles of ikebana, the Japanese art of flower arrangement. The organization was founded in 1956 with the purpose of uniting the peoples of the world through their mutual love of nature and enjoyment of ikebana. Today its membership includes approximately 10,000 persons in over sixty counties and 175 chapters.

**The Institute for the International
Education of Students (IES)**
33 North LaSalle Street, 15th Floor
Chicago, IL 60602
Telephone: (800) 995- 2300
E-mail: Info@IESabroad.org
Web site: www.iesabroad.org

The Institute for the International Education of Students (IES), founded in 1950, blends elements of foreign higher education with American university requirements, and encourages university students to explore the unique elements of each country's culture. IES works with more than 500 colleges and universities to enroll more than 1,800 students in twenty academic programs in twelve cities throughout Europe, Asia, Australia, and South America, including Tokyo and Nagoya, Japan.

Japan-U.S. Community Education and Exchange (JUCEE)
1440 Broadway, Suite 501
Oakland, CA 94612
Telephone: (510) 267-1920
Fax: (510) 267-1922
E-mail: info-us@jucee.org

Japan-U.S. Community Education and Exchange (JUCEE) was established with the aim of building a global participatory society, bringing together and supporting individuals and community organizations that wish to work on issues of common concern through international internships, training and education, and collaborative projects.

**The Japanese American Cultural
and Community Center (JACCC)**
244 South San Pedro Street, Suite 505
Los Angeles, CA 90012
Telephone: (213) 628-2725
Fax: (213) 617-8576
E-mail: info@jaccc.org

The Japanese American Cultural and Community Center (JACCC) is the largest ethnic cultural center in the United States. It is a nonprofit organization established to preserve and encourage the appreciation of Japanese and Japanese American heritage and cultural arts.

The Japanese American Network
231 East Third Street, Suite G-104
Los Angeles, CA 90013
E-mail: janet-info@janet.org
Web site: www.janet.org

The Japanese American Network is a partnership of Japanese American organizations encouraging the use of the Internet and other interactive communications technologies to exchange information about Japanese Americans, including culture, community, history, news, events, social services, and public policy issues.

The Japan Association for Cultural Exchange (ACE Japan)
4th Floor, Akasaka 1-chome Mori Building
1-11-28 Akasaka, Minato-ku
Tokyo 107-0052, Japan
Telephone: 81-3-5562-4422
Fax: 81-3-5562-4423

The Japan Association for Cultural Exchange (ACE Japan) is a nonprofit organization operated under the jurisdiction of Japan's Ministry of Foreign Affairs with the goal of promoting programs in international cultural exchange. ACE Japan maintains a network of relations, including the Japan Foundation (see following entry) and other cultural exchange organizations in Japan and overseas and assists in facilitating their programs and disseminating pertinent information.

The Japan Foundation
New York Office
Carnegie Hall Tower
152 West 57th Street, 39th Floor
New York, NY 10019
Telephone: (212) 489-0299
Fax: (212) 489-0409
Web site: www.jfny.org/jfny/index.html

Established in 1972, the Japan Foundation was the first specialist organization for international cultural exchange in Japan, and it carries out a broad variety of cultural-exchange programs, ranging from academic (including Japanese language instruction) to the arts, publication, audio-visual media, sports, and culture.

The Japan Foundation: Center for Global Partnership (CGP)
United States:
Carnegie Hall Tower
152 West 57th Street, 39th Floor
New York, NY 10019
Telephone: (212) 489-1255
Fax: (212) 489-1344
E-Mail: info@cgp.org

Japan:
Ark Mori Building, 20th Floor
1-12-32 Akasaka
Minato-ku, Tokyo 107-6021, Japan
Telephone: 81-3-5562-3541
Fax: 81-3-5572-6324
Web site: www.cgp.org/cgplink/

The CGP was established in 1991 to help achieve closer relations between Japan and the United States, and to contribute to a better world through the cooperative efforts for both countries.

Japan Information Network
Web site: www.jinjapan.org/jd/index.html

Japan Information Network maintains a comprehensive online directory of major organizations in Japan. The listings contain brief descriptions of each organization, its activities, and information on how they may be contacted.

Kansai Gandai University, Asian Studies Program
Center for International Education
16-1 Kitakatahoko-cho, Hirakata City
Osaka 573-1001, Japan
Telephone: 81-72-851-6751
Fax: 81-72-850-9011
E-mail: inquiry@khc.kansai-gaidai-u.ac.jp
Web site: www.kansai-gadai-u.ac.jp/bekka/index.html

The Asian Studies Program at Kansai Gandai University accommodates international students wishing to pursue Japanese language and Japan/Asian studies.

Keizai Koho Center Fellowships Program (KKC)
Attn.: Program Coordinator
6628 Frost Lake Lane
Kingstowne, VA 22315
Telephone: (703) 921-0824
Fax: (703) 924-0162
E-mail: LSWKKC@aol.com

The Keizai Koho Center (KKC) offers fellowships to visit Japan in cooperation with the National Council of Social Studies. K-12 educators in the Unites States and Canada involved in social studies education—among them, classroom teachers, supervisors, specialists, and school administrators, as well as college and university faculty—are eligible to apply for KKC's eighteen fellowships.

The Laurasian Institution
Web site: www.laurasian.org
E-mail: tli@laurasian.org

San Francisco Office:
TLI Development Office
3025 Bolero Court
Pleasanton, CA 94588
Telephone: (888) 310-4164 (toll-free) or (925) 463-1393

Seattle Office:
12345 Lake City Way, NE #151
Seattle, WA 98125
Telephone:(425) 398-1153
Fax: (425) 398-8245

Tokyo Office:
5-5-17 Shimomeguro
Meguro-ku, Tokyo 153-0064; Japan
Telephone: 81-3-3712-6176
Fax: 81-3-3712-8975

The Laurasian Institution is a nongovernmental, nonprofit organization that offers a variety of international and cross-cultural educational programs. Its Japan program is designed for precollege students and provides study tour experience. The program curriculum focuses on four themes: art, business, society, and culture.

National Association of Japan-America Societies (NAJAS)
733 15th Street, Suite 700
Washington, DC 20005
Telephone: (202) 783-4550
Fax: (202) 783-4551
E-mail: najas@us-japan.org

The National Association of Japan-America Societies (NAJAS) is a private, nonprofit, nonpartisan organization offering educational, cultural, and business programs about Japan and U.S.-Japan relations to the general public through its member Japan-America Societies.

United States–Japan Foundation (USJF)
154 East 32nd Street
New York, NY 10016
Telephone: (212) 481-8753
Fax: (212) 481-8762
E-mail: info@us-jf.org

Tokyo Office:
Reinanzaka Building 1F
1-14-2 Akasaka
Minato-ku, Tokyo 107-005 Japan
Telephone: 81-3-3586-0541
Fax: 81-3-3586-1128
E-mail: JDU05456@nifty
Web site: www.us-jf.org

The United States–Japan Foundation (USJF) focuses on promoting stronger ties between the United States and Japan through greater mutual understanding, increasing awareness of policy issues, and addressing common concerns in the Asia-Pacific region through the U.S.-Japan perspective.

GOVERNMENT

Embassy of Japan
2520 Massachusetts Ave NW
Washington, D.C. 20008
Telephone: (202) 238-6700
Fax: (202) 328-2187
Web site: www.embjapan.org/

Consulates General of Japan
Agana, Guam:
P.O. Box AG
Agana, Guam 96932
U.S.A.
Telephone: (671) 646-1290
Fax: (671) 649-2620
Web site: www.cgj-hagatna.org

Anchorage:
3601 C Street, Suite 1300
Anchorage, AK 99503-5925
Telephone: (907) 562-8424

Fax: (907) 562-8434
E-mail: cgjpnak@ptialaska.net
Web site: www.embjapan.org/anchorage/

Atlanta:
100 Colony Square Building, Suite 2000
1175 Peachtree Street NE
Atlanta, GA 30361
Telephone: (404) 892-2700
Fax: (404) 881-6321
E-mail: info@cgjapanatlanta.org
Web site: www.cgjapanatlanta.org

Boston:
Federal Reserve Plaza, 14th Floor
600 Atlantic Avenue
Boston, MA 02210-2285
Telephone: (617) 973-9772
Fax: (617) 542-1329
E-mail: japan@tiac.net
Web site: www.embjapan.org/boston/

Chicago:
Olympia Centre, Suite 1100
737 North Michigan Avenue
Chicago, IL 60611-2656
Telephone: (312) 280-0400
Fax: (312) 280-9568
E-mail: jicc@xsite.net
Web site: www.jchicago.org

Denver:
1225 17th Street, Suite 3000
Denver, CO 80202-5505
Telephone: (303) 534-1151
Fax: (303) 534-3393
Web site: www.embjapan.org/denver/

Detroit:
400 Renaissance Center, Suite 1600
Detroit, MI 48243
Telephone: (313) 567-0120
Fax: (313) 567-0274
E-mail: ryouji@globalbiz.net
Web site: www.embjapan.org/detroit/

Honolulu:
1742 Nuuanu Avenue
Honolulu, Hawaii 96817-3294
Telephone: (808) 543-3111
Fax: (808) 543-3170
Web site: www.embjapan.org/honolulu/

Houston:
Wells Fargo Plaza, Suite 5300
1000 Louisiana Street
Houston, TX 77002-5013
Telephone: (713) 652-2977
Fax: (713) 651-7822
E-mail: cjapanho@concentric.net
Web site: www.cgjhouston.org/

Kansas City:
1800 Commerce Tower
911 Main Street
Kansas City, MO 64105-2076
Telephone: (816) 471-0111
Fax: (816) 472-4248
E-mail: cgjkc@swbell.net
Web site: www.embjapan.org/kansascity/

Los Angeles:
350 South Grand Avenue, Suite 1700
Los Angeles, CA 90071-3459
Telephone: (213) 617-6700
Fax: (213) 617-6727

Web site: www.embjapan.org/la/

Miami:
Brickell Bay View Centre, Suite 3200
80 SW 8th Street
Miami, FL 33130-3047
Telephone: (305) 530-9090
Fax: (305) 530-0950
E-mail: cgjmia@netrunner.net
Web site: www.embjapan.org/miami/

New Orleans:
639 Loyola Avenue, Suite 2050
New Orleans, LA 70113-3140
Telephone: (504) 529-2101
Fax: (504) 568-9847
E-mail: cgjpnola@communique.net
Web site: www.embjapan.org/neworleans/

New York:
299 Park Avenue, 18th Floor
New York, NY 10171-0025
Telephone: (212) 371-8222
Fax: (212) 319-6357
Web site: www.ny.cgj.org/index.html

Portland:
Wells Fargo Center, Suite 2700
1300 SW 5th Avenue
Portland, OR 97201
Telephone: (503) 221-1811
Fax: (503) 224-8936
Web site: www.embjapan.org/portland/

San Francisco:
50 Fremont Street, Suite 2300
San Francisco, CA 94105-2236
Telephone: (415) 777-3533

Fax: (415) 777-0518
E-mail: cgjinf3@pacbell.net
Web site: www.embjapan.org/sf/

Seattle:
601 Union Street, Suite 500
Seattle, WA 98101-4015
Telephone: (206) 682-9107
Fax: (206) 624-9097
Web site: www.embjapan.org/seattle/

TOURISM

Fodor's Travel Publications
Web site: www.fodors.com

Fodor's Web site provides brief guides for several major cities in Japan. Each online guide provides an overview of the city and a map; recommends sights, activities, restaurants, hotels, shopping, nightlife, art exhibits; and gives travel tips. A resource section with maps, Web links, and information on purchasing Fodor's extensive travel guidebooks are also available at this site.

Japan Association of Travel Agents (JATA)
Zen-Nittu Kasumigaseki Building
3-3 Kasumigaseki 3-chome, Chiyoda-ku
Tokyo 100-0013, Japan
Telephone: 81-3-3592-1271
Fax: 81-3-3592-1268
Web site: www.jata-net.or.jp/english

The Japan Association of Travel Agents (JATA) seeks to improve the quality of services provided to travelers to and from Japan. It contributes to the development of the travel and tourism industries by disseminating information, encouraging cooperation among members, and developing businesses and legal dealings that will benefit the membership and the industry at large.

Japan National Tourist Organization (JNTO)
2-10-1 Yurakucho, Chiyoda-ku
Tokyo 100-0006, Japan

New York Office:
Japan National Tourist Organization
One Rockefeller Plaza, Suite 1250
New York, NY 10020
Telephone: (212) 757-5640
Fax: (212) 307-6754
E-mail: info@jntonyc.org

Los Angeles Office:
Japan National Tourist Organization
515 South Figueroa Street, Suite 1470
Los Angeles, CA 90071
Telephone: (213) 623-1952
Fax: (213) 623-6301
E-mail: info@jnto-lax.org

Chicago Office:
Japan National Tourist Organization
401 North Michigan Avenue, Suite 770
Chicago, IL 60611
Telephone: (312) 222-0874
Fax: (312) 222-0876
E-mail: jntochi@mcs.net

San Francisco Office:
Japan National Tourist Organization
360 Post Street, Suite 601
San Francisco, CA 94108
Telephone: (415) 989-7140
Fax: (415) 398-5461
E-mail: sfjnto@webjapan.com

Toronto Office:
Japan National Tourist Organization
165 University Avenue
Toronto, Ontario
Canada M5H 3B8
Telephone: 416-366-7140
Fax: 416-366-4530
E-mail: jnto@interlog.com

The Japan National Tourist Organization (JNTO) engages in a range of overseas tourism promotions encouraging individuals and companies to visit Japan on business, to hold conferences and meetings in Japan, or to simply deepen their understanding of Japanese history, culture, customs, and its people through travel.

Japan Travel Bureau (JTB)
Web site: www.jtb.co.jp/eng

The Japan Travel Bureau (JTB) provides information on travel to and around Japan, whether the visit is for business or for pleasure.

Lonely Planet Publications
150 Linden Street
Oakland, CA 94607
Telephone: (800) 275-8555 (toll-free) or (510) 893-8555
Fax: (510) 893-8563
E-mail: info@lonelyplanet.com
Web site: www.lonelyplanet.com

Lonely Planet's Web site provides a thorough online guide to travel in Japan, including when to go (as well as how to get there and how to get around), money and costs, events and attractions, activities (both popular and off-the-beaten-track), plus overviews of the history, culture, and environment of the region. A resource section with Web links, information on purchasing Lonely Planet guidebooks, and access to travelers' postcards with tips and useful current information are also available at this site.

Annotated Bibliography of Recommended Works on Japan

The books, CD-ROMS, periodicals, and Web sites noted below are organized in accordance with the subjects of the individual chapters. Every effort has been made to include accurate and readable sources that should assist those readers who want to know more about Japan. The resources included in this section are, for the most part, general works on Japan. For more specialized titles on Japan please consult either the individual References sections at the ends of the chapters or the bibliographies in the titles. Note that Japan-related videos are excluded from this bibliography, primarily because so few are applicable to general audiences. However, several entries here and in the individual References cite a variety of special-topic videos.

GEOGRAPHY AND HISTORY

Beasley, W. G. *The Japanese Experience: A Short History of Japan.* Berkeley: University of California Press, 1999. 299 pp. (hardcover and paperback).

This is a concise and well-done history of Japan. Cultural, economic, geographical, political, and social topics are addressed.

Collcut, Martin, Mariius Jansen, and Isao Kumakura. *The Cultural Atlas of Japan.* New York: Facts on File, Inc., 1988. 204 pp. (hardcover).

This attractive reference book is a historical and cultural account of Japan that addresses archeology, geography, history, and contemporary issues.

Ellington, Lucien, ed. *Education about Asia.* Ann Arbor: Association for Asian Studies. www.aasianst.org/eaa-toc.htm

This eighty-page illustrated magazine, published three times a year, contains articles on Japanese history as well as pieces on contemporary Japan for general readers.

Rysaku, Tsunoda, W. M. Theodore De Bary, and Donald Keene, eds. *Sources of Japanese Tradition.* New York: Columbia University Press; Vol. 1, 2001, 520 pp.; Vol. 2, 1964, 406 pp. (first edition of Vols. 1 and 2 available in paperback; revised Vol. 1 available in hardback only).

This is a superb collection of primary-source documents for the reader who wants to understand Japan through the conceptualizations of Japanese themselves. The editors do an excellent job of providing context for the literary, philosophical, and political excerpts that are included.

Shirokauer, Conrad. *A Brief History of Chinese and Japanese Civilizations.* New York: Harcourt Brace Jovanovich College Publishers, 1989. 673 pp. (paperback).

This history survey is notable because the author does a good job of depicting the effect of Chinese culture upon Japan. The book is also noteworthy for excellent art illustrations.

Stanley-Baker, Joan. *Japanese Art.* Farnborough, Hampshire, U.K.: Thames & Hudson, 2000. 233 pp. (paperback).

This is a well-written survey of Japanese art from prehistoric times to the present. The book is illustrated with examples from all the arts.

Varley, Paul. *Japanese Culture.* Honolulu: University of Hawaii Press, 2000. 384 pp. (paperback).

This is a classical cultural history of Japan that has been through several editions.

Yamamoto, Tsunetomo. *Hagakure: The Book of the Samurai.* Translated by William Scott Wilson. New York: Kodansha, 1983. 180 pp. (paperback).

There has been considerable interest in samurai in the West. This classic book of advice on appropriate samurai behavior, written by a samurai in 1716, is indispensable for an understanding of Japan's warrior class.

JAPAN'S ECONOMY

Ennis, Peter, ed. *The Oriental Economist Report.* New York: Toyo Keizai America.

This 16–20 page newsletter is clearly written and provides up-to-date information on a variety of Japan-related topics. The editors do a particularly good job of relating political issues to economics.

Jobs in Japan

www.jobsinjapan.com

This is a comprehensive and useful database for job seekers in Japan. It also contains tips on working in Japan.

Katz, Richard. *Japan: The System That Soured.* Armonk, NY: M. E. Sharpe, 2001. 530 pp. (hardcover).

This is a somewhat challenging but very accurate analysis of why many of the characteristics of Japan's economic system that fostered success now contribute to Japan's lingering problems.

Macpherson, W. J. *The Economic Development of Modern Japan: 1868–1941.* New York: Cambridge University Press, 1996. 105pp. (paperback).

There are few readable surveys on Japanese economic history. The above book is a good general introduction. For the period after World War II consult the history readings and Katz.

Mak, James, Shyam Sunder, Shigeuyuki Abe, and Kazuhiro Igawa. *Japan: Why It Works, Why It Doesn't: Economics in Everyday Life.* Honolulu: University of Hawaii Press, 1998. 219 pp. (paperback).

The multiple contributors to this accessible book use examples from daily life in explaining positive and negative aspects of Japan's economy. Readers who are seeking a better understanding of Japan's economy should read this book and the Katz work.

Revzin, Philip, ed. *The Far Eastern Economic Review.* Hong Kong: Dow Jones.

This weekly magazine provides comprehensive coverage of economic, political, and social Asian issues and includes much Japan content.

JAPANESE INSTITUTIONS

Benjamin, Gail. *Japanese Lessons: A Year in a Japanese School through the Eyes of an American Anthropologist and Her Children.* New York: New York University Press, 1998, 241 pp. (hardcover and paperback).

Benjamin is both an expert on Japanese education and a past client of the schools. Her book is very readable and is especially useful for readers who want to learn more about elementary schools in Japan.

Curtis, Gerald. *The Logic of Japanese Politics.* New York: Columbia University Press, 1999, 303 pp. (hardcover).

The book is an interesting discussion of political elites in Japan and recent electoral reform efforts.

Earhart, Byron. *Religions of Japan: Many Traditions within One Sacred Way.* Prospect Heights, IL: Waveland Press, 1998. 142 pp. (paperback).

This is an excellent short overview of religion in Japan and is highly recommended.

Ellington, Lucien. *Education in the Japanese Life-Cycle: Implications for the United States.* New York: Edwin Mellen Press, 1992. 241 pp. (hardcover).

Japanese education from preschool through the adult years is addressed in this general survey.

Encyclopedia of Japan. CD-ROM. New York: Kodansha, 1999.

This CD-ROM utilizes the research of 1,100 scholars and is a tremendous comprehensive resource on all aspects of Japan. It contains over 12,000 entries and 2,500 color photographs augmented by movie and sound clips. Fully utilizing the immense resources of Kodansha's nine-volume *Encyclopedia of Japan* and two-volume *Japan: An Illustrated Encyclopedia,* it is an essential reference for anyone with a professional, academic, or general interest in Japan.

Fukuzawa, Rebecca Erwin, and Gerald K. Letendre. *Intense Years: How Japanese Adolescents Balance School, Family, and Friends.* New York: Routledge/Falmer, 2001. 135 pp. (hardcover).

This is an excellent treatment of the often stressful lives of Japanese junior high students.

Stockwin, J. A. A. *Governing Japan: Divided Politics in a Major Economy.* London: Blackwell Publishers, 1998. 269 pp. (paperback and hardcover).

Stockwin's text is a broad overview of post–World War II Japanese politics.

JAPANESE SOCIETY

Association for Japanese Language Teaching. *Japanese for Busy People,* Vols. 1–3. New York: Kodansha America, Inc., 1995, 1996, 1997 respectively. (paperback).

These three books, each well over 200 pages, along with audio-cassettes and workbooks, comprise a self-contained Japanese language course. Videotapes are also available.

Hendry, Joy. *Understanding Japanese Society.* New York: Routledge, 1995. 240 pp. (paperback).

Hendry's book is a good general introduction to Japanese society and includes substantial information on recent societal change.

Japanese Cookbook for Kids

www.jinjapan.org/kidsweb/cook.html

This Web site provides basic information about Japanese cuisine (e.g., the word for "meal" in Japanese is *gohan*) and explains many Japanese dietary and dining customs. Recipes include rice and miso soup; *hanbagu,* similar to meatloaf in patty form; *nikujaga,* a meat and vegetable stew; sushi (of course); *okonomiyaki,* a fried pancake; and *yakisoba,* a fried noodle dish, with a separate lesson on noodle making.

Japanese Recipe Collection

www.bento.com/tf-recp.html

The Japanese Recipe Collection is published on the Tokyo Food Page. The Web site has been published in Tokyo since 1994, and it currently logs around 250,000 page views per month. The Tokyo Food Page is published in Tokyo by Lobster Enterprises and Yamato Tomato Planning. Included are recipes for grilled miso chicken, *tori no mizutaki* (chicken stew), *shabu-shabu* (quick-cooked beef), *tonkatsu* (pork cutlet), *hiyashi-chuuka* (cold Chinese-style noodles), and many more.

Japan Times Online

www.japantimes.co.jp/

This is the online version of the oldest English-language Japanese newspaper. It is a good source for information about politics and international affairs.

Japan Travel expert

www.businessinsightjapan.com/cgi-bin/expwww/exp.cgi

This is an excellent site for domestic travel in Japan, sponsored by the online magazine *Japan Insight Japan.*

Jim Breen's Japanese-English Dictionary Server

www.csse.monash.edu.au/~jwb/wwwjdic.html

This easy-to-use site accesses Japanese words and kanji. It also has the capability to translate Japanese Web pages into English.

Jolivet, Muriel. *Japan: The Childless Society.* New York: Routledge, 1997. 240pp. (hardcover and paperback).

The author does a good job in depicting the relatively new dilemma Japanese women face concerning motherhood and other possible social roles.

Kabuki Story (Japan Festival Award 1999)

www.lightbrigade.demon.co.uk/

This site details a project for schools exploring Edo-period Japan via *kabuki*, one of its major artforms. You, too, can participate.

National Sumo Association

www.sumo.or.jp/index_e.html

This is the attractive official homepage of Japan's national sumo association. It is included for the small but growing audience of American afficionados of the sport.

News on Japan

www.newsonjapan.com

This is a superb site for keeping up with the latest news from Japan on a wide variety of topics ranging from business to the arts.

Nipponia

www.jinjapan.org/nipponia/

This is the online version of a very well-done quarterly on Japanese contemporary culture. Back issues of Nipponia are also available at the site.

Reid, T. R. *Confucius Lives Next Door: What Living in the East Teaches Us about Living in the West.* New York City: Vintage, 2000. 176 pp. (paperback and hardcover).

This is a very readable book about the connection between Confucianism and how Japanese and other East Asians act. Although the book is recommended, the author does tend to cast Japanese behavior in an overly positive manner at times.

Rosenberger, Nancy. *Gambling with Virtue: Japanese Women and the Search for Self in a Changing Nation.* Honolulu: University of Hawaii Press, 2001. 277pp. (paperback).

This is a very good book on how Japanese women's lives have changed over the past three decades.

Rowley, Michael. *Kanji Pict-o-graphix.* Berkeley: Stonebridge Press, 1992. 216 pp. (paperback).

This offers an elemental and somewhat unorthodox introduction to the Chinese characters that constitute as integral part of written Japanese.

Schauwecker's Guide to Japan

www.japan-guide.com

This site is quite comprehensive and covers both contemporary and traditional Japan. The site developers envision it as a starting point for online research on Japan for tourists, students, cooks, and others. There is even a pen pal section.

Shilling, Mark. *The Encyclopedia of Japanese Pop Culture.* New York: Weatherhill, 1997. 343 pp. (paperback).

This book provides a delightful introduction to a side of Japan that, for most Westerners, is unfamiliar (to say the least).

Trends in Japan

www.jinjapan.org/trends/index.html

Readers can find a wide range of information on this site from various Japanese news sources. The site is part of the Japan Information Network homepage, which is sponsored by the Ministry of Foreign Affairs.

Vukov, Elaine. *Japanese Literature for the High School Classroom.* New York: Japan Society, 2001. 61 pp. (monograph).

Although intended for high school students, this annotated bibliography is a wonderful introduction to all periods of Japanese literature.

Index

About the Author

Lucien Ellington is editor of the journal *Education about Asia* and codirector of the Asia Program at the University of Tennessee at Chattanooga. His books include *Japan: Tradition and Change* and *Education in the Japanese Life Cycle*. He has conducted institutes on Japan throughout the United States and has codirected nine study tours of the country.